THE SERVANT OF GOD

STUDIES IN BIBLICAL THEOLOGY · 20

THE SERVANT OF GOD

W. ZIMMERLI
J. JEREMIAS

REVISED EDITION

WIPF & STOCK · Eugene, Oregon

Wipf and Stock Publishers
199 W 8th Ave, Suite 3
Eugene, OR 97401

The Servant God
Revised Edition
By Zimmerli, Walther and Jeremias, Joachim
Copyright©1965 SCM Press
ISBN 13: 978-1-60899-034-4
Publication date 8/20/2009
Previously published by SCM Press, 1965

Copyright © SCM Press 1965
First English edition 1965 by SCM Press
This Edition published by arrangement with SCM-Canterbury Press

This English translation of the article Παῖς Θεοῦ *from Kittel's* Theologisches Wörterbuch zum NT *was drafted by Harold Knight and afterwards completed by the editorial staff of the publisher, with help both from Professor Jeremias and his assistants in Göttingen.*

CONTENTS

Preface to the Second Edition 7
Abbreviations 9

Zimmerli

I THE עֶבֶד יהוה IN THE OLD TESTAMENT 11

1 The Profane Use of the Title עֶבֶד 11
  i עֶבֶד = the slave 11
  ii The עֶבֶד in the service of the king 12
  iii עֶבֶד as a description of political submission 14
  iv עֶבֶד as a humble self-description 14
  v The sanctuary servants 14

2 עֶבֶד in Religious Usage 15
  i עֶבֶד as the humble self-description of the pious in the presence of his God 15
  ii 'Servants of Yahweh' in the plural as denoting the pious 18
  iii עֶבֶד יהוה in the singular as a description of Israel 19
  iv עֶבֶד יהוה as a title for specially distinguished figures 20
  v The Suffering Servant of Deutero-Isaiah 25

Zimmerli

II TRANSLATIONS IN THE LXX 37

1 The עֶבֶד Translations in the LXX 37
2 The Translation of Servant of God Passages in Deutero-Isaiah 42

Jeremias

III Παῖς Θεοῦ IN LATE JUDAISM IN THE PERIOD AFTER THE LXX 45

1 The Twofold Meaning of Παῖς Θεοῦ 45
  i Παῖς Θεοῦ = 'child of God' 45
  ii Παῖς Θεοῦ = 'servant of God' 46

2 THE PERSISTENCE OF THE O.T. RELIGIOUS
  USAGE OF עֶבֶד יהוה   47
    i Παῖς Θεοῦ as self-descriptive of the worshipper   47
    ii The plural 'servants of God'   48
    iii The collective linguistic use   49
    iv Παῖς Θεοῦ as a title of honour for outstanding instruments of God 49
    v 'Servant of God' as denoting the Messiah   51

3 INTERPRETATIONS OF THE DEUTERO-ISAIAH
  'SERVANT OF GOD' PASSAGES   52
    i Hellenistic Judaism   53
    ii Palestinian Judaism   55
      (a) The collective interpretation   55
      (b) Application to the prophet Isaiah   57
      (c) Messianic exegesis   59

Jeremias

IV Παῖς (Θεοῦ) IN THE NEW TESTAMENT   80

  1 Παῖς (Θεοῦ) AS A PREDICATION OF JESUS   81
    i The origin of the predication   81
    ii The meaning of the predication   86
    iii The semantic change from 'servant of God' to 'child of God'   86

  2 CHRISTOLOGICAL INTERPRETATIONS OF THE
    SERVANT TEXTS OF DEUTERO-ISAIAH IN THE
    NEW TESTAMENT   88
      i The evidence   88
      ii The historical setting in the life of the early church   94

  3 CAN JESUS HAVE REFERRED THE SERVANT
    PASSAGES OF DEUTERO-ISAIAH TO HIMSELF?   99

Bibliography   107
Index of Authors   113
Index of Biblical References   117

PREFACE TO THE SECOND EDITION

The book has been thoroughly revised for the second edition. Most of the changes occur in Professor Jeremias' contribution. The following are to be noted:

In ch. III (Παῖς Θεοῦ in Late Judaism in the period after the LXX), the Qumran texts have been given due attention. The result is, however, negative; they show no trace of a collective application of the servant of Deutero-Isaiah to the Essene community, nor of an individual application to the Teacher of Righteousness (pp. 57, 59). Further, *Test. B.* 3.8 (1st ed., pp. 57f.) and *Siphra Lev.* as quoted by Raymundus Martini (pp. 73f. below) had to be struck off the list of Late Jewish applications of servant passages to the Messiah on grounds of textual criticism.

In ch. IV (Παῖς [Θεοῦ] in the New Testament), the designation of Jesus as παῖς [Θεοῦ] in Acts is no longer derived from Deutero-Isaiah, but from the custom in the O.T. and in Late Judaism of qualifying eminent men of God as 'servants of God' (p. 86). The association of (παρα-)διδόναι ('to deliver') in the active and passive with Isa. 53 has been restated in more precise terms (pp. 96f.). The connexion of Phil. 2.7 with Isa. 53 has been clarified (pp. 97-9). Finally, in the last section supplementary evidence has been adduced which goes to show that Jesus referred the chapter about the Suffering Servant to himself.

The numbers of the footnotes were left unaltered wherever possible for the convenience of readers who may wish to compare the German and the first English editions. This accounts for a few gaps in numbering and some *a*- and *b*-numbers.

The authors wish to thank Dr Christoph Burchard for his very careful and painstaking work in translating the alterations and preparing the manuscript for press.

Göttingen, June 1964

LIST OF ABBREVIATIONS

'A	Aquila's translation
'Αλλ	The column of the *Hexapla* called ἄλλος
AOB	H. Gressmann, *Altorientalische Bilder zum AT*², 1927
ATANT	*Abhandlungen zur Theologie des Alten und Neuen Testaments*
BFT	*Beiträge zur Förderung christlicher Theologie*
BHK	*Biblia Hebraica*, ed. R. Kittel* ²(1909); ³(1929 ff.)
BJRL	*Bulletin of the John Rylands Library*
BWANT	*Beiträge zur Wissenschaft vom Alten und Neuen Testament*
DT	*Deutsche Theologie*
ET	*Expository Times*
FRL	*Forschungen zur Religion und Literatur des AT und NT*
GCS	*Die Griechischen Christlichen Schriftsteller der ersten drei Jahrhunderte*
HNT	*Handbuch zum NT*
HSAT	*Die Heilige Schrift des AT*
HUCA	*Hebrew Union College Annual*
JAOS	*Journal of the American Oriental Society*
JBL	*Journal of Biblical Literature*
JEH	*Journal of Ecclesiastical History*
JQR	*Jewish Quarterly Review*
JTS	*Journal of Theological Studies*
Meyer	*Kritisch-Exegetischer Kommentar über das NT*, begründet von H. A. W. Meyer
MGWJ	*Monatsschrift für Geschichte und Wissenschaft des Judentums*
M.T.	Massoretic Text
NGG	*Nachrichten von der Gesellschaft der Wissenschaften zu Göttingen*
NKZ	*Neue kirchliche Zeitschrift*
OTS	*Oudtestamentische Studiën*
PG	*Patrologia Graeca*
PL	*Patrologia Latina*
RB	*Revue Biblique*
RE	*Realencyclopaedie für protestantische Theologie und Kirche*
RGG	*Die Religion in Geschichte und Gegenwart*
RTP	*Revue de Théologie et de Philosophie*
Σ	Symmachus' translation
SAB	*Sitzungsberichte der Preussischen Akademie der Wissenschaften zu Berlin*
SAH	*Sitzungsberichte der Heidelberger Akademie der Wissenschaften*
SBT	*Studies in Biblical Theology*
S.-B.	H. L. Strack-P. Billerbeck, *Kommentar zum Neuen Testament aus Talmud und Midrasch*, I, 1922; II, 1924
s.v.	*sub voce*
Θ	Theodotion's translation
TB	*Theologische Blätter*
TbB	*Theologische Bücherei*
TLZ	*Theologische Literaturzeitung*
TR	*Theologische Rundschau*
TSK	*Theologische Studien und Kritiken*
TWNT	*Theologisches Wörterbuch zum NT*
TZ	*Theologische Zeitschrift*
v.l.	*varia lectio*
ZAW	*Zeitschrift für die alttestamentliche Wissenschaft*
ZDMG	*Zeitschrift der Deutschen Morgenländischen Gesellschaft*
ZDPV	*Zeitschrift des Deutschen Palästina-Vereins*
ZNW	*Zeitschrift für die neutestamentliche Wissenschaft*
ZST	*Zeitschrift für systematische Theologie*
ZTK	*Zeitschrift für Theologie und Kirche*

I

THE עֶבֶד יהוה IN THE OLD TESTAMENT

1. THE PROFANE USE OF THE TITLE עֶבֶד

The noun עֶבֶד is probably not to be derived from the verb עבד, 'to work', contrary to what is commonly thought;[1] rather it must be considered a primitive noun from which the verb has been secondarily derived. The noun hardly ever implies 'work'.[2] The primary meaning of the word has to do with a specific personal relationship. Not 'the idle' but אָדוֹן 'the Lord' is the counterpart expressed or unexpressed of עֶבֶד.[3] עֶבֶד is the one who belongs to a master. The whole rich development of the עֶבֶד idea begins with this sense of belonging. The suffix or construct formations but also the less frequent loose link with לְ all point not to the object that is produced by the worker but to the Lord who bids the work be done.[4] In particular, the following chief modes of employment of the word עֶבֶד can be distinguished:

(i) עֶבֶד = *the slave*, the man who is characterized above all by the fact that he belongs to another.[5] The slave appears to be the one who has completely become property. But O.T. law can point to the fact that in Israel limits are set to this victimization.

---

[1] So the 1st edition, following Noeldeke, review of F. Delitzsch, 'Prolegomena eines neuen hebr.-aram. Wörterbuchs zum A.T.', *ZDMG*, 40, 1886, 741; W. J. Gerber, *Die hebr. Verba denominativa*, 1896, 14–16; Lindhagen, 41–42.

[2] So, for example, in Job 7.2 or in I Kings 9.22 where in Origen's supplement the נָתַן עֶבֶד of the O.T. is translated by ἔδωκεν εἰς πρᾶγμα.

[3] This is beautifully clear in Lev. 25, where v. 39 forbids that a brother who has fallen into bondage should be given עֶבֶד-work, while v. 40 assumes as a matter of course that he will work (עבד).

[4] Thus one can indeed speak verbally of an עֹבֵד אֲדָמָה (Gen. 4.2; Zech. 13.5; Prov. 12.11; 28.19) but never of an עֶבֶד אֲדָמָה in the sense of a tiller of the soil. The verb עבד with the meaning 'serve' as derived from the noun should be termed secondary. For its usage see Gerber, loc. cit. in n. 1. The obvious weakness of the work of Lindhagen (cf. especially n. 41) lies in the unnoticed confusion of the noun עֶבֶד and the verb עבד on which in fact is based his memorandum of the עֶבֶד passages in the O.T.

[5] Most plainly in the enumerations of possessions, for example in Gen. 20.14; 24.35; 30.43; 32.5, and elsewhere, or in the extremely unsentimental כַּסְפּוֹ הוּא of Ex. 21.21 (cf. also Lev. 22.11). Cf., for instance, R. de Vaux, *Ancient Israel*, 1961, 80–90.

The Servant of God

The slave has rights as a human being. Thus, in contradistinction to Babylonian law, for example, any injury done to a slave must be compensated by his release.[6] In O.T. slave law there are no punishments by mutilation.[7] The slave who has escaped from another master is not to be surrendered.[8] This greater dignity and freedom of the slave were assisted by the fact that the slave shared in the common cultic life in O.T. faith, directed as it was to community and the people of God.[9] Furthermore, Israel itself was conscious from the start that it owed its own whole existence to an act of deliverance from Egypt, the 'house of bondage' (Ex. 20.2; Deut. 5.6; 6.12, etc.). Lev. 25.42 is able to show how clearly Israel's consequent sense of belonging to Yahweh can assure to her slaves at least the right to live. Gen. 24 narrates the finest slave story in the O.T. The name of its hero is never indicated, but he is referred to simply as עֶבֶד אַבְרָהָם or more briefly as הָעֶבֶד.[10] His action is determined wholly by the cult-communion of the house of his master. God is for him 'the God of my master Abraham' (vv. 12, 27, 42, 48). Within that setting an utterly free type of service is possible; the עֶבֶד acts in his business of wooing a bride for Abraham's son as effectually as though Abraham himself were present. He is the full representative of his master and remains nevertheless the submissive, nameless servant who does not even permit himself the humanly very understandable respite at the scene of his successful mission (vv. 54ff.).

(ii) *The* עֶבֶד *in the service of the king.* The need of repelling the professional army of the Philistines made it necessary in Israel, from the time of Saul onwards, for the king, who normally had at his disposal only a voluntary army, to form for himself a paid standing army.[11] Whoever entered the latter seceded from

---

[6] Ex. 21.26f.; cf. *Codex Hammurabi*, § 199, 213.
[7] *Codex Hammurabi*, § 205, 282.
[8] Deut. 23.16; cf. *Codex Hammurabi*, § 15–20.
[9] Sacrifice, Deut. 12.12, 18; sabbath, Ex. 20.10; Deut. 5.14; passover, Ex. 12.44; circumcision, Gen. 17.13, 27. In Lev. 22.11, although the עֶבֶד title is missing, the fact is very clearly expressed.
[10] עֶבֶד אַבְרָהָם vv. 34, 52, 59; הָעֶבֶד vv. 5, 9, 10, 17, etc.; v. 2 represents him as עַבְדּוֹ זְקַן בֵּיתוֹ הַמֹּשֵׁל בְּכָל־אֲשֶׁר לוֹ. The reader of the extant Abraham stories as a whole will think of Eliezer, mentioned in Gen. 15.2.
[11] I Sam. 14.52; cf. especially A. Alt, *Die Staatenbildung der Israeliten in Palästina*, 1930, 33f.; E. Junge, *Der Wiederaufbau des Heerwesens des Reiches Juda unter Josia*, 1937, 8–22.

The Servant of God in the Old Testament

natural tribal membership and became עֶבֶד הַמֶּלֶךְ.[12] It would not be appropriate to speak in this matter of slavery, since service with the king probably was based upon a firm agreement whereby the king too bound himself to reciprocal duties.[13] The עֶבֶד was spoken of in this connexion because here again a clear relationship of belonging, which superseded all previous relationships of the kind, was what determined the status of these royal servants. With the increasing elaboration of the monarchy and the creation of further groups of officials the use of the עֶבֶד-idea was extended. All functionaries dependent on the king could be summarily designated 'servants of the king'.[14] Finally, the bearer of an important unique office at the court, whose functions unfortunately are not made plain in the sole reference to him, II Kings 22.12 (II Chron. 34.20), seems to have carried the title עֶבֶד הַמֶּלֶךְ in a very special sense.[15]

---

[12] עַבְדֵי שָׁאוּל I Sam. 18.5; 22.9 etc.; עַבְדֵי אִישׁ־בֹּשֶׁת בֶּן־שָׁאוּל II Sam. 2.12; עַבְדֵי דָוִד II Sam. 2.13, 15, 17, etc.

[13] I Sam. 22.7; the king's right—an ambiguous title—overshadows the voluntary nature of the עֶבֶד, but there is talk of recompense in I Sam. 8.14f. Here and in what follows we may compare with the Arab. *bai'*-covenant (J. Pedersen, *Der Eid bei den Semiten*, 1914, 52–63). On the other hand, it is hardly correct to characterize the עֶבֶד-relationship outright, hence every slave relationship, as 'a בְּרִית-relationship of a *bai'* type' (Lindhagen, 53). However much in Israel the religious עֶבֶד-relationship can be fitted into the בְּרִית-relationship of Israel, the religious עֶבֶד-statements receiving a special stamp, the בְּרִית- and the עֶבֶד-relations are originally different structures.

[14] Thus already in the time of Saul an עֶבֶד seems to have had special charge of the flocks, I Sam. 21.7. The steward Ziba is termed עֶבֶד in II Sam. 9.2 (cf. v. 9)—is that an early form of the household office עַל־הַבָּיִת I Kings 4.6; 16.9? He himself again has עֲבָדִים at his disposal. The counsellors of Saul are so named in I Sam. 16.15. The circle of those courtiers not involved in the war at the time of David is called עֶבֶד II Sam. 11.9, 13; also David's counsellor (II Sam. 15.34) and ambassadors are so named (II Sam. 10.2–4). A comparison of the parallel texts II Kings 19.23 and Isa. 37.24 shows that עֶבֶד can be simply replaced by מַלְאָךְ. In I Kings 11.26 Jeroboam, Solomon's overseer of labour, is called עֶבֶד; cf. II Chron. 13.6.

[15] If Jeroboam named in the inscription of the fine seal found in Megiddo שמע עבד ירבעם were one of the kings of this name (*AOB*[2], *fig.* 578, cf. K. Galling, 'Beschriftete Bildsiegel des I. Jahrtausends', *ZDPV* 64, 1941, 121–202 No. 17), if the עזיו and אחז of the seal inscriptions Galling No. 85 and 125, especially 1a, should mean King Uzziah and Ahaz, then possibly we should have here further allusions to this courtly title which is perhaps directly cited on the seal Galling No. 43 (ליאוניהו עבד המלך). Cf. further p. 32, n. 92; D. Diringer, *Le iscrizioni antico-ebraiche palestinesi*, 1934, 229–31; Lindhagen, 36–39.

(iii) עֶבֶד *as a description of political submission.* More widely and indefinitely עֶבֶד is used to express quite generally the idea of political submission.[16] In this connexion even kings can be described as עֶבֶד (II Sam. 10.19; cf. II Kings 18.24). But always עֶבֶד denotes one who is subject and belongs to a master. There is always latent therein the implication of humiliation which at times comes out unexpectedly in plain lament (Lam. 5.8).

(iv) עֶבֶד *as a humble self-description.* From the language of the court self-reference as עֶבֶד has penetrated as an expression of humility into everyday polite speech.[17] Here at times words may be added which emphasize overmuch the element of meekness.[18]

(v) *The sanctuary servants.* Perhaps the sanctuary servants should be mentioned as a special group. According to Josh. 9.23 Joshua dooms the Gibeonites to be עֶבֶד לְבֵית אֱלֹהַי.[19] But if we regard the O.T. as a whole, what strikes us is how plainly עֶבֶד suggests a personal relationship. Parallels to the formula often to be found in Carthaginian inscriptions, עֶבֶד of the house of God,[20] are lacking in the O.T.[21] This is significant, not merely for an answer to the question about the emergence of a temple

---

[16] Thus the Gibeonites come with the formula of subjection עֲבָדֶיכָם אֲנַחְנוּ Josh. 9.11; cf. I Kings 20.32; II Kings 10.5. For the fuller formula of subjection and demand for help II Kings 16.7: עַבְדְּךָ וּבִנְךָ אָנִי, see *TWNT*, II, 270, 13.

[17] L. Köhler, 'Archaeologisches', *ZAW*, 40, 1922, 43f.; I. Lande, *Formelhafte Wendungen der Umgangssprache im AT*, 1949, 68–71; for courtliness in diplomatic intercourse, *TWNT*, II, 270, n. 40–42. Alongside the polite self-reference of the speaker stands the polite reference to a third party by the speaker as עַבְדְּךָ.

[18] For example Hazael, II Kings 8.13; 'thy servant the dog' or II Sam. 9.8, Mephibosheth, 'What is thy servant that you should have turned to such a dead dog as myself?' Cf. J. A. Knudtzon, *Die El-amarna-Tafeln*, 1915, 60, 6f.; 71, 17f.; 85, 64. For the *ardu/amtu* of the Amarna letters see Lindhagen, 7–30. Further Lande (op. cit. in n. 17), 74–76. The formula עבדך כלב, in the Lachish letters 2.5.6, ed. H. Torczyner, *The Lachish Letters*, 1938, 36f., 92f., 104f.

[19] Is the now intervening 'hewers of wood and drawers of water' a gloss or original? Probably the sanctuary in Gilgal is in question. M. Noth, *Das Buch Josua* (Handbuch z. AT, I, 7)², 1953, 53–59.

[20] עבד בת צדתנת *Corpus Inscriptionum Semiticarum*, I, 1, 1881, No. 247–9, עבד בת אשמן 252, cf. 250f., 253f.

[21] In the enumeration of the sanctuary servants of Ezra 2 and Neh. 7, where a mention of such people would be most expected, we have a group of בְּנֵי עַבְדֵי שְׁלֹמֹה Ezra 2.55, 58; Neh. 7.57, 60; 11.3, who from the time of Solomon must have been appointed to a specific temple service. But it is significant that they are characterized at this late period by their once personal relation as בְּנֵי עַבְדֵי שְׁלֹמֹה.

capitalism, but equally for the appraisement of עֶבֶד-passages in the O.T. עֶבֶד is a person who belongs to a person.

2. עֶבֶד IN RELIGIOUS USAGE

In the religious usage of עֶבֶד are to be found the same three constructions of phrase as in profane usage, together with the construct formation עֶבֶד יהוה,[22] the grouping with a suffix in all three persons, more seldom the combination with לְ.[23]

(i) עֶבֶד *as the humble self-description of the pious in the presence of his God.* The connexion with secular usage can be seen most plainly in the pious man's meek description of himself as he stands in the presence of his God. Just as the inferior, in speaking to the superior, refers to himself humbly as 'thy servant' in the third person, this manner of speech is all the more appropriate when man stands in the presence of God.[24] In this connexion the expression can assume varying emphases. First, in many passages the simple, humble confession of the lowly status of the speaker before his great Lord can be uppermost.[25] Next, from this expression of humble submission can be heard a certain claim. As

---

[22] Thus twenty-one times. Plur. עַבְדֵי יהוה. Only in later times is to be found also during the process of the displacement of the Yahweh name עֶבֶד הָאֱלֹהִים, I Chron. 6.49; II Chron. 24.9; Neh. 10.29; Dan. 9.11. Once in an older text we can recognize the penetration of the Father-God title; in Gen. 50.17 the brothers in the presence of Joseph describe themselves as עַבְדֵי אֱלֹהֵי אָבִיךָ; in the Aram. Dan. Darius describes Daniel as עֲבַד אֱלָהָא חַיָּא, 6.21; elsewhere the three friends are described as עַבְדוֹהִי דִּי אֱלָהָא עִלָּיָא, 3.26. In the Aram. Ezra 5.11 we find in the address to the Persian governor the Jews representing themselves as עַבְדוֹהִי דִּי אֱלָהּ שְׁמַיָּא וְאַרְעָא.

[23] עַבְדִּי 62 times; עֲבָדִי 17 times; עַבְדְּךָ 92 times; עֲבָדֶיךָ 20 times; עַבְדּוֹ 23 times; עֲבָדָיו 16 times. Combination with לְ: sing. Isa. 44.21; 49.5f.; plur. 56.6; Lev. 25.55.

[24] Cf. esp. Baudissin, *Kyrios*, III, 524–55. The similarity between this polite mode of address and the language of religious worship stands out most clearly in those passages where one wonders whether the speaker is aware that he stands in the presence of the divine Lord. In Gen. 18.3, 5 the original text may well have implied that Abraham did not yet recognize Yahweh among his three visitors and hence offered his greetings in the style of polite speech. But the M.T. by its vocalization אֲדֹנָי in v. 3 wishes to express the idea that Abraham is aware of his encounter with God. Clearly any change in the style of address was not thought necessary.

[25] Moses, Ex. 4.10; Num. 11.11; Deut. 3.24. Curiously enough the עֶבֶד-title is missing in Abraham's strong expressions of self depreciation, Gen. 18.27. If H. Torczyner is right in his proposed change of text (בַּעֲבוּר עַבְדְּךָ וְכָלְבָּךְ) 'Dunkle

The Servant of God

in the mouth of Ahaz the formula of subjection turned into the request 'I am thy servant and thy son: come up, and save me' (II Kings 16.7), so the same thing can happen in addressing God. He who confesses allegiance to a master withdraws himself from the dominion of all other possible masters, and so with inner justification can request the master whose allegiance he owns to be careful for his part to preserve his power and to protect his servant. In this sort of situation the honour of the divine Lord is at stake.[26] If in this supplicating approach to the Lord man's own performance is stressed (but I am your worshipper) then the self-description עֶבֶד acquires a strongly active tone. If, on the contrary, the already experienced favour of God is emphasized, then the name עֶבֶד marks the attitude of thankful self-surrender.[27]

What has so far been shown is in no way peculiar to the O.T. These features of pious self-description as עֶבֶד (Babylonian *ardu*) are to be found in exactly the same way in the world surrounding Israel. But three further points are to be noted which characterize the O.T. encounter with God and render intelligible how the O.T. understanding of עֶבֶד could undergo its own peculiarly rich development.

O.T. faith springs from the encounter with Yahweh the jealous Lord (Ex. 20.5; 34.14; Deut. 4.24; 5.9; 6.15; Josh. 24.19; Nahum 1.2). When Ashurbanipal owns himself the servant of Nebo,[28] but

---

Bibelstellen', in *Festschr. K. Marti*, = ZAW, Beiheft 41, 1925, 275), then we should have here in the language of prayer the use of the formula of humility common in profane speech: your servant and dog. Since this type of humble self-expression, which is really de-personalizing, occurs nowhere else in O.T. religious language—is it merely an accident?—there must be doubts about Torczyner's reconstruction of the text.

[26] Ps. 143.11f. 'Quicken me, O Lord, for thy name's sake . . . destroy all them that afflict me; for I am thy servant.' Cf. the Babylonian: 'Quicken thy servant, who wishes to exalt thy power and praise thy greatness among all men', W. Schrank, *Babylonische Sühnriten*, 1908, 56.

[27] Thus for example the inscription on a votive pillar of Malta: 'To our Lord Melkart, the Lord of Tyre, from your devotees your servant (עבדך) Abdosir and my brother Osirshamar, son of Osirshamar, son of Abdosir, for he has heard their voice. May he bless them.' *Corpus Inscriptionum Semiticarum*, I, 1, 1881, No. 122.

[28] J. Pinckert, *Hymnen und Gebete an Nebo*, 1920, 16ff. The text is not quite certain in line 5. But that does not affect the fundamental principle here asserted.

The Servant of God in the Old Testament

at the next New Year's feast again grasps the hands of his land-god Ashur and is again invested by him with his sovereign rights, this self-description as the servant of Nebo cannot be understood in an exclusive sense. In Israel, on the other hand, the self-description of the pious man as עֶבֶד יהוה is characterized by its total claim. The thought 'no man can serve two masters' embraces not merely the moment of the worshipful turning towards God but the whole of life. Alongside it no other עֶבֶד-status is conceivable. The seriousness of this attitude becomes manifest on both sides: Yahweh claims the total obedience of his servant and the latter even in the hour of bitterest trial may claim the protection of this exclusive allegiance.

O.T. faith is aware of a primal inclination of Yahweh to Israel arising from the free grace of Yahweh. In regard to the development of the expression עֶבֶד יהוה this implies that this inclination cannot be realized conclusively in the sphere of individual piety or even in that of any local cult. It stands related to the event of Israel as a whole. The individual can become the servant of Yahweh only in so far as he is a member of Israel; for the will of Yahweh is directed toward Israel. It has become manifest in the deliverance from Egypt and the conclusion of the covenant which followed from it and of which Israel speaks from the earliest times. The servant status of the pious man is to be understood from within the sphere of this relationship which was created not by man but by Yahweh.

O.T. faith realizes that the encounter with Yahweh took place in the midst of history and that it points to an historical goal. Thus the servant character remains not within the timeless sphere of individual piety but gains special importance where Yahweh in his historical meeting with his people calls individuals to some special service.

If we turn now from these conclusions to consider again the humble self-description of the pious which occurs in the O.T., we shall find intelligible the note of ardent trust in the expression. The עֶבֶד state is not one which the pious man has attained through his own achievement or which rests on sacrifices and good works alone. The self-description עַבְדְּךָ gains its security from being felt to be an echo of a call which originally was uttered by the mouth of Yahweh himself. Thus, in Num. 12.7f. Yahweh says in

The Servant of God

emphatic and repeated affirmation of Moses: 'My servant Moses'.[29] But it is also to be heard on the lips of the simple anonymous man of prayer: 'Let thy merciful kindness (חֶסֶד) be for my comfort, according to thy word unto thy servant' (Ps. 119.76). The petitioner dares, on the strength of a word from Yahweh which was directed to him, to approach Yahweh as a servant. The word which the O.T. worshipper hears becomes, however, again and again a word of commanding guidance on the part of the covenant God.[30] 'I have gone astray like a lost sheep; seek thy servant, for I do not forget thy commandments' (Ps. 119.176; cf. vv. 17, 23, 135, 140). The servant is he who is obedient to the command of God. But the עֶבֶד יהוה will also have enemies who are especially sinister because they at the same time embody enmity to Yahweh. Hence the title עַבְדְּךָ may explicitly or implicitly be contrasted with the counter word 'my enemies' (thy, Yahweh's, enemies). 'Let them curse, but bless thou: when they arise let them be ashamed; but let thy servant rejoice' (Ps. 109.28).[31]

(ii) *'Servants of Yahweh' in the plural as denoting the pious.* The expression עֶבֶד יהוה on account of its inner depth acquires great force in the O.T. It is not merely a conventional formula for the individual pious man.[32] It can be freely used in the plural to denote the pious as a whole.[33]

---

[29] As also of Caleb, Num. 14.24, further of David, Isaiah, Eliakim, Nebuchadnezzar etc. It is significant that as against עַבְדְּךָ occurring 92 times in the mouth of the petitioner, עַבְדִּי occurs in the mouth of Yahweh as many as 62 times (in the plural 20 עֲבָדַי to 17 עֲבָדֶיךָ).

[30] Cf. for example Ps. 50 or the torah Psalms 15 and 24.

[31] It is not necessary in this connexion to discuss the problem of the 'enemies' in the Psalms.

[32] In the world of the ancient Near East surrounding Israel the עֶבֶד title seems to have been mainly used in this formula of humble self-description and in the giving of names. The Malta inscription quoted in n. 27, p. 16, above, may perhaps give us some idea of the rigidity of this type of formula. Although two benefactors are there named they do not dare to use the formula in the plural but say clumsily 'Thy servant and my brother'. As for the giving of names cf. especially the rich material in Baudissin, *Kyrios*, III, 531–48. For Ras Shamra see Lindhagen, 30–31. For O.T. giving of names M. Noth, *Die israelitischen Personennamen im Rahmen der gemeinsemitischen Namengebung*, 1928, 137–8. In Karatepe *'ztwd* is denoted as עבד בעל (A. Alt, 'Die phönikischen Inschriften von Karatepe', in *Die Welt des Orients*, 1949, 272–87).

[33] Ps. 113.1 and 135.1f. mention the worshipping community in the temple or the circle of priests, 134.1 mentions a vigil. Ps. 112.1 LXX (παῖδες), 'A, Σ, Θ (δοῦλοι) and 134.1 LXX (δοῦλοι) seem to use the description 'your servants' absolutely and the construct state עַבְדֵי יְ is misunderstood (αἰνεῖτε, παῖδες, κύριον). The Hebrew text knows nothing of the absolute use.

The Servant of God in the Old Testament

Synonymous parallels may elucidate for us their inner meaning. Servants of Yahweh are those who 'seek refuge in him' (Ps. 34.22), who 'love his name' (Ps. 69.36)—here the possession of the land of Yahweh's inheritance is ascribed to the servants of Yahweh, his saints (= those who are bound to him in חָסָד, Ps. 79.2). Or most briefly and pregnantly: 'his people' (Ps. 105.25; 135.14). Here plainly an allusion to divine election is linked with the עֶבֶד idea.³⁴ In Trit. Isa. the cleavage of the community into servants and enemies of Yahweh is strongly emphasized (Isa. 65.13ff.). Further, the two poles of the עֶבֶד idea are clearly recognizable. Isa. 56.6 describes obedience to the laws of the covenant as the basis of the עֶבֶד status, while 65.9, by equating servants of Yahweh and 'elect', lays all the emphasis on the divine election. These elect are the visible pledge of the gracious favour of Yahweh. 'So will I do for my servants' sake' is his own gracious promise (Isa. 65.8).

(iii) עֶבֶד יהוה *in the singular as a description of Israel*. This humble self-description of the individual saint leads to the characterization of Israel in the singular as the עֶבֶד יהוה which probably started with Deutero-Isaiah.³⁵ The latter formulates most of his words of promise in the style of the priestly oracles of deliverance.³⁶ The promise given by the priest to the suppliant corresponds closely in style to the lament with which the suppliant approaches his God.³⁷ Thus the oracle takes up the liturgical word usual in such individual laments, 'I am thy servant', and embeds it in the quite new context of the comforting divine assurance: 'But thou, Israel, art my servant, Jacob whom I have chosen, seed of Abraham my friend; thou whom I have taken from the ends of the earth, and called thee from the chief men thereof, and said unto thee, Thou art my servant, I have chosen thee, and not cast thee away.'³⁸

---

³⁴ Lindhagen, 153–5.
³⁵ If we take the mention in Jer. 30.10 (see p. 20, n. 41, below) as original then we find the beginning of this development in Jer. In that case the slender amount of testimony to this impressive new use in Jer. is striking. Is it that Jer. found it in a tradition of prophetic language unknown to us and used it only incidentally? The striking freshness which the phrase has in Deut. Isa. seems to me to point to the fact that its manifestation here is an innovation.
³⁶ Begrich, *Heilsorakel*, 81–92, and *Studien*, 6–19, 137, 140f.
³⁷ H. Gunkel-J. Begrich, *Einl. in die Ps.*, 1933, § 6, cf. also § 4.
³⁸ Isa. 41.8ff. Cf. further 44.1f.; 45.4. In the exhortatory word 44.21. In a brief order 48.20.

The Servant of God

The title is transformed in the mouth of Yahweh. No longer does there stand in the foreground the humble confession of the people crushed in exile (conceived by this prophet in full personal terms as an individual figure), but the powerful, gracious use of it by Yahweh. In statements which go far beyond the concept master-servant and are not levelled out, the idea of belonging utterly to Yahweh by grace is brought to expression. Israel the עֶבֶד יהוה has been created by Yahweh (44.2, 21), chosen by him (41.8f.; 44.1; 45.4), fetched from the ends of the earth (41.9), and is the seed of Abraham the friend of God (41.8). With the formula already found in the Babylonian oracles of favour, she is urged to be fearless (44.2). Yahweh promises her help, indeed, the help of ransom secured to the blood relation (48.20).[39] There is no talk of any initiative to be taken by the servant Israel herself. If 42.19 refers to Israel then she is even declared to be utterly blind (cf. 43.8). The witnessing to the power of Yahweh which she is summoned to undertake[40] is that of a passive recipient of a gift. 'To return'—that is the sole activity to which the people is summoned (44.22); to return in view of the saving deed which Yahweh alone has accomplished.[41]

(iv) עֶבֶד עבד *as a title for specially distinguished figures.* Yahweh made contact with his people Israel in history, and held them to history as the place where he is near and where responsible decision is made. Hence it is not surprising that O.T. faith again and again sees in history figures whom it recognizes pre-eminently as

---

[39] J. J. Stamm. *Erlösen und Vergeben im AT*, 1940, 27–45.
[40] 43.10. It is debatable whether here by עֶבֶד Israel is meant or an individual figure alongside the people.
[41] The style of Deut. Isa. is echoed in Jer. 30.10 (par. 46.27f.), cf. p. 19, n. 35. In Ezek. 28.25; 37.25 it is a question whether by the servant is meant the patriarch Jacob or the people. In the similar expression in Ps. 136.22, which uses the name Israel, it is clear on the other hand that the people is indicated. This is the text where Lindhagen most dangerously misleads. Since in his examination he does not distinguish noun and verb, he is unable to see the narrowly defined limits within which alone the singular עֶבֶד title is used for Israel. The abundant use of the verbal עבד for Israel conceals them from him. Consequently the whole arrangement of his study gives the impression that the references to the servant of Yahweh apply to Israel in the first instance (the major section goes under the heading 'Israel as Yahweh's Servant', 82–233), and only secondarily do individual pious men bear the title עֶבֶד יהוה (233–62 deals with the nucleus of pious as עֶבֶד יהוה, 262–88 with 'The Servant as Individual Members of the People of Israel'). The real state of affairs for the substantive use of עֶבֶד is exactly the opposite.

servants of Yahweh. We must now consider these outstanding representatives of the עֶבֶד יהוה status. It is to be expected from the outset that profane courtly usage, which is also aware of these pre-eminent and marked עֶבֶד figures as contrasted with the general use of the title, will not have been without influence.

(a) Israel finds the beginnings of its history embodied in the figures of the patriarchs. In them the gracious character of Yahweh's revelation,[42] which began long before Israel was a people, is expressed most clearly. Thus it is to be understood that wherever the fathers are spoken of as servants of Yahweh, the idea of a gracious relationship to Yahweh is clearly presupposed. The patriarchs are pledges of the divine will to save. Yahweh promises blessing to Isaac for the sake of Abraham his servant.[43] In a specially dark hour for the people Moses implores Yahweh by reminding him of the oath which he sware to the fathers whom he names.

(b) Moses stands on the threshold of the people's history. Forty times in the M.T. the name of עֶבֶד is given to him. Two pre-Deuteronomic passages do so with especial emphasis. In Num. 12.7f. Moses is differentiated by a divine explanation from those prophets who know God only in a dream or vision. 'Not so is my servant Moses, who is faithful in all mine house. With him I speak mouth to mouth . . . wherefore then were ye not afraid to speak against my servant Moses?' Moses is the vizier, the true steward of Yahweh. We are reminded of the faithful servant of Abraham (cf. p. 12). In Ex. 14.31 (J), after Israel had been saved at the Red Sea by the leadership of Moses, 'then they believed Yahweh and Moses his servant'. Moses is only Yahweh's servant. But in what he powerfully accomplished Yahweh was so obviously present that the people's responsive faith submits to Moses and to Yahweh in him. An essential feature of the biblical revelation comes out here. God's history is not transcendental heavenly history. It stoops to earth and

[42] So at least according to the popular tradition which is especially manifest in Gen. Otherwise with the prophets: Hos. 12.3ff.; Jer. 9.4; Isa. 43.27.
[43] Gen. 26.24, cf. Ps. 105.6, 42. Only in the speech of Abraham's servant is Isaac called 'servant of Yahweh' (Gen. 24.14). In the mention of the name Jacob, the difficulty is in each case to decide whether the patriarch Jacob is designated, or the people called after him. See n. 41. Cf. in I Chron. 16.13 the distorted quotation from Ps. 105.6.

The Servant of God

appoints men with their deeds and words as its signs. Moses, Yahweh's servant, embodies in his activity such a part of divine history. Obedience or disobedience to his word is decisive for men's attitude to Yahweh. Moses is much more emphatically than the patriarchs an active servant-figure. He shapes the law (Josh. 1.2, 7; II Kings 18.12; Mal. 4.4, etc.), orders particular matters with regard to the possession of the land (Josh. 1.13, 15; 8.31), prescribes cultic matters (II Chron. 1.3; 24.6), and promises coming peace in the land (I Kings 8.53, 56). But behind it all stands the election of Yahweh who appoints to him and Aaron their service.[44]

(c) The further series of servants of Yahweh can be clearly divided into two lines of development. First, the king, who has to perform an outstanding service in Israel. 'By the hand of my servant David I will save my people Israel out of the hand of the Philistines and out of the hand of their enemies', is Yahweh's word in the certainly pre-Deuteronomic text of II Sam. 3.18. The king is the servant of Yahweh with the special duty of saving the people of God out of the hand of their enemies—but not every king. From the promise to Nathan we see a second development: David, in virtue of a special bond of grace, is the pre-eminent king of the holy people. Hence in the Deuteronomic history, where the description of David as עֶבֶד יהוה is especially frequent, the blameless obedience of David can be strongly emphasized, and also the duty of the servant in regard to meritoriousness. But only in appearance. The same Deuteronomic history especially stresses the basic fact of divine election[45] which again shows the Davidic monarchy to be a pure gift of grace. I Kings 11.34 combines the two factors into a tense duality: 'David my servant, whom I chose because he kept

---

[44] Cf. the parallel statement in Ps. 105.26. In the after-glow of the story of Moses, Joshua also can once (Josh. 24.29 = Judg. 2.8), as the one who completes the work of Moses, be called 'Servant of Yahweh'. In the case of Caleb the faithful informant (Num. 14.24), on the other hand, the thought of obedience is stressed.

[45] I Kings 11.13, 32 names, in conjunction, David and the chosen city of Jerusalem as the pledge of Yahweh's fidelity. H. J. Kraus, *Die Königsherrschaft Gottes im Alten Testament*, 1951, 58f., believes that this double election has its cultic background in a 'royal Zion feast'. However, cf. against this view, among others, H. Gese, 'Der Davidsbund und die Zionserwählung', *ZTK*, 61, 1964, 10–26. I Kings 11.36 and II Kings 8.19 mention the will of Yahweh to give David a lamp. II Kings 19.34 and 20.6 formulate most strongly the significance of David as the divinely ordained symbol of salvation: 'For my . . . and my servant David's sake' Yahweh wills to help.

The Servant of God in the Old Testament

my commandments and my statutes.' The more their history runs into disaster the more intensely O.T. faith clings to the figure of David, the servant of God, as a token of promise. It waits for the day when this servant will again be king (Ezek. 34.23f.; 37.24f.). It reminds Yahweh of the oath which he sware to his chosen servant David (Ps. 89.3; cf. v. 20). It speaks of the indissoluble bond which Yahweh made with his servant David (Jer. 33.21f., 26).[46] Immediately after the exile we see the same hope flare up. The post-exilic successor of David, Zerubbabel, who in Zech. 3.8 is described with the secret messianic title צֶמַח, gains here and in Hag. 2.23, from the mouth of Yahweh, the additional title of honour עַבְדִּי.[47] Jer. 25.9; 27.6; 43.10, show[48] that the description of a king as עֶבֶד יהוה, even in the context of prophetic declaration of judgement, can have a peculiar emphasis. In Nebuchadnezzar the stern holiness of Yahweh appointed, with limited mission, a royal servant who was foreign to Israel. Here too the divine will expresses itself through the servant in human form. Whoever resists Nebuchadnezzar, resists Yahweh (Jer. 27–29).

(*d*) The line of prophets stands beside that of kings. The prophet is Yahweh's word-messenger. The office of messenger existed in the royal service too.[49] The report of David's embassy to Hanun (II Sam. 10.2ff.) shows clearly how closely the honour of the messenger is bound up with that of the king. From I Kings 18.36 we can see that the same thing applies to the servant of God. Elijah prays on Carmel: 'Yahweh God of Abraham, Isaac and Israel, let it be known this day that thou art

---

[46] How closely the cause of Yahweh, and that of his royal servant of the lineage of David, are bound up together is shown by the statement about Sennacherib's messengers, who speak against the Lord 'and against his servant Hezekiah' II Chron. 32.16 (still more strongly expressed, without the use of עֶבֶד in I Chron. 28.5; 29.23; II Chron. 13.18). Yahweh's honour is involved in the affair of Hezekiah. Cf. what was said about Ex. 14.31 on p. 21.

[47] An unknown Davidite; Ps. 89.39, 50. Cf. also I Kings 8.30, 36 (corrected text), 52, 59.

[48] But the pre-hexaplar LXX reads עַבְדִּי only in the second passage (δουλεύειν αὐτῷ לְעָבְדוֹ). The statement about Nebuchadnezzar sounds so peculiar that it is not likely to be a new formation of later times. Since intrinsically it fits best with the oracles of Jeremiah its invention by the latter is the most satisfactory supposition.

[49] For the alternation of עֶבֶד and מַלְאָךְ see p. 13, n. 14 above. Isa. 44.26 (amended text) shows a corresponding parallel for the office of the prophetic messenger of God, Job 4.18 for that of heavenly messenger.

The Servant of God

God in Israel, and that I am thy servant, and that I have done all these things at thy word.' Yahweh's history is again present in the midst of men through his authorized messenger. The knowledge of God depends upon the knowledge of his servant. In the Deuteronomic writing of history, the prophet gains an almost instrumental significance. Constantly his teaching reveals the course of history as a redemption of the divine pledges made in prophecy.[50] Thus Ahijah of Shiloh (I Kings 14.18; 15.29), Elijah (II Kings 9.36; 10.10) and Jonah ben Amittai—as prophet of good things—(II Kings 14.25) are described as servants of Yahweh.[51] In the wider range of Deuteronomic writing the usual formula of ' "my" ("thy", "his") servants the prophets' has crystallized into a cliché. It becomes a firm mode of thought employed mostly in a specific type of theological context. These messengers are the great admonishers of the people[52] sent by Yahweh, without intermission. In all these passages there comes to the fore a definite active mission on the part of the servant. The parallel with the royal court can be specially clearly seen here. To the heavenly court of Yahweh belong these servants who perform his commissions on earth. Job 4.18 adds the thought of the heavenly messengers with their appointed tasks.[53]

In the older narratives (especially of Elisha) seer and prophet are given the probably pre-exilic title[54] אִישׁ הָאֱלֹהִים.[55] The subsequent replacement of this by עֶבֶד might well have been due to the desire to see the weaker אלהים supplanted by יהוה,[56] but even more the unrelated אִישׁ supplanted by עֶבֶד which expresses more sharply the sense of fully belonging to God.[57] On the

---

[50] G. von Rad, *Studies in Deuteronomy*, 1953, pp. 74ff. The thought was then taken up by Deut. Isa. and made an important pillar of his argument against the idols of the heathen (Isa. 41.22f., 26f.; 42.9 etc.).

[51] In Isa. 20.3, Isaiah too is called 'my servant' by Yahweh.

[52] II Kings 9.7; 17.13, 23; 21.10; 24.2; Jer. 7.25; 25.4; 26.5; 29.19; 35.15; 44.4; Ezek. 38.17; Amos 3.7 (probably a later addition); Zech. 1.6; Dan. 9.6, 10; Ezra 9.11.

[53] I Kings 22.19ff. shows both circles of the heavenly court in a peculiar connexion. The name עֶבֶד is not mentioned here.

[54] Noth (loc. cit. in n. 32).

[55] LXX II Chron. 24.6 translates Moses' title עֶבֶד יהוה by ἄνθρωπος τοῦ Θεοῦ.

[56] For the late development see n. 22.

[57] אִישׁ can also express the idea of belonging to a collective, e.g., in the plural, the men of Kirjath-jearim (I Sam. 7.1), of Jabesh (I Sam. 11.5, 10). Such a use is inconceivable with עֶבֶד, cf. p. 14, n. 21.

The Servant of God in the Old Testament

other hand, the older writing prophets clearly avoid[58] the use of עֶבֶד as a description of their office. An attempt has been made to explain this by suggesting that the word עֶבֶד implies 'the bondage of man's will to the will of God', whereas the prophets 'demand a free decision for obedience to the will of God'.[59] This explanation is not convincing. A more adequate suggestion is that the description of oneself or others as עֶבֶד יהוה is rooted in the cultic style of the sanctuaries (cf. the Psalms) and of popular piety—shaped by courtly style. The older writing prophecy stands in strong opposition to this type of piety and avoids its terminology.[60] It is significant that the terminology in the Deuteronomic sections of Jer. and especially in Deut. Isa.,[61] whose close affinity with popular prophecy and the Psalms is becoming ever plainer, gains more and more ground.

(e) In the framework of the book of Job, the latter is several times named by Yahweh 'my servant' (1.8; 2.3; 42.7f.). Here, in the frame of wisdom theology, the writer speaks freely of a 'servant of Yahweh' outside the borders of Israel. What is correctly displayed in Job's fidelity is, despite the fact that in Job's own words the name of Yahweh is avoided, the best biblical awareness of Yahweh's immovable connexion with his creation (cf. for instance, 14.13–15). Further, the active obedience of the servant of God is here vigorously stressed. Job's fear of God, which was vividly depicted in the introduction, proves itself in faithful obedience, since in spite of all the temptation of Satan he does not renounce God with a curse. Hence God acknowledges Job by graciously naming him his own servant (עֶבֶד) as against the calumniating speech of Satan (1.8; 2.3), and the self-righteous speeches of the friends (42.7f.).

(v) *The Suffering Servant of Deutero-Isaiah*. The O.T. usage of עֶבֶד יהוה reached its fulfilment in the suffering servant passages in Deutero-Isaiah.

---

[58] Amos 3.7 is probably secondary; Isa. 20.3 seems to be a report at third hand, cf. O. Procksch, *Isaiah I*, 1930, 255. Isa. 37.35 comes from the Isaiah legend; thus 22.20 remains, if genuine (it is not the prophet himself, however, but the court official, Eliakim, who is given the title עֶבֶד in a prophetic utterance).
[59] Baudissin, *Entwicklung*, 8.
[60] Cf. the terms 'covenant', 'election', the patriarchal theology.
[61] The passages in Isa. which have the religious use of עֶבֶד seem likewise to come from the groups of pupils.

The Servant of God

Since in 1892 Duhm took from their context the passages Isa. 42.1–4; 49.1–6; 50.4–9 and 52.13–53.12, and referred them to a later time as songs depicting the fate of an unknown teacher of the torah, the question of their connexion with Deutero-Isaiah has been much discussed.[62] Closer examination has shown how intimately they[63] are related to Deut. Isa., as regards diction, style, and pattern of structure.[64] This applies least to 52.13–53.12 where the middle portion (53.1–11a), in particular, stands out as a song of thanksgiving by the community, with characteristic style and peculiarity of diction.[65] Even in content it goes beyond the matter of the first songs. But it is impossible to free it from the framework of Yahweh's word (52.13–15; 53.11b, 12), which for its part is inseparable from 49.7. But the latter is more strongly Deutero-Isaian in style, and in thought is not far removed from 50.4–9. So 52.13–53.12, the final mystery of which is not yet cleared up, appears firmly attached to the whole cycle of songs and is, like the other songs, to be interpreted in the light of Deutero-Isaiah's message.

(a) How is the figure of the עֶבֶד to be explained? In the history of exposition there have been from early times two main opposing contentions. Consideration of the present text of 49.3, and of the otherwise predominant use of the עֶבֶד title in Deut. Isa. (cf. p. 19 above), pointed inevitably to the collective interpretation of Israel as a whole.[66] In contrast with that stands the idea of an individual figure suggested by the songs.[67] Reflection on the religious use of the עֶבֶד concept in the O.T. where, except for the unambiguous

---

[62] A full history of recent exposition is given by North in the first part of his book, also by H. H. Rowley, 'The Servant of the Lord in the Light of Three Decades of Criticism', in: *The Servant of the Lord and Other Essays on the Old Testament*, 1952, 3–57.
[63] To them should probably be added 42.5–9; 49.7, 8–13. Cf. Begrich, *Studien*, 74f., 131–51.
[64] Cf. Gressmann, 'Analyse'; also Köhler and Begrich, *Studien*. Mowinckel, 'Komposition', does not pay sufficient attention, in his counter-argument, to the conclusions established in regard to style and genre.
[65] A separate origin for 52.13–53.12, has been argued even in recent times by Elliger, Volz and Sellin.
[66] The text was already modified in that sense in the LXX 42.1 (see pp. 42f.). Cf. in the middle ages the Jewish exegesis by Rashi, Ibn Ezra, Kimchi; and later J. Wellhausen, *Israelitische und jüdische Gesch.*, 1894, 117–18. See Giesebrecht, Budde, *Ebed Jahve-Lieder*, 34, Eissfeldt, 268, and others.
[67] The oldest piece of evidence is probably Isa. 61.1ff. Cf. also W. Zimmerli, 'Zur Sprache Tritjs's', in *Festschr. L. Köhler*, 1950, 69–71 (reprinted in W. Zimmerli, *Gottes Offenbarung. Gesammelte Aufsätze*, 1963, 226–8). LXX particularly for 52.13ff., cf. p. 43 below. Cf. further the question of the eunuch, Acts 8.34. More recently, see n. 70.

The Servant of God in the Old Testament

collective application in Deut. Isa., the individual application predominates (cf. pp. 20ff.), is not itself decisive. The suggestion of an individual meaning might well commend itself to us from 49.5f. If the words of God here, which answer a complaint of the servant, refer to an originally more limited mission of the עֶבֶד to Israel and to its later expansion to cover the gentiles, then there are insuperable difficulties in the way of the collective interpretation.[68] In the יִשְׂרָאֵל of 49.3 we shall have to see an early, but in the text a secondary *midrash*[69] made in a collective sense while the original text will have to be interpreted in an individual sense. But in that case, what kind of an individual is meant? The use of the עֶבֶד title elsewhere in the O.T. apart from its application to the great figures of early times (patriarchs and Moses), suggests two main lines of development: the Messiah-King (see p. 22) and the prophets (see p. 23). Attempts have been made to solve the עֶבֶד riddle by means of both these types.[70] A closer study of the character of the servant's office, the means of its fulfilment described

---

[68] The reckless adjustment of the text by Giesebrecht, 44f., will convince as little as the tortured reinterpretation of Budde (in Kautzsch ad loc.). Again, the recent attempts at collective interpretation by Eissfeldt and H. Wheeler Robinson, 58-62, do indeed give us important information about the conception of the people as a collective personality but do not really get to grips with the text of Deut. Isa. Finally the assertion that the issue ought not to be presented as a stark alternative (e.g., A. Bentzen, *Introduction to the O.T.*, II, 1949, 113. 'Ebed Yahweh is both the Messiah and Israel and Deutero-Isaiah and his band of disciples', *inter alia*) seems to me to serve only to befog the whole problem. J. Lindblom, *The Servant Songs*, tries another way to combine both tendencies of interpretation by understanding the songs as 'allegorical pictures'. 42.1-4; 49.1-6; 50.4-9 and 53.2-13 depict an individual figure, but they mean Israel. This is brought out by the interpretations which either follow the songs (in 42.4-9; 49.7; 50.10f.) or precede it (in 52.13-53.1). Rowley finds in the songs a development from collective toward individual understanding.

[69] For the possibility of such interpretations cf. LXX of 42.1. J. A. Bewer has shown in 'The Text-critical Value of the Hebrew MS Ken. 96 for Isaiah 49.3', in *Jewish Studies in Memory of G. A. Kohut*, 1935, 86-88; also in 'Textkritische Bemerkungen', in *Festschrift für A. Bertholet*, 1950, 67-68, that the MS Kennicott 96 in which יִשְׂרָאֵל in 49.3 is absent cannot be adduced as evidence of sound tradition. The gloss goes back behind all the textual evidence at our disposal (cf. also M. Burrows, *The Dead Sea Scrolls of St Mark's Monastery*, I: *The Isaiah Manuscript and the Habakkuk Commentary*, 1950, plate 40, line 30).

[70] For the kingly line the following have been thought of: Uzziah: see J. W. C. Augusti, 'Über den König Usia nebst einer Erläuterung Is 53', in *Magazin für Religionsphilosophie, Exegese und Kirchengeschichte*, 3, 1795, 282-99; K. Dietze, *Ussia, der Knecht Gottes*, 1929; Hezekiah: L. Itkonen, 'Dtjs metrisch untersucht', *Annales Academiae Fennicae*, 14, 1916; Jehoiachin: E. Sellin, *Studien zur Entstehungsgeschichte der jüdischen Gemeinde*, 1901, 284-97, also *Das Rätsel des deuterojesajanischen Buches*, 1908, 144-50; Zerubbabel: E. Sellin, *Serubbabel*, 148-92; the Messiah: Gressmann, *Messias*, 337ff., J. Fischer, *Isaias 40-55 und die Perikopen vom Gottesknecht*, 1916, 165. Kaiser, *Der königliche Knecht*, also emphasizes the royal traits, but finds Israel behind the עֶבֶד.

The Servant of God

in 50.4ff. (ear, tongue), and unmistakable points of contact with Jeremiah's and Ezekiel's narratives of their call, seem to recommend a prophetic basis.[71] The features suggesting kingly action (execution of judgment, 42.1, 3f., release of captives, 42.7; 49.9 and the sharp sword, 49.2), can also be understood from a prophetic point of view.[72]

(b) What individual prophetic figure may have determined the character of the עֶבֶד? The supposition is very strong that in the songs something of the mission of Deutero-Isaiah has been reflected,[73] and there receives an interpretation which transcends the framework of his life and dares by faith to attain an ultimate insight.[74] (See *TWNT*, IV, 616, 30ff.[75]) The striking element of objectification and concealment under the anonymous title עֶבֶד יהוה may well imply that the prophet did not wish to be misunderstood simply in subjective-biographical terms.[76] The figure

---

For the prophetic line the following have been thought of: Moses: E. Sellin, *Mose*, 108–13; Isaiah: C. F. Stäudlin, *Neue Beiträge zur Erläuterung der bibl. Propheten*, 1791; Jeremiah: C. J. Bunsen, *Vollst. Bibelwerk für die Gemeinde*, vol. 2, 1860, 438; Ezekiel: R. Krätzschmar, *Ezechiel*, 1900, among others. For the whole history of these types of exegesis see North.

[71] We have already referred to the high valuation of the prophets' word which illuminates history (Deut. Isa. uses for them the עֶבֶד title in 44.26 [amended text]) as a trait akin to that of the Deuteronomist; cf. n. 50.

[72] Whether the passion features may be claimed as something distinctive of kings, thus coming to Deut. Isa. from the ritual of the suffering atoning king, or had influenced the whole class of individual songs of lament, has been much discussed recently. See Dürr, Engnell, Bentzen and Gressmann, *Ursprung* (329–33), who argues on the basis of the Tammuz ritual. One wonders whether it would be easier and more likely to suppose that these timeless traits of a ritual king-liturgy should reach the O.T. from Babylonian cultic life, which Deutero-Isaiah passionately rejected, rather than from the prophetic confessions of Jeremiah (n. 75), which arose out of the trials of a specific historical mission. This is not to exclude the possibility that at individual points old cultic formulae may have exerted an influence and moulded language *via* Psalmody, already extant in Canaan and cultivated at the time of the kings. But such formulae can hardly have constituted the real impulse to the formation of the image of the servant in the mind of Deutero-Isaiah, with his passionate faith in historical decision.

[73] First impressively substantiated by Mowinckel in *Knecht*, then later rejected by himself in his 'Komposition'.

[74] Cf. the analogy of the kingly line, and see G. von Rad, 'Erwägungen zu den Königspsalmen', *ZAW*, 58, 1940–1, 216–22.

[75] This is suggested also by the parallelism with Jeremiah's confessions. They too, similarly interspersed into the literary framework of Jeremiah's book, show the inner vision on which the duty of obedience rests, the inescapability of the prophet's mission, and especially the path of suffering which prophecy involved. But that which with Jeremiah remains in the darkness of mystery (20.14ff.) with Deutero-Isaiah reaches a characteristically ultimate answer which rounds off O.T. insights.

[76] That the confessions of Jeremiah too show the struggle against his duty is shown by G. von Rad, 'Die Konfessionen Jeremias', *Evangelische Theologie*, 3, 1936, 265–76.

The Servant of God in the Old Testament

is called עֶבֶד. As in the story of the servant in Gen. 24 (cf. p. 12 above), the omission of any proper name is meant to express the fact that the true essence of this mysterious figure lies in its belonging to another—here Yahweh.[77] Thus it becomes plain that the link is not with a thing but with a person (see p. 15). The reference to a servant occurs mostly in passages where the word of Yahweh makes a decisive call (42.1; 49.3, 6; 52.13; 53.11; only 49.5 in the third person). The servant has been fashioned by Yahweh (42.6; 49.5, 8) from his mother's womb (49.5; cf. v.1). He is the chosen one on whom Yahweh's favour has been focused (42.1), whom the hand of Yahweh has seized (42.1). He has been called by Yahweh (42.6; 49.1) in truth (i.e., validly, 42.6). His name has been named with all the solemnity of a name-giving.[78] To this decisive election is added equipment for service. Yahweh endows his servant with his Spirit.[79] He touches and makes ready for his use those organs which are of especial importance for the fulfilment of the prophet's mission: the ear (50.4f.), and the mouth (49.2; 50.4).[80]

(c) In what does the duty of this servant messenger consist? In the introductory words of 42.1-4, where Yahweh offers his servant a wider sphere of public service and which gives Yahweh's call to the prophet as something turned outwards,[81] there occurs three times, in an absolute sense, the word מִשְׁפָּט to indicate the content of the servant's preaching (42.1, 3, 4). Our whole interpretation of the servant's task will turn on our understanding of these words. Is it here suggested that the duty of the servant is to

---

[77] Do we not find there perfectly expressed the state which Jeremiah had differently suggested in one of his confessions? 'When I found thy words I devoured them. Thy word was a joy and it became the delight of my heart that I am called by thy name, O Lord' (15.16).

[78] 49.1. For הִזְכִּיר שֵׁם see Ex. 20.24; 23.13; Josh. 23.7. Cf. W. Schottroff, 'Gedenken' im Alten Orient und im Alten Testament (Wissenschaftliche Monographien zum Alten und Neuen Testament, 13), 1964.

[79] 42.1. Here there is a connexion with a saying from the old popular type of prophecy (cf. II Kings 2.9) which had fallen into the background with the great writing prophets. Cf. P. Volz, Der Geist Gottes, 1910, 24, 62–69. In the rendering of the saying in Isa. 61.1 (cf. n. 67) we find also the thought of the anointing of the prophet, which can likewise be attested in the older type of prophecy (cf. I Kings 19.16). Cf. E. Kutsch, Salbung als Rechtsakt im Alten Testament und im Alten Orient (ZAW, Beiheft 87), 1963, 62.

[80] Cf. Jer. 1.9; Isa. 6.7 and Ezek. 3.1ff.

[81] A N.T. analogy is the juxtaposition of the word at the baptism addressed to Jesus himself in Mark 1.11; Luke 3.22; and the address to the bystanders in Matt. 3.17. More expressly in Matt. 17.5 (Mark 9.7, Luke 9.35).

spread abroad[82] the truth,[83] 'the only valid religion since Yahweh is the only God',[84] 'the true law in which Yahweh's Spirit has found perfect expression'?[85] In that case the servant might be thought of simply in terms of a missionary whose task it was to convert men everywhere to this true and timeless insight—a work which it is difficult to conceive as practicable for a single individual, and against which the objections of those who support the collective idea are justified. Or should we not see here rather in strict historical connexion the suggestion of an instruction in judgment and right (in 42.4 the parallelism of מִשְׁפָּט and תּוֹרָתוֹ) which is rooted in the accompanying divine execution of judgments in history? It cannot be denied that this second line of understanding is far nearer to what we know of prophecy in general than the first, which would make of Deutero-Isaiah a teacher of religion in quite a new style.

What then is the history with which the proclamation of מִשְׁפָּט coheres, and wherein by reason of its content it is rooted? In Isa. 42.2f. the content of this proclamation of מִשְׁפָּט is indicated by means of three images, which possibly stemmed from the sphere of law-symbolism and leave no doubt about the historical place where the proclamation is made. The pictures of the herald who, contrary to custom, does not cry aloud, of the bruised reed which symbolizes the death sentence, and which contrary to expectation does not break, and of the smoking flax never quite extinguished, are designed to express the surprising act of grace by which Yahweh establishes justice.[86] Isa. 42.7 speaks more clearly of the release of captives, and in 49.5f. it is quite openly stated that, in concrete terms, it is a question of the restoration of the preserved of Israel, i.e., of the exiles, and of the gathering together of the people (v. 5 should read יִשְׂרָאֵל לוֹ יֵאָסֵף). The passage 49.8ff de-

---

[82] On מִשְׁפָּט cf. further *TWNT*, III, 932; J. Pedersen, *Israel, its life and culture*, I-II, 1946, 348–52. Oddly enough K. Fahlgren, *ṣᵉdākā nahestehende und entgegengesetzte Begriffe im A.T.*, 1932, 120–38, which treats of מִשְׁפָּט, does not speak of Isa. 42.1–4.

[83] Volz, ad loc.

[84] Budde in Kautzsch, ad. loc.

[85] W. Hertzberg, 'Die Entwicklung des Begriffes משפט im A.T.', *ZAW*, 41, 1923, 41, n. 1.

[86] The images of the sword and the arrow (49.2) are meant to express the idea that the Word of God in the mouth of the prophet has the power of penetration (cf. Jer. 23.29). They ought not in sentimental fashion to be set over against 42.2f. (against Volz, ad loc.).

The Servant of God in the Old Testament

scribes this restoration, in harmony with the joyful tones of Deutero-Isaiah's message elsewhere, as a return journey through a now transformed desert blessed with water, and as a new taking possession of the devastated promised land. At the same time it becomes clear that in all that, not only is there intended an external historical restitution but an establishment of justice which will transform Israel both outwardly and inwardly. The eyes of the blind shall be opened (42.7; cf. the blind people 43.8); darkness will be pierced with light (49.9); Israel will again find her God and will recognize his faithfulness (hence the call to return 44.22). Thus Yahweh marvellously establishes his justice for a people which had dejectedly complained of the loss of its right (40.27).

But that does not exhaust this process. Isa. 49.5f. reports a mighty expansion of the mission of the servant which will be made clear to him just when he despairs of the success of his efforts.[87] Already in 42.1f. it is stressed that the judgement, מִשְׁפָּט, though obviously concerning Israel in the first instance, shall be proclaimed to all peoples even to the farthest isles.[88] In 49.5f. what is there suggested incidentally becomes a full and direct statement: the servant will be a light for the whole earth.[89] His activity, which takes place against the background of Yahweh's vindication of Israel,[90] soon to be historically manifested, destroys

---

[87] In a striking parallel (Jer. 12.1-6) the downcast prophet is 'comforted' by Yahweh's reference to an increased burden.
[88] The parallel in Jeremiah's call, who is from the beginning appointed as a prophet to the nations (1.5, 10), although at first his activity is limited to Judah, must not be overlooked at this point.
[89] Cf. also in 42.6 אוֹר גּוֹיִם, which is, however, not an assured reading (Ziegler, *Untersuchungen*, 54). If the associated בְּרִית עָם which occurs again alone in 49.8 is to be understood as a synonymous phrase, then the scope of the servant's mission is here widened as is also the covenant category stemming from Israel's history; he becomes a בְּרִית for the peoples. In this there is in view the thought of the covenant as a gift of grace; cf. Begrich, 'Berith', *ZAW*, 60, 1944, 1-11 and *TWNT*, I, 34, n. 73. The idea of the covenant can hardly be interpreted here in a narrow juristic way. It includes the two points: first, the fact that Yahweh's salvation extends to the ends of the earth (49.6); and second, that consequently every knee should bow and every tongue confess Yahweh's power (45.23f.).
[90] At this point should be mentioned the declaration about Cyrus. This proclamation is in a certain sense a further development of the announcement in Deuteronomic-Jeremianic circles concerning the royal servant Nebuchadnezzar. The only difference is that in Deut. Isa. the title עֶבֶד is replaced by the clearly military-political title מָשִׁיחַ. From this point of view it is unlikely that the עֶבֶד should be understood in a kingly-messianic sense. The substitution theories, e.g., of Hempel, which see in the עֶבֶד proclamation a substitute for the disappointed expectation centred in Cyrus, rest at

the still apparently triumphant world of idols.[91] It glorifies the sole honour of Yahweh and thus becomes the light and salvation of the whole world.[92]

(*d*) The passages 49.7; 50.4-9; and 52.13-53.12 make it clear that the servant passed through a vale of suffering. The lot of Jeremiah repeats itself in the experience of the servant of Yahweh. But while as a result of his confessions and the tale of woe, written no doubt by Baruch, the sufferings of Jeremiah are brought into the full light of biographical openness, Deutero-Isaiah reports with a noticeable objectivity and aloofness. In what

---

the decisive point—the supposed experience of disillusionment—on very uncertain ground. But no more may the Cyrus expectation, as Begrich, *Studien*, 144f., wishes, be interpreted as the scanty remnant of a disappointed eschatological hope. It represents—not as a logical necessity but for a daring faith in Yahweh—the true historical manifestation of the saving nearness of Yahweh. In Isa. and Jer. too, such interpretations of historical phenomena can be recognized.

[91] The speeches of rebuke and judgment against the idols 41.1-5, 21-29; 43.8-13; 44.4-6 etc., are to be understood against the background of Yahweh's imminent fulfilment of the right in history. They are not meant to express 'monotheistic insights' —static, timeless and divorced from history—but to glorify triumphantly the truth which is soon to be actualized historically in judgments which will thus assume eschatological dimensions. The speech against the escaped of the nations (45.20) shows that the healing of the nations will be realized by a judgement shattering not only the idols but also their worshippers; cf. Begrich, *Studien*, especially ch. 3 'Das Verhältnis Dtjs's zur religiösen Überlieferung'.

[92] Begrich, *Studien*, supp. I, 161-6, would like to translate הוֹצִיא מִשְׁפָּט 42.1 as 'make known the judgement'. Thus he would see in the servant the one who proclaims publicly Yahweh's gracious judgments on Israel, and he inquires further whether we should not recognize in 42.1-4 the book of the duties of the above mentioned (p. 13) עֶבֶד הַמֶּלֶךְ. The latter would thus be a herald whose office it would be to make known the righteous judgments of the king through the symbolism which is transparent in 42.2f. Thus Begrich claims that the choice of the title עֶבֶד יהוה is to be understood by analogy with this office. Against this last hypothesis it must be pointed out that Begrich clearly does not take sufficiently into account to what an extent Deut. Isa. is here dependent on older linguistic usage in the description of the prophets, and the fact that he is in no way coining new phrases. Also Begrich's suggested translation of הוֹצִיא מִשְׁפָּט can hardly be justified. If it might be considered for the הוֹצִיא מִשְׁפָּט of 42.1 it is utterly impossible for the synonymous שִׂים מִשְׁפָּט of 42.4; and above all for the parallelism of מִשְׁפָּט and תּוֹרָה. Here it must be a question of the establishment of a universal judgement overlapping the individual case (cf. the מִשְׁפַּט הַמֶּלֶךְ of I Sam. 8, or the formula in II Kings 17.27 אֶת הוֹרָה מִשְׁפַּט אֱלֹהֵי הָאָרֶץ akin to 42.4). But the views of Begrich may well be correct in so far as this execution of justice stands in the closest relation to the gracious judgements of Yahweh, taking concrete shape in the history of Israel, which it is the office of the servant as messenger of joy to announce, and that it finds in those disclosures its guarantee, and that in consequence the proclamation of salvation to the peoples radiates from this revelation through history to which Israel, by its experience of grace, remains the true witness (43.10; 44.8).

does the suffering of the servant consist? Was he persecuted by his own people? The visible opposition of the exiles (45.9f.) to the announcement that Cyrus had been sent by Yahweh as the anointed and saviour of Israel, might seem to lend colour to such a proposition. Did the Babylonian power pit itself against the proclaimer of the power of Yahweh? The formula, 'servant of rulers', coined in antithesis to the 'servant of Yahweh' (49.7), and the allusion (49.7; 52.15) to the forthcoming astonishment of kings might be regarded as pointing in that direction. Did the servant fall sick?[93] The songs give us no definite information. As in the psalms of lament, multiple competing images give us oblique indication. Also the question whether 53.8–10 speaks of the death of the servant,[94] or whether it suggests only the imminent and ineluctable but not yet fulfilled necessity of his dying,[95] is wrapped in an obscurity which we cannot with certainty pierce. With this is involved the further point that 52.13–53.12, after echoing clearly traits from the earlier songs, unmistakably abandons the realm of the biographical, on the basis of which we thought we could understand what the servant's office was, and gives a picture of the true servant of Yahweh which far transcends the personal experience of the prophet. Thus it is not by chance or by ineptitude that Isa. 53 has again and again been understood as alluding to the figure of the one that is to come.[96]

Thus it is at this point that the account of the servant diverges from the account of Jeremiah given in his confessions, and goes beyond them to express in a twofold way a final word about the office of and promise to the true עֶבֶד יהוה. Jeremiah's confessions ended on a note of unrelieved darkness,[97] but the servant of

[93] Duhm, ad loc., explains the נָגוּעַ of 53.4 as referring to the leper.
[94] See Elliger; Sellin, 'Lösung'. In this case the text must come from a later hand.
[95] Begrich, *Studien*.
[96] H. W. Wolff, 36, formulates the idea of a prefiguration of the coming one to express the prophet's sense of transcendence over his own specific office. G. von Rad (' "Gerechtigkeit" und "Leben" in den Ps.' in *Festschr. A. Bertholet*, 1950, 424f.) has pointed out that in the speech of the psalmist about the 'righteous', we meet with such images, conceived in the ultimate daring of faith, to transcend the empirical. He speaks of the prototype of the just (צַדִּיק). On the analogy of Ps. 2 (n. 74) we might refer to the royal messianic line.
[97] In the cursing of his own birth the tormented messenger of God cries out in the final word of his confessions (20.14ff.). The sole ray of light which illuminates the darkness lies in the prophet's surmise that he does not bear his pain alone but that it is a sharing of the pain of Yahweh. This is directly asserted in the word to Baruch (45.4f.) and may be indirectly recognized in 12.7ff.

The Servant of God

Yahweh comes to rest in the recognition of the deep meaning in his pain. His suffering is vicarious.[98] In the context of this deepest insight which—and here the reserve of the language reaches its climax—is uttered not by the servant himself, but by a fellowship of believers gripped by this event,[99] the servant's own reaction to his sorrows, as compared with that of Jeremiah, is utterly different. Here is the fulfilment of the עֶבֶד attitude: the עֶבֶד יהוה bears in obedience and surrender what Yahweh ordains for him (53.6, 10). In words which are reminiscent of Ezekiel he confesses his unresisting obedience.[100] The image which Jeremiah uses in his confessions of the sheep led to the slaughter, and which in Jer. 11.19 is meant to express the unsuspecting innocence of the prophet encircled by threats,[101] is now deepened to express the servant's passive readiness to bear his pain (Isa. 53.7).

(e) What is the source of such a surrender? Is it simply the result of insight into the hidden meaning of a personal experience of sorrow? Or is it merely blind obedience? Here is the second point at which Deutero-Isaiah goes beyond Jeremiah; for he reaches the triumphant recognition that Yahweh will vindicate his servant beyond death and the grave. Alongside the confession of utter submission to the Lord, which is proper to the consciousness of the O.T. עֶבֶד, stands the liberating insight of faith in the ultimate fidelity of Yahweh to the servant whom he has called. Or to express it by means of the two concepts which are implied in the servant's profession of trust (49.4): the servant knows that he will receive from Yahweh his right (מִשְׁפָּט) and his reward (פְּעֻלָּה).

---

[98] Stamm: 68–75: vicarious suffering. The use of the common sacrificial idea אָשָׁם in 53.10, and the use of the image of the slaughtered animal (suggested of course by Jeremiah) imply perhaps that the thought of sacrifice is not far away. Yet here too everything is again left in great uncertainty. One may wonder whether, in view of the obvious contacts between Deut. Isa. and Deuteronomic material, there may not be a reference to Moses, that great servant of Yahweh, who was more than a prophet (Bentzen, 64–67, following H. S. Nyberg). Deut. 3.26 reports of him, after he had prayed to be permitted to enter the land of Canaan: 'But Yahweh was angry with me for your sakes.' Nothing is said here of any guilt incurred by Moses which Num. 20.12 seems to imply. Moses bears the anger of Yahweh against his people. There is, however, nothing about a *voluntary* action. On Ex. 32.30 see Stamm, 71.

[99] 53.1–11a is set in the context of two passages which illuminate the whole: 52.13–15; 53.11b–12. The second passage takes up the theme of substitution in connexion with 53.1–11a.

[100] 50.5. Is there a side-glance here at Jeremiah who rebelled in his prophetic suffering (15.19)? See Ezek 2.8, etc., for מרה in connexion with the prophet's call.

[101] In Jer. 12.3 it is applied as a bitter word of revenge against enemies (omitted in the LXX).

The Servant of God in the Old Testament

Right is the key-word which governs 50.7ff. In face of the bitter humiliations which he has known, the servant here confesses his firm trust in Yahweh: 'The Lord Yahweh will help me; therefore shall I not be confounded; therefore have I set my face like a flint, and I know that I shall not be ashamed.' Then the speech breaks out into an apostrophe, and an appeal such as is made by an accused person in a court of law[102]—a favourite mode of expression with Deutero-Isaiah: 'He is near that justifieth me; who will contend with me? Let us stand together; who is mine adversary? Let him come near to me. Behold they shall wax old as a garment; the moth shall eat them up.'[103] As the Lord's servant Job, in the face of all the frustrations of the present, knows that at last Yahweh will manifest his righteousness, so here the servant of the Lord. In 52.13–53.12, on the other hand, it reaches a climax in the thought of Yahweh's reward to his servant. Even greater emphasis, externally, is laid on this whole circle of ideas by the fact that this ultimate goal is expressed not merely in terms of the subjective faith of the servant, but in the words of Yahweh himself, who after the community's words of 53.1–10a himself speaks and gives his concluding pledge to his servant. By the image of the dividing of the conquered spoil[104] is expressed the vindication which Yahweh will procure for his servant beyond death and the grave (53.12).[105] If in Isa. 53 we seek a didactically formulated expression of what is implied in salvation from death,[106] which is clearly the theme here, we shall be disappointed. There is no such expression. What is said is concealed beneath the image. On the other hand, the promise that Yahweh himself will uphold his servant against death and the grave—and thus show that the servant belongs inseparably to him—is unmistakably ratified.

(f) But finally, in all this is it a question of a mere private happening between the servant and his Lord? It is very striking how

---

[102] Begrich, *Studien*, 19–42, 48–49.
[103] Isa. 51.8. The same image of Yahweh's eschatological vindication of right against his enemies.
[104] 40.10f. seems also to connect war booty and reward. Again 9.3 illustrates the joy of the eschatological day of salvation by picturing the joy of dividing the spoil.
[105] In 10b the astonished onlookers were already speaking of the granting of posterity to him who was obviously given over to death.
[106] For this whole circle of problems cf. Ch. Barth, *Die Errettung vom Tode in den individuellen Klage- und Dankliedern des A.T.*, 1947.

in Yahweh's speech introducing his final words (52.13ff.) there is an emphasis on the effect which the encounter between Yahweh and his servant produces on a wider public. Kings and the great ones of the earth will be astonished at it (52.14f.). Isa. 49.7 may suggest what Yahweh intends by this public character of the happening. 'Kings shall see and arise, princes shall prostrate themselves—because of Yahweh's fidelity and his choice of thee.' Thus, finally, this vindication and recompense of the servant shall redound to the honour of Yahweh and to the fuller recognition of his fidelity by the whole world. In that the work of the servant is consummated.

II

TRANSLATIONS IN THE LXX

1. THE עֶבֶד TRANSLATIONS IN THE LXX

עֶבֶד occurs 807 times in the M.T.[107] The following equivalents[108] are to be found in the LXX: παῖς (παιδίον, παιδάριον) 340 times; δοῦλος, (δουλεία,[109] δουλεύων) 327 times; οἰκέτης (οἶκος) 63 times; θεράπων (θεραπεία, θεραπεύων) 46 times; υἱός once; ὑπηρέτης once. Further there are 56 places where there is a misunderstanding or a free translation. The rendering by these various Greek equivalents does not follow the same principles in all the O.T. books, but at different points discloses different principles—a fact which clearly implies a plurality of translators. Since the 272 passages where עֶבֶד appears in relation to Yahweh are not distinguished by any special type of translation, we must survey the translations of all the עֶבֶד passages together.

(a) A first important layer of translation is to be found in the books Gen. to Josh. Not that these books show uniformity in the translations they offer. It is strikingly clear even that in Gen. a different hand must have been at work from that which was at work in Ex.[110] In Gen. the παῖς title is the rule. Of 88 עֶבֶד texts, 79 are translated by παῖς, and οἰκέτης occurs five times. In Ex., on the other hand, θεράπων prevails. Of 43 עֶבֶד texts, 23 are translated by θεράπων; only 8 by παῖς and 6 by οἰκέτης. The Egyptian courtiers called παῖδες in Gen. are here denominated

---

[107] 800 times in Heb., 7 times in Aram. text.
[108] Text of Rahlfs. In Judg. text B, in Dan. the LXX, and not the Theodotion text of the great manuscripts are used for the statistics. See on Isa. Ziegler, *Isaias*.
[109] The numerous δουλία-passages to be found in Swete are throughout considered by Rahlfs as itacism and written in the form δουλεία.
[110] The conclusion by F. Baumgärtel, J. Herrmann and F. Baumgärtel: *Beiträge zur Entstehungsgeschichte der Septuaginta*, 1923, 55, that Gen., as contrasted with the rest of the Pentateuch, occupies a special position, is thus thoroughly confirmed by an examination of the translation of עֶבֶד.

θεράποντες.¹¹¹ In the subsequent Hexateuch writings the renderings, which in Gen. and Ex. are so characteristically distributed, are mixed: Lev. παῖς 3 times; οἰκέτης 4 times; Num. θεράπων 4 times; παῖς 5 times; οἰκέτης once; Deut. παῖς 9 times; οἰκέτης 8 times; θεράπων 4 times; only Josh. shows again a predominance of παῖς 13 times, though of course θεράπων (3 times) and οἰκέτης (3 times) are not absent. What, however, in spite of these differences characterizes the books of the Hexateuch and unmistakably differentiates them from the following five narrative books is the almost complete absence of δοῦλος. Of the 88 texts of Gen. and the 11 of Num., not a single one is translated by δοῦλος; of the 15 δοῦλος examples in the remaining 4 books of the Hexateuch, 10 can be discounted as referring to Egypt, the house of bondage (οἶκος δουλείας). In Lev. 25.44 the foreign slave is denoted by δοῦλος. Ex. 21.7 (misunderstood in the LXX) seems also to point in this direction. Deut. 32.36 belongs to the Song of Moses, which also in v. 43, the second occurrence of עֶבֶד in the Heb. text of the Song of Moses, shows a peculiarity in the Greek translation. Josh 24.29 (LXX v.30) seems to be determined by the parallel Judg. 2.8. There remains Josh. 9.23, where in the curse on the Gibeonites δοῦλος occurs. Hence it is clear that δοῦλος has been used quite rarely only in connexion with the special hardships of slavery. Throughout the whole slavery law (Ex. 21.7 excepted) we have παῖς (Ex. 21.2, 5, 20, 32) and οἰκέτης (Ex. 21.26f.) and also in formulae of submission (Josh. 9.8f., 11). As regards the courtly style of self-reference we find παῖς in Gen. 18.3, 5, and elsewhere, and οἰκέτης in Ex. 5.16 in the same verse with παῖς. Hence the usage passes over into humble discourse in the presence of Yahweh. Here, too, Jacob can call himself παῖς (Gen. 32.10) or Moses (Ex. 4.10) θεράπων of God. Also where the title is used independently, Moses the servant of Yahweh is described as θεράπων (Ex. 14.31; Num. 12.7), the patriarchs as οἰκέται (Ex. 32.13) and Caleb (Num. 14.24) like Moses (Josh. 1.13; 12.6, and elsewhere) as παῖς κυρίου. Here again, what is

---

111 In Gen. only in 45.16 is the court of Pharaoh פַּרְעֹה וַעֲבָדָיו translated Φαραω καὶ ἡ θεραπεία αὐτοῦ. And in 50.17 in humble self-reference the title θεράπων is used in connexion with the name of the God of the fathers: τῶν θεραπόντων τοῦ θεοῦ τοῦ πατρός σου.

Translations in the LXX

really striking is the complete avoidance of the name δοῦλος which later in Judg. to IV Βασ. just as exclusively governs religious terminology.

The Song of Moses still requires a brief notice. It is remarkable in that v. 36 is the only text in the Hexateuch where the religious δοῦλος idea is met with. But on the other hand v. 43 is the only text where עֶבֶד is translated υἱός. Thus, with unusual emphasis both aspects of the עֶבֶד are underlined. Has Deut. 32 the same translation history as the rest of the Hexateuch?

(b) Alongside the Hexateuchal group of writings which can be characterized only negatively stands the group Judg. to IV Βασ., which can plainly be described by positive features. Here only the two words παῖς and δοῦλος are used to translate עֶבֶד. And, indeed, here is to be noted the neat distinction by which παῖς is used to denote only the category of the free servants of the king who place themselves at his disposal by their own decision (soldiers, ministers, and officials, cf. p. 13). On the other hand, δοῦλος expresses true essential slavery.[112] It denotes, therefore, one who is compelled to be a serf even were he a king (II Βασ. 10.19). Naturally, this word is employed in the contemptuous speech of a Saul (I Βασ. 22.8) or even of a Nabal against David (I Βασ. 25.10) even where it refers to one who objectively considered would be in the position of a παῖς. These considerations lead us to conclude that in the whole field of courtly speech, whether one is speaking of himself or another,[113] the δοῦλος title is used. If the עֶבֶד הַמֶּלֶךְ of IV Βασ. 22.12 is described as δοῦλος τοῦ βασιλέως then it must mean that his office is misunderstood in the sense of a menial service. As a rule the distinction is so carefully maintained throughout the whole five books that where there is an apparent deviation the question must seriously be raised whether the translator has not desired to express a slight nuance not contained in the Heb. text (II Βασ. 12.18f.; 15.34; doubtfully 21.22). In accordance with what has already been said, we see that in humble

---

[112] The slaves of Ziba (II Βασ. 9.10, 12; 19.17) who was himself a παῖς of the house of Saul, 9.2; the Egyptian slave of an Amalekite (I Βασ. 30.13).
[113] Ahimelech of the servants of Saul, I Βασ. 22.14, called in an objective narrative παῖδες, 6f., or Ziba in courtly self-description, represented as παῖς in the same verse, II Βασ. 9.2.

The Servant of God

self-description in prayer to God the petitioner constantly refers to himself as δοῦλος. The fact that for the great individual figures of Israelite history, for Moses and Joshua as well as for the figures of the kingly line,[114] the δοῦλος title is used without exception betrays plainly that the translator wished to view even these great men of history not after the pattern of the free kingly ministry, but after that of the humble slave.

(c) The two groups of writings, Gen. to Josh.[115] and Judg. to IV Βασ. show us two phases in the translation history of the LXX. The second of these is plainly recognizable by the determination to achieve a more precise apprehension of the facts in the translation of עֶבֶד. This is expressed in the careful distinction between παῖς and δοῦλος. The first phase is more difficult to explain. It has been suggested that the rule of translation here is based on the fact that the ambiguous παῖς[116] best corresponds to the ambiguous עֶבֶד. This purely linguistic explanation may perhaps illuminate the facts so far as Gen. is concerned. Nevertheless, it should be made clear that the ambiguity of the two terms lies in different directions, and that their equivalence is in no sense material and substantial. But whence comes the use of θεράπων in Ex.? And why the unmistakable avoidance of the harsh δοῦλος when the promiscuous use of παῖς, οἰκέτης and θεράπων becomes the rule (Ex.–Josh.)? The fact that even in the translation of the religious עֶבֶד phrase δοῦλος is avoided, and only παῖς, οἰκέτης and θεράπων,[117] which is fairly far removed from the O.T. attitude, are used, may well indicate that the translation of the Hexateuch in Hellenistic Judaism shows us a

---

[114] The verse III Βασ. 8.59 LXX (B), in which, as against M.T., Israel itself seems to be understood by the servant, may be considered as an error through homoioteleuton, cf. Rahlfs.

[115] It may be considered established that Josh. was among the writings first translated and that the Hexateuch, which is beginning to be very problematical as a literary quantity for O.T. criticism (M. Noth, *Überlieferungsgeschichtliche Studien*, I, 1943, 253), is to be thought of for the translation period as a continuous whole.

[116] P. Katz (*Philo's Bible*, 1950, 6, n. 1 and Appendix I, 141–6), has shown in regard to the translation of שָׁמַיִם, for example, that such rules of translation are recognizable. As regards the use of παῖς and δοῦλος in Philo, ibid. 83–87.

[117] *TWNT*, III, 132, 12ff. Just like θεραπεία, θεράπων and θεραπεύειν are also predetermined by heathen cultic usage. This must be maintained in spite of the objections of J. Barr, *The Semantics of Biblical Language*, 1961, 254. With regard to θεραπεύω, cf., in addition to the passages quoted in *TWNT*, III, 128.37ff., W. Dittenberger, *Orientis Graeci inscriptiones selectae*, 1903–5, 90.40, and Dionysius Halicarnassensis, II.21. On θεραπεία, cf. I Βασ. 15.23 B.

Translations in the LXX

first phase of biblical translation which betrays the uninhibited influence of the Greek feeling for the nearness of God and man.[118] The translation of the section Judg. to IV Βασ. which took place somewhat later shows the growing awareness of the specific O.T. consciousness of the distance between God and man, and the fact that man belongs to God. In the exclusive use of the harsher δοῦλος idea in religious speech the scandal of the austere sovereignty of God is carried over into the image of man in the Greek Bible.[119]

(d) Broadly speaking, the later biblical books no longer give the clear picture presented by the two big groups of writings in the earlier part of the LXX. The patterns distinguished above begin to get confused. A general survey shows that the translation of עֶבֶד by θεράπων, the most daring and farthest from the Hebrew, recedes altogether. Apart from the mention in Isa. 54.17,[120] this translation now appears only in Job where again it is predominant.[121] The Pss. as a whole adopt δοῦλος, which occurs fifty-three times as opposed to παῖς, three times.[122] In Ezekiel all five religious references to עֶבֶד are translated δοῦλος (Jacob, David, and the prophets) as also are the five in the Dodekapropheton (Moses, David, the prophets) and the two in Ezra (the prophets and the Jerusalem community).[123] On the other hand, there is Isaiah. In Proto-Isa. all three, in Deut. Isa. fourteen of the twenty religious עֶבֶד texts are translated by παῖς. In Isa.: Isaiah himself, Eliakim and David; in Deut. Isa.: Israel the prophetic servant.[124] Dan. is to be linked with it where

---

[118] Also παῖς and οἰκέτης express a stronger familiar relationship of the servant than δοῦλος.

[119] The later variants even in the Hexateuch put δοῦλος. Cf. for example Codex Ambrosianus on Josh. 1.1, 15; Alexandrinus on 14.7.

[120] In the form θεραπεύοντες (κύριον) which may point to a verbal understanding of עבדי יהוה.

[121] Nine out of the total twelve עֶבֶד instances are translated by θεράπων, five of which give the predication of Job as servant of God. Only 1.8 translates by παῖς in the religious sense. LXX (A) assimilates here too while A together with LXX (V) in 42.8 replaces the first of the three instances of θεράπων by παῖς.

[122] ψ 85.16 in humble self-description in prayer; 112.1 in the description of the community gathered for worship; 17.1 in the prelude of David to a psalm.

[123] At both points in the transcription in I Εσδρ., the δοῦλος is replaced by παῖς. Cf. II Εσδρ. (Ezra) 5.11; 9, 11 with I Εσδρ. 6.13; 8.82.

[124] It is quite striking that in the translation of Trit. Isa. there is a deviation into the use of δοῦλος pure and simple. We have established above (p. 19) that in Isa. 56–66 the separation of the pious obedient to God from the impious godless was sharply expressed. Does this explain the fact that in the Greek translation, against

The Servant of God

all twelve references (seven of which are religious) are translated by παῖς.[125] In Jer. the confusion of expressions is especially striking. While the formula 'my servants the prophets' in the first half of the book (7.25; 25.4) is translated by δοῦλος, παῖς occurs later 26.5 ('Ιερ. 33.5); 35.15 (42.15); 44.4 (51.4). In 46.27 (26.27) Jacob is called δοῦλος and then, just beside this, in v. 28, παῖς. That there is a special problem behind the relation of the LXX to Jer.[126] is suggested by the frequent omission of a word corresponding to עֶבֶד in the older MSS. The later ones are accustomed to add δοῦλος. The confusion of patterns reaches its climax in Neh. and Chron., where it is no longer possible to see any principle behind the alternation of παῖς and δοῦλος.[127] In Neh. 1.7f. Moses is called παῖς (II Εσδρ. 11.7); in 9.14 δοῦλος (II Εσδρ. 19.14) of God. In Nehemiah's humble self-description before God we find in 1.11 (II Εσδρ. 11.11) παῖς and δοῦλος in the same verse. The feeling for the specific content of the terms seems here to have completely vanished. The translation of עֶבֶד יהוה by ἄνθρωπος τοῦ θεοῦ in II Chron. 24.6 has been mentioned in n. 55.

2. The Translation of Servant of God Passages in Deutero-Isaiah

The phraseology of Isa. 42.1 Ιακὼβ ὁ παῖς μου, ἀντιλήμψομαι αὐτοῦ· Ισραηλ ὁ ἐκλεκτός μου, προσεδέξατο αὐτὸν ἡ ψυχή μου shows that the LXX understands the introductory words of the

---

three examples of δοῦλος (56.6; 63.17; 65.9) we find the form δουλεύων six times (65.8, 13–15)? This form brings out more the active obedience of the servant. Only once is עֶבֶד translated by σεβόμενος (66.14; φοβούμενος Origen and Lucian).

[125] Theodotion translates six times by δοῦλος (each time a religious use of עֶבֶד); only in 3.28 (Δαν. 3.95) is παῖς maintained in religious use.

[126] P. Volz, *Der Prophet Jeremia* (Komm. zum A.T., X)², 1928, L; W. Rudolph, *Jeremia* (Handbuch zum A.T., II, 12)², 1958, xxf.

[127] A comparison with the parallel texts in I–IV Baσ. enables us to recognize as a general tendency a strong penetration of παῖς texts. The clearly distinguishable differentiation of παῖς and δοῦλος in Judg. to IV Baσ. is in the process completely obscured, without suggesting any conscious plan. Cf. for example Nathan's discourse of promises in II Sam. 7 with I Chron. 17. In seven of the ten comparable texts παῖς has replaced the δοῦλος which occurs in II Sam. alone. So then in Yahweh's speech about David we find jumbled up together παῖδά μου (17.4) and τῷ δούλῳ μου (17.7) or in the humble self-description before God, τοῦ παιδός σου 17.25 alongside of τὸν δοῦλόν σου 17.26. Again, in I Chron. 18.6f. where the parallel II Sam. 8.6f. showed a fine differentiation of παῖς and δοῦλος, παῖς is uniformly used.

Translations in the LXX

servant songs in the narrower sense to refer to Israel (see n. 66). The destruction of the threefold parallelism evident in the Heb. text up to v. 4 as a result of the addition of the proper names speaks against the originality of the LXX text. The latter, however, is not only important because it unmistakably shows in what sense it was interpreted and hence is an early witness to the collective interpretation, but also because it shows the secondary penetration into the text of interpretative expansions. In 49.3 too this type of penetration seems at least possible (n. 69). In this sense then we must take the LXX interpretation of the passages 42.1–4 (similarly 5–9) and 49.1–6 (with the connecting 7, 8–13). The translation of 50.4–9 gives no plain indication of the interpretation of the translator.

On the other hand, 52.13–53.12 of the LXX might well be taken to refer to an individual figure.[128] The striking rendering of צֶאֱצָא (53.2) by παιδίον, familiar from the messianic statement of 9.6 (cf. the correctly rendered ῥίζα likewise reminiscent of the messianic text 11.1), raises the question whether the LXX version does not imply a messianic significance. Ἀνέτειλε[129] which can be reconstructed in 53.2 may point in the same direction.[130] If so, the Greek translator must have seen in Isa. 52.13–53.12 the description of a messianic figure whose coming he awaits. This last idea is confirmed by the translation of 52.14f. as a future,[131] which is a clear deviation from the Heb. text. The contemptuous aversion of the many from the servant (v. 14) as also the amazed surrender of peoples and kings (v. 15) is an event which is to take place only in the future. The perfect tenses used in the description of the servant's passion (53.1ff.)— where in deviation from the Heb. text several present tenses are interpolated[132]—will then have to be understood as prophetic perfects. Further, we shall ask whether the repeated solemn key-word δόξα, 52.13, 14b, 14c; 53.2, which has no full equivalent in the Heb. text, does not carry the decisive imprint of

---

[128] Cf. Euler, 85–91.
[129] ἀνηγγείλαμεν which appears in the versions is no doubt to be called, with Ziegler *Isaias* ad loc. and p. 99, a textual corruption; v. 2 is to be read ἀνέτειλε μὲν ἐναντίον αὐτοῦ ὡς παιδίον. For an attempt at interpretation see Euler, 22–23.
[130] ἀνατολή as a translation of the messianic צֶמַח. See *TWNT*, I, 354f.
[131] ὃν τρόπον ἐκστήσονται... οὕτως ἀδοξήσει... οὕτως θαυμάσονται...
[132] V. 2 οὐκ ἔστιν εἶδος; v. 4 φέρει... ὀδυνᾶται; v. 8 αἴρεται.

43

The Servant of God

interpretation.¹³³ Here a figure is mentioned which by its child-like nearness to God possesses a secret δόξα. Of course in the sight of men the παῖς appears as a humbled and dishonoured person. Judged by human standards he has no glory.¹³⁴ But by a word of God¹³⁵ the παῖς becomes aware of his secret glory—nay, more than aware. Through his humiliation and death, consequent upon the ignorance of mankind, God leads him to exaltation and glorification.¹³⁶ In this way insight is granted to a number of men that they may apprehend the glory of the παῖς and the meaning of his passion. In 53.1ff. they express their new recognition. Of course against too strong an emphasis on the thought of δόξα it may be objected that the phrasing of 52.13 ὑψωθήσεται καὶ δοξασθήσεται is a common mode of expression which is to be found also in 10.15; 33.10 and which therefore must not be over-estimated. The echoing of a word which has once been made resonant for the purpose of translating similar statements is a stylistic feature characteristic of 53.¹³⁷ Hence the δόξα phrase ought not perhaps to be singled out as the special interpretative element of the LXX translation. It is plain, however, that the LXX, too, thinks of a passion of the παῖς which leads him to death.¹³⁸ The exaltation following upon this death, the description of which is indebted to the store of images in the Heb. text,¹³⁹ goes, however, beyond the latter in suggesting that judgement is passed on the godless in retribution for their murder of the παῖς.¹⁴⁰ As distinct from the interpretation of the *Targums* which gives us the thought of judgement here too,¹⁴¹ judgement according to the LXX is executed not by the παῖς but by God himself.

---

[133] Cf. Euler, 101–7.
[134] 52.14b: οὕτως ἀδοξήσει ἀπὸ ἀνθρώπων τὸ εἶδός σου καὶ ἡ δόξα σου ἀπὸ τῶν ἀνθρώπων.
[135] The whole of 52.14 has been shaped by the LXX as a word of God to the servant.
[136] 52.13 συνήσει. . . ὑψωθήσεται. . . δοξασθήσεται.
[137] Also Ziegler, *Untersuchungen*, 24–25.
[138] 53.8b: ὅτι αἴρεται ἀπὸ τῆς γῆς ἡ ζωὴ αὐτοῦ, ἀπὸ τῶν ἀνομιῶν τοῦ λαοῦ μου ἤχθη εἰς θάνατον.
[139] The φῶς of 53.11 has now been confirmed by the Heb. text, see *The Dead Sea Scrolls* (op. cit. in n. 69), plate 44, line 19.
[140] 53.9: καὶ δώσω τοὺς πονηροὺς ἀντὶ τῆς ταφῆς αὐτοῦ καὶ τοὺς πλουσίους ἀντὶ τοῦ θανάτου αὐτοῦ.
[141] See Hegermann, 86f.

III

Παῖς Θεοῦ IN LATE JUDAISM IN THE PERIOD AFTER THE LXX[142]

Παῖς (τοῦ) θεοῦ occurs only seldom in late Jewish literature after 100 B.C., namely in Wisd. 2.13; 9.4; 12.7, 20; 19.6; Bar. 1.20; 2.20, 24, 28; 3.36; Ps. Sol. 12.6; 17.21; I Esd. 6.13, 27; 8.82; in Philo[143] and Josephus[144] only once (Philo, Conf. Ling. 147; Josephus, Ant. 10.215); finally in the later Greek translations of the O.T. (Isa. 42.1 Θ v.l., cf. p. 54; Jer. 30.10 Θ; Δαν. 3.95 Θ; Deut. 34.5 'Αλλ).

1. THE TWOFOLD MEANING OF Παῖς Θεοῦ

In most cases it is quite clear from the context and linguistic usage whether the meaning 'child of God' or 'servant of God' is intended. II Macc. 7.34 (see below) and Bar. 3.36 (cf. p. 47 below) are disputed passages.

(i) *Παῖς Θεοῦ = 'child of God'*. The plural παῖδες θεοῦ, meaning 'children of God', occurs in four passages in Wisd. as a description of the people of Israel (12.7, 20; 19.6) or of the pious (9.4).[145] It has the same meaning in the one place where it occurs in Philo (Conf. Ling. 147).[146] Again in II Macc. 7.34, where the children of Israel are called οἱ οὐράνιοι παῖδες, we should presumably translate 'children of God'[147] rather than 'servants of God'.[148] The singular παῖς θεοῦ with the meaning

---

[142] Towards the end of the second century B.C. almost the whole of the O.T. already existed in the LXX translation. The evidence both of the Prologue to Ecclus. and Ep. Ar. points to this date. Therefore 100 B.C. is the starting point for the following treatment of παῖς θεοῦ.
[143] Leisegang, Index, 619.
[144] Schl. Theol. d. Judt., 50.
[145] The meaning 'children of God' results from the interchangeability of παῖδές σου (9.4; 12.20) and υἱοί σου (9.7; 12.19, 21). This is confirmed by what is said below, p. 46, on 2.13.
[146] καὶ γὰρ εἰ μήπω ἱκανοὶ θεοῦ παῖδες νομίζεσθαι γεγόναμεν, none the less 'of his Logos'. The context shows that the meaning is 'children of God'.
[147] As also O. Michel, Der Brief an die Hebräer (Meyer, 13)[11], 1960, on 2.10.
[148] Thus the v.l. οἱ δοῦλοι αὐτοῦ; cf. 7.33.

'child of God' is only found once, Wisd. 2.13.[149] Here the godless say of the just παῖδα κυρίου ἑαυτὸν ὀνομάζει. In view of the linguistic usage of the LXX (cf. p. 37) the translation 'servant of God' seems the obvious one.[150] But in the following verses it is further stated that the righteous boasts of God as his father (2.16) and in 2.18 he is described as υἱὸς θεοῦ.[151] Since, moreover, in Wisd. we find that the plural phrases παῖδες θεοῦ and υἱοὶ θεοῦ are interchangeable, the translation 'child of God' must be regarded as the right one.[152] Now in 5.1ff. Wisd. depicts the righteous in terms derived from Isa. 52.13ff. (cf. p. 55). This means that the suffering servant of Deut. Isa. has become in Wisd.—by means of the dual significance of παῖς—the child of God who in spite of all suffering and misery knows himself to be safe with his Father and rejoices in the fact. The rare appearance of παῖς θεοῦ with the meaning 'child of God' is only partially explained by the fact that Hellenistic Judaism prefers for 'child of God' υἱὸς τοῦ θεοῦ (occasionally τέκνον τοῦ θεοῦ). The real reason for this rarity is that late Judaism less frequently uses the image of a child[153] than that of a servant[154] to describe the relation of the individual or the people to God.

(ii) Παῖς Θεοῦ = 'servant of God'. Παῖς θεοῦ more frequently means 'servant of God' in the period subsequent to 100 B.C., which concerns us. This meaning is certainly present in Bar. 1.20; 2.28; Deut. 34.5 Ἀλλ where Moses is called παῖς of God, since the description of Moses as 'servant of God' is established linguistic usage (cf. n. 183). The same applies to the denotation of the prophets, Bar. 2.20, 24; I Esd. 8.82 by the stereotyped formula (cf. n. 167) τῶν παίδων σου τῶν προφητῶν. When παῖδες is used of the three men in the fiery furnace (Δαν. 3.95 Θ;[155]

---

[149] Possibly Bar. 3.36 should be added; see p. 47.
[150] So K. Siegfried in E. Kautzsch, *Apokryphen und Pseudepigraphen*, I, 1900, 483, cf. Wolff, 41.
[151] Cf. 5.5: πῶς κατελογίσθη (the just) ἐν υἱοῖς θεοῦ; ask the sinners at the last judgement.
[152] So also the commentaries by O. F. Fritzsche, *Kurzgefasstes Handbuch zu den Apokryphen des A.T.*, 6, 1860, ad loc.; P. Heinisch, *Das Buch der Weisheit*, 1912, 51; F. Feldmann, *Das Buch der Weisheit*, 1926, ad loc.; J. Fichtner, *Weisheit Salomos* (Handbuch zum A.T., II, 6), 1938, ad loc.; further Dalman, I, 31, n. 1; Bousset, 48, 54; S.-B., I, 219; Dalman, *WJ*, 278. Cf. the Syriac of Wisd. 2.13, 18: ברה דאלהא = 'Son of God'.
[153] See S.-B., I, 219f., 371f.
[154] Cf. Bousset, 54; Schl. *Theol. d. Judt.*, 50.
[155] Also Josephus, *Ant.* 10.215.

The Servant of God in Late Judaism

3.93 Θ δοῦλοι [of God]), the meaning 'servant of God' is again assured. As for I Esd. 6.13 (δοῦλοι II 'Εσδρ. [Ezra] 5.11), 27, the context makes this meaning clear. The meaning of παῖς (of God) can only be doubtful now in those texts mentioned below in n. 177 where the phrase is used collectively; since however in Bar. παῖς θεοῦ is otherwise always used with the meaning 'servant of God' (1.20; 2.20, 24, 28), this meaning is to be accepted for Bar. 3.36: 'Ιακὼβ τῷ παιδὶ αὐτοῦ, and thence also for Ps. Sol. 12.6; 17.21; in Luke 1.54 a comparison with 1.69 yields the same conclusion. This survey shows that in passages where παῖς θεοῦ has the meaning 'servant of God' the O.T. usage of עֶבֶד יהוה, with its various implications, persists.

2. The Persistence of the O.T. Religious Usage of עֶבֶד יהוה

The O.T. עֶבֶד יהוה lives on not only in the Greek παῖς θεοῦ, and the following survey, therefore, must not be confined to παῖς θεοῦ but must (especially in view of the great significance of the expression עֶבֶד יהוה for the N.T.) include the occurrence of עֶבֶד (of God); טַלְיָא (of God);[156] מְשָׁרֵת (of God); שַׁמָּשׁ (of God);[157] διάκονος θεοῦ;[158] δοῦλος θεοῦ; θεράπων θεοῦ;[159] οἰκέτης θεοῦ;[160] ὑπηρέτης θεοῦ;[161] ὑποδιάκονος θεοῦ.[162] Allowing for the fact that the phrase 'my servant', so frequent in the mouth of God in the O.T., now appears only rarely[163] because the time of the revelation ended with the death of the last writing prophet, we can discern the essentially unchanged persistence of the O.T. עֶבֶד יהוה—with, of course, characteristic shifts of emphasis.

(i) *Παῖς Θεοῦ as self-descriptive of the worshipper.* The very old humble self-description of the worshipper in the presence of his God as עַבְדְּךָ (cf. p. 16) continues to be used without

---

[156] Gen. 18.3 syr^pal; Isa. 52.13 syr^pal; Jer. 30.10 syr^pal.
[157] For נַעַר cf. n. 194.
[158] Only in Josephus, *Bell.* 3.354.
[159] Only in Philo, Leisegang, *Index*, 384.
[160] Only I Esd. 4.59; Ecclus. 36.17(22) א A (cf. n. 169).
[161] Only in Philo, Leisegang, *Index*, 802.
[162] Only in Philo, Leisegang, *Index*, 804.
[163] IV Ezra 7.28f.; 13.32, 37, 52; 14.9; Syr. Bar. 70.9, cf. p. 51. Each of these passages deals with the designation of the Messiah as 'my (God's) servant'.

The Servant of God

modification.[164] But it can hardly be an accident that in the Greek renderings (as distinct from the LXX where παῖς alternates with δοῦλος) for the period after 100 B.C., examples of παῖς (of God) are wanting, and only δοῦλος and διάκονος (of God) are attested (cf. nn. 166, 183, 184); the worshipper's awareness of the distance of God is intended to be unequivocally expressed.

(ii) *The plural 'servants of God'*. Likewise the plural 'servants of God', as in the O.T. (cf. p. 18),[165] remains current as a description of the Israelites[166] and the prophets.[167] A new fact is that in contrast with O.T. usage where it appears relatively seldom, and almost always in late writings,[168] the phrase 'servants of Yahweh' occurs with increasing frequency[169] as a description of the

---

[164] עֲבָדֶיךָ (of God): Ecclus. 36.17 (22) and the 16th Berakha of the *XVIII Blessings* (Palestinian recension); Shema' benediction אֱמֶת וְיַצִּיב 1 (W. Staerk, *Altjüdische liturgische Gebete*[2] [Kleine Texte, 58, ed. H. Lietzmann], 1930, 6). עבדכה (of God): frequently in the Qumran texts. עֲלֶיךָ in humble address to God, Gen. 18.3 syr[pal] (*Targ. Onkelos and Jonathan* I: עבדך [= Heb.]; in the *Samaritan Targ.* [pub. A. Brüll, 1879]: שמשכן). δοῦλος (of God): Wisd. 9.5; Δαν. 3.33, 44 Θ (also LXX); 9.17 Θ (LXX: παῖς); II Macc. 8.29. οἰκέτης (of God): I Esd. 4.59. διάκονος (of God): Josephus, *Bell.* 3.354. Examples preserved in Latin, Syriac, Ethiopian, Arabic and Armenian translations only: IV Ezra 5.45, 56; 6.12; 7.75, 102; 8.6, 24; 10.37; 12.8; 13.14; those preserved in the Syriac only: *Syr Bar.* 14.15; 48.11; 54.6; preserved in the Latin only: Pseudo-Philo, *Ant. Bibl.* 18.4; 25.6; 27.7 (twice); 42.7; 47.1f.

[165] Israelites: cf. Lindhagen, 82ff.; prophets: ibid., 277–80. Cf. p. 24 above.

[166] *Jub.* 23.30; *Syr. Bar.* 14.15. παῖδες (of God): I Esd. 6.13; *Sib.* V, 68 (on II Macc. 7.34 see p. 45). δοῦλοι (of God): II Macc. 7.34 v.l.; 8.29; Philo, *Migr. Abr.* 45. According to Josephus, *Ant.* 11.101, the Jews in the Cyrus edict are designated δοῦλοι τοῦ θεοῦ; and ibid., 90, they call themselves: δοῦλοι τοῦ μεγίστου θεοῦ. The expression δοῦλος θεοῦ is, however, infrequent in Josephus (cf. Schl. *Theol. d. Judt.*, 49f.). The predominance of δοῦλος both in the self-description of the worshipper (n. 164) and in the designation of the Israelites as the servants of God is significant. עבדים (of God): *Mekhilta Ex.* 22.20; *Siphre Num.* 15.41 §115; and further in prayers (cf. n. 164). עבדיא (of God): *Targ.* Isa. 48.20. משרתים (of God): *Mekhilta Ex.* 22.20.

[167] παῖδες (of God): I Esd. 8.82; Bar. 2.20, 24 (in all three places, τῶν παίδων σου [of God] τῶν προφητῶν [as a formula; cf. *Ιερ.* 33.5; 42.15; 51.4]). δοῦλοι (of God): Δαν. 9.6, 10 Θ (LXX: παῖδες θεοῦ), cf. Rev. 11.18. ὑπηρέται (of God): Philo, *Decal.* 178. ὑποδιάκονοι (of God): ibid. עבדיא (of God): *Targ.* Isa. 50.10. Also in the Qumran texts the prophets are repeatedly called 'servants of God'; see 1QpHab. 2.9; 7.5; 1QS 1.3; 4QpHos.[b] 2.5.

[168] Lindhagen, 233–62.

[169] παῖδες (of God): Josephus, *Ant.* 10.215 (of the three men in the fiery furnace as Δαν. 3.93, 95 LXX; 3.95 Θ). δοῦλοι (of God): II Macc. 7.6 (= LXX Deut. 32.36), 33; 8.29; *Ps. Sol.* 2.37; 10.4; Philo, *Det. Pot. Ins.* 146; *Rer. Div. Her.* 7; Josephus, *Ant.* 11.90, 101; Δαν. 3.85 Θ. θεράποντες (of God): Philo, *Det. Pot. Ins.* 62. עבדיא (of God): *Targ.* Isa. 42.19 (n. 219); 44.26 (n. 221). The description of the pious as οἰκέται (of God), Ecclus. 36.17 (22) א A, is original, as the Heb. text (עבדיך) shows. The reading ἱκετῶν (suppliants) instead of οἰκετῶν is a scribal error.

The Servant of God in Late Judaism

pious. The priests too are described in this way[170] after the O.T. pattern.[171] Further, proselytes[172] are now at times so named, as are parents[173] and the angels.[174]

(iii) *The collective linguistic use.* The new collective use of the singular עֶבֶד יהוה as a description of Israel, first clearly to be seen in Deut. Isa. (cf. p. 19),[175] also persists after 100 B.C. both in Hellenistic and Palestinian Judaism. But examples of the use of the title 'servant of God' for Israel, if we exclude O.T. quotations and late translations of the O.T.,[176] are not numerous.[177]

(iv) Παῖς Θεοῦ *as a title of honour for outstanding instruments of God.* Finally עֶבֶד יהוה, in accordance with general oriental and pre-exilic usage, continues to be used as a title of honour for outstanding instruments[178] of God (cf. pp. 20ff.), though apart

[170] θεράποντες (of God): Philo, *Spec. Leg.* I, 242; in the same book the high priest is called (ibid. 116) ὑποδιάκονος (of God). λειτουργοὶ θεοῦ: *Spec. Leg.* IV, 191.
[171] Cf. Lindhagen, 107-20.
[172] עֲבָדִים (of God): *Mekhilta Ex.* 22.20. מְשָׁרְתִים (of God): ibid. The LXX in translating Isa. 66.14 עֲבָדִים (of God) by σεβόμενοι αὐτόν (א A) or φοβούμενοι αὐτόν (B) is thinking no doubt of the proselytes.
[173] ὑπηρέται (of God): Philo, *Decal.* 119.
[174] δοῦλοι (of God): *Ps. Sol.* 18.12. θεράποντες (of God): Philo, *Fug.* 67. ὑπηρέται (of God): Philo, *Mut. Nom.* 87; *Som.* I, 143. ὑποδιάκονοι (of God): Philo, *Spec. Leg.* I, 66; *Abr.* 115. מְשָׁרְתִים (of God): *Heb. Enoch* 1.8; 4.1; 6.2f.; 19.6; 40.1. שַׁמָּשׁין (of God): *Mekhilta Ex.* 20.23 par. B. *Rosh Ha-shana* 24b; *Targ.* Isa. 6.2, etc. In *Spec. Leg.* I, 31 Philo calls the heavenly bodies ὑποδιάκονοι θεοῦ. In B. *Chul.* 60a the sun is described as one of the שַׁמָּשׁין of God.
[175] Isa. 41.8, 9; 44.1, 2, 21 (twice); 45.4; 48.20; 49.3; to which must be added as the tenth instance LXX Isa. 42.1: Ἰακὼβ ὁ παῖς μου (M.T. only עַבְדִּי), see p. 54. Further, outside Deut. Isa., in the Heb. text Jer. 30.10 (missing in the LXX, though Θ offers παῖς); 46.27f. (= LXX Ιερ. 26.27: δοῦλος, v. 28: παῖς); Ps. 136.22 (= LXX ψ 135.22: δοῦλος); on Ezek. 28.25 and 37.25 cf. n. 41. Also without Heb. equivalent: LXX III Βασ. 8.34 BA; 16.2A; ψ 134.12 א A (in all three places: δοῦλος). In all these instances 'Jacob' and 'Israel' have collective significance. Since the application of this title to the people ('my servant Israel', 'Jacob' [collectively]) is not certainly attested in the O.T. before Deut. Isa. in all those passages the influence of Deut. Isa. is to be assumed. Cf. Bentzen, 63, and n. 35 above.
[176] E.g., Jer. 30.10 Θ: σὺ δὲ μὴ φοβοῦ, παῖς μου Ἰακώβ (syr[pal] עַלַּיִי; *Targ.* עַבְדִּי). For the translation and the understanding of the collective servant texts of Deut. Isa. (enumerated in n. 175) in late Palestinian Judaism, see pp. 55f. below. We shall remark here that *Targ.* Isa. (following the Heb. text) 41.8, 9; 44.1, 2, 21 (twice); 45.4; 49.3 retains the phrase 'servant of God' and understands it to mean Israel collectively; only in 48.20 has the *Targ.* replaced the singular of the Heb. text by the plural.
[177] Bar. 3.36: Ἰακὼβ τῷ παιδὶ αὐτοῦ καὶ Ἰσραὴλ τῷ ἠγαπημένῳ ὑπ' αὐτοῦ (cf. LXX Isa. 44.2: παῖς μου Ἰακὼβ καὶ ὁ ἠγαπημένος Ἰσραὴλ ὃν ἐξελεξάμην); *Ps. Sol.* 12.6: Ἰσραὴλ παῖδα αὐτοῦ (of God); 17.21: Ἰσραὴλ παῖδά σου (of God); cf. Luke 1.54 (reference to Isa. 41.8) and p. 80 below; for rabbinical examples cf. n. 213.
[178] G. Sass quite rightly stresses ('Zur Bedeutung von δοῦλος bei Paulus', ZNW, 40, 1941, 24-32) that the title 'servant of God' in the O.T. and the N.T. conveys the

The Servant of God

from scriptural quotations,[179] almost exclusively in ancient formulae, especially prayers. Examples are few. In Philo this usage is altogether absent.[180] In Josephus we find only the description of Moses as δοῦλος θεοῦ,[181] and of the three men in the fiery furnace as παῖδες τοῦ θεοῦ.[182] In the whole of the *Mishnah* the title 'servant of God' appears only three times and then only in the three confessional formulae of the high priest on the Day of Atonement; in these three texts the formula is: ככתוב בתורת משה עבדך (*Yoma* 3.8 [= *T. Yoma* 2.1]; 4.2; 6.2). This title of honour is firmly established only for Moses,[183] less frequently it is used for David,[184] occasionally for Noah,[185] Abraham,[186] Isaac,[187] Jacob,[187a] Joseph,[187b] Aaron,[188]

---

thought of divine election. The decisive point is not the readiness to serve on the part of the human being concerned, but the divine appointing.

[179] *Siphre Deut.* §27 on 3.24 produces a long list of these figures described as 'servants of God' in the O.T.

[180] It is significant for Philo that he replaces the expression Ἀβραὰμ τοῦ παιδός μου (LXX Gen. 18.17) by Ἀβραὰμ τοῦ φίλου μου (*Sobr.* 56). Cf. Katz (loc. cit. in n. 116).

[181] Josephus, *Ant.* 5.39.

[182] Josephus, *Ant.* 10.215.

[183] παῖς (of God): Bar. 1.20; 2.28 (both texts in one and the same prayer of penitence). δοῦλος (of God): Josephus, *Ant.* 5.39 (prayer), cf. Rev. 15.3. θεράπων (of God): Wisd. 10.16 (poetic praise of the divine wisdom), cf. I *Cl.* 51.3, 5; 53.5; *Barn.* 14.4. *servus* (of God): Pseudo-Philo, *Ant. bibl.* 20.2. עֶבֶד (of God): IV Ezra 14.31 Syr. (Ezra's last words to the people); see further l. 9 above (formula for the confession of sins). The later Greek translations call Moses δοῦλος (of God): Ex. 4.10 Ἀ; Josh. 1.15 Ἀ, Σ, Θ; Δαν. 9.11 Θ; only Deut. 34.5 Ἀλλ has παῖς κυρίου.

[184] The description of David as 'servant of God' is to be found solely in prayers (with the exception of the later O.T. translations); I Macc. 4.30 (τοῦ δούλου σου Δαυίδ); 1QM 11.2 (דויד עבדכה); IV Ezra 3.23 and the 15th Berakha of the *XVIII Blessings* (Babylonian recension), v.l. (+ עבדך) דוד; an old Musaph prayer which is interpolated on the days of the new moon into the 17th (16th) benediction of the *XVIII Blessings* reads: זכרון משיח בן דוד עבדך (W. Heidenheim, שפת אמת, 1886, 21; S. R. Hirsch, סדור תפלות ישראל, *Israels Gebete*, 1921, 146, 274, 624); and the prayer of the passover *haggada* וּבַמָּקְהֲלוֹת before the fourth cup reads דוד בן־ישי עבדך משיחך. Cf. Luke 1.69; Acts 4.25; *Did.* 9.2 (in all three places παῖς [of God]); these early Christian usages, too, come from prayers. The later Greek translations of the Bible always call David δοῦλος (of God): III Βασ. 11.36 Ἀ, Σ; 14.8 Ἀ; ψ 35.1 Ἀ, Σ; Isa. 37.35 Ἀ, Σ, Θ.

[185] IV Ezra 3.11 Armenian (prayer).

[186] II Macc. 1.2 Ἀβραὰμ καὶ Ἰσαὰκ καὶ Ἰακὼβ τῶν δούλων αὐτοῦ (of God) τῶν πιστῶν (blessing); Syr. Bar. 4.4 (divine discourse); Pseudo-Philo, *Ant. bibl.* 6.11: *serve Dei* (Ambraham); 7.4: *puerum meum Abraham* (twice, divine discourse).

[187] Cf. n. 186; Δαν. 3.35 Θ (= LXX): διὰ Ἰσαὰκ τὸν δοῦλόν σου (prayer).

[187a] Cf. n. 186; 4Q Test. Levi[b] 2.10 (ed. J. T. Milik, *RB*, 62, 1955, 400).

[187b] Pseudo-Philo, *Ant. bibl.* 43.5 (*puer meus* [of God]).

[188] Heb. *Enoch* 2.3: משרת (of God).

The Servant of God in Late Judaism

Elijah,[189] and the three men in the fiery furnace.[190] In the mouth of non-Jews the title 'servant of God' is applied to Zerubbabel[191] and, following the O.T. text, to Daniel[192] and the three men in the fiery furnace.[193] In *Heb. Enoch* Meṭaṭron, the heavenly vicegerent, bears the title עֶבֶד (of God).[194]

(v) *'Servant of God' as denoting the Messiah*. Besides all this, 'servant of God' is met with denoting the Messiah. In the O.T. itself the Messiah is five times called 'my servant': Ezek. 34.23f.; 37.24f. (all four texts: עַבְדִּי דָוִד) and Zech. 3.8 (עַבְדִּי צֶמַח).[195] Subsequently, in IV Ezra 7.28; 13.32, 37, 52; 14.9 'my servant' (throughout'); 7.28 v.l., 29; *Syr. Bar.* 70.9 ('my servant, the Messiah');[196] *Targ.* Isa. 42.1; 43.10; 52.13; *Targ.* Zech. 3.8 (in all four texts עבדי משיחא); *Targ.* Ezek. 34.23f.; 37.24f. (in all four texts עבדי דוד). This exhausts the examples. Quite striking is the complete absence of the denotation of the Messiah as 'servant of God' in the whole of the rest of rabbinic literature, apart from quotations. With regard to the reason for this silence cf. p. 76 below. Thus in

---

[189] The third benediction after the reading of the prophets in the worship service: 'make us to rejoice, Yahweh, our God, בּאֵלִיָּהוּ הַנָּבִיא עַבְדֶּךָ' (Hirsch, op. cit. in n. 184, 342).
[190] Josephus, *Ant.* 10.215: τοὺς παῖδας τοῦ θεοῦ. See n. 169.
[191] I Esd. 6.27: τὸν παῖδα τοῦ κυρίου Ζοροβάβελ; cf. n. 195.
[192] Δαν. 6.20 Θ: ὁ δοῦλος τοῦ θεοῦ τοῦ ζῶντος (vocative).
[193] Δαν. 3.95 Θ (παῖδες of God); 3.93 Θ (δοῦλοι of God).
[194] 1.4; 10.3; 48 C 1, D 1 (17th of the 70 names). D 9. Also in later times the Meṭaṭron keeps the title עֶבֶד יהוה (cf. Odeberg, *3 Enoch*, part II, 28). If he is called נַעַר, Heb. Enoch 2.2; 3.2; 4.1, this word as elsewhere (examples in Odeberg, *3 Enoch*, part II, 173) is the equivalent of עֶבֶד in the meaning 'servant'. Cf. also n. 256.
[195] Cf. further Hag. 2.23 where Zerubbabel is called עַבְדִּי (LXX: τὸν δοῦλόν μου) and receives the promise that he shall be 'as a signet'.
[196] In the passages alluded to in IV Ezra the description of the Messiah fluctuates in the different versions. The rival terms are 'my son' (throughout *Lat.* and *Syr.*; *Eth.* 13.52; 14.9; *Sahidic* translation 13.32), 'my child' (*Arab.*, edition by G. H. A. Ewald, 1863, 7.28), 'my young man' (ibid. 13.32, 37, 52; 14.9; *Arab.*, edition by J. Gildemeister, 1877, 13.37; *Eth.* 13.37) and 'my servant' (*Arab.*, ed. J. Gildemeister, 13.32, 52; 14.9; *Eth.* 7.29). All these translations go back to the παῖς of the Greek source, which lies behind the surviving translations of IV Ezra. Cf. B. Violet, *Die Apokalypsen des Esra und des Baruch in deutscher Gestalt* (GCS, 32), 1924, 74f.: 'No Christian would ever have changed υἱός to παῖς but the opposite might easily have happened'. This conclusive proof has met with general consent. Cf. Harnack, 'Die Bezeichnung Jesu als "Knecht Gottes"', 212f.; A. v. Gall, *Βασιλεία τοῦ θεοῦ*, 1926, 417; Gressmann, *Messias*, 383f.; J. Jeremias, 'Erlöser und Erlösung', 110f.; ''Ἀμνὸς τοῦ θεοῦ', 120, n. 29; Buber, 113; Torrey, 'The Messiah', 260. J. Drummond had already correctly judged the state of affairs in *The Jewish Messiah*, 1877, 285–9; and Bousset had independently recognized the truth (53) on the basis of IV Ezra given by B. Violet, *Die Esra-Apokalypse (IV. Esra)*, I (GCS, 18), 1910. *Syr. Bar.* 70.9 calls the Messiah עַבְדִּי, the Greek text lying behind the Syriac also probably reads παῖς; this may be assumed because of the state of affairs in IV Ezra.

The Servant of God

the whole of the O.T. and late Jewish literature the description of the Messiah as God's servant occurs without exception only in the form 'my servant' and only in the mouth of God. We have here a biblical phrase which was in use up to the end of the first century A.D., then disappeared and survived only in quotation. 'Servant of God' as a real title for the Messiah never existed in Judaism, as is shown by its restriction to divine discourse.

3. INTERPRETATIONS OF THE DEUTERO-ISAIAH 'SERVANT OF GOD' PASSAGES

With reference to the N.T. it is of special importance to note how late Judaism interpreted the *'ebed* passages of Deut. Isa. If we except three places where historical figures are named עַבְדִּי by God (Isa. 20.3: Isaiah; 22.20: Eliakim; 37.35: David), in the whole book the singular 'servant of God' occurs only in chapters 41–53, the number of occurrences being nineteen: 41.8, 9; 42.1, 19 (twice); 43.10; 44.1, 2, 21 (twice), 26 (but cf. n. 221); 45.4; 48.20; 49.3, 5, 6; 50.10; 52.13; 53.11. For the investigation of the interpretation of these passages in late Judaism it is essential that various all too common sources of error should be avoided. First it must be borne in mind that, like the distinction between Proto-, Deutero- and Trito-Isaiah, so also the modern delimitation of the servant songs is completely unknown to that period. Hence the study must not be limited to the latter or to Isa. 53. Then it must be realized that the atomistic character of exegesis at that time does not permit us to presuppose a uniform interpretation of the *'ebed*; *Targ.* Isa., for example, explains certain servant passages as applying to the people, others as referring to the prophets and yet others as speaking of the Messiah (pp. 67ff. and n. 291). The conception of the *'ebed* as it is formulated in modern research 'does not exist at all in Jewish interpretation'.[197] Interpretations of single passages must therefore not be generalized. Further, careful distinction must be made between mere allusions and applications of isolated words in other connexions, whatever they may be, on the one hand, and deliberate exegesis on the other.[198]

---

[197] Cf. Fischel, 54.
[198] Rightly stressed by Moore, I, 229, 541; III, 166, n. 255 (on I, 551); cf. further Schlatter, *Das A.T. in der johanneischen Apokalypse*, 50; K. G. Kuhn, *Der tannaitische Midrasch Sifre zu Numeri* (Rabbinische Texte, II, 3), 1959, 527; Sjöberg, *Der Menschensohn im äthiopischen Henochbuch*, 119. Fischel, 59, n. 24, sought to establish rules for the distinction between mere allusion and deliberate exegesis.

The Servant of God in Late Judaism

The latter alone has real weight. Finally, it must not be forgotten that the Diaspora, partly as a result of divergent readings in the LXX, developed its own special traditions of exegesis; Hellenistic and Palestinian statements must not be placed on the same level.

(i) *Hellenistic Judaism*. (a) While the LXX predominantly renders Deutero-Isaiah's עֶבֶד יהוה by παῖς,[199] though δοῦλος does appear three times,[200] subsequently, however, δοῦλος completely disappears in references to the servant of God based on Deut. Isa. The servant is consistently called παῖς in Jewish Hellenistic literature subsequent to the composition of the LXX.[201] That remains so until A.D. 100. As a result of its ambiguity the phrase παῖς θεοῦ could be understood either as 'servant of God' (thus the LXX) or as 'child of God' (thus Wisd., cf. p. 45 above). The further the distance from the original Hebrew text the more the second conception ('child of God') prevailed in the Jewish Hellenistic understanding of Isa. 40ff.

Only after the beginning of the second century does the picture change, and that radically. Aquila (cf. n. 263) always calls Deutero-Isaiah's servant δοῦλος.[202] The question as to what determined his choice of word is answered by the observation that he also renders עֶבֶד by δοῦλος outside Isa. 40ff.[203] Thus he is merely following his strictly practised translation technique of rendering Heb. roots everywhere by the same Greek roots.[204] Hence for his translation of עֶבֶד by δοῦλος in Isa. 40ff. we may ascribe to him no other motive than the desire for accurate translation.[205] His example was followed by his successors. Theodotion also renders עֶבֶד by δοῦλος. Accordingly he calls

---

[199] 41.8, 9; 42.1, 23 א; 43.10; 44, 1, 2, 21 (twice), 26; 45.4; 49.6; 50.10; 52.13; also plural οἱ παῖδές μου for Heb. עֲבָדַי 42.19a.

[200] 48.20; 49.3, 5; also plural οἱ δοῦλοι τοῦ θεοῦ for Heb. עֶבֶד יהוה, 42.19b; and εὖ δουλεύοντα for Heb. עֲבָדִי, 53.11.

[201] J. Jeremias, ''Ἀμνὸς τοῦ θεοῦ', 118–21.

[202] Preserved in Isa. 41.8, 9; 42.1; 49.6; 52.13.

[203] There seem to be four exceptions to this rule, but cf. Hegermann, 29f.

[204] Aquila practises this principle with such astonishing consistency that one is led simply to suppose that before beginning his translation he prepared for himself a Heb.-Greek lexicon. Cf. *Septuaginta*, ed. A. Rahlfs, 1935, I, x.

[205] The supposition expressed by Euler (88) with reservations, by Zolli (229f.), and by J. Jeremias, 'Zum Problem der Deutung von Jes. 53 im palästinischen Spätjudentum', in *Aux sources de la tradition chrétienne. Mélanges offeris à M. Maurice Goguel*, 1950, 115f., that Aquila's disinclination to render עֶבֶד by παῖς is connected with anti-Christian tendencies, cannot therefore be maintained; Hegermann, 29f.

The Servant of God

the servant of God δοῦλος in all the extant servant passages in Isa. 40ff. (41.8, 9; 42.1; 49.6); only in 42.1 Θ a v.l. reads παῖς (= LXX).²⁰⁶ The translation of the Jewish Christian Symmachus, following the model of Aquila, renders עֶבֶד as δοῦλος.²⁰⁷

(*b*) The exegesis of Deutero-Isaiah's servant of God in Hellenistic Judaism was determined by the fact that the LXX had extended the collective interpretation which the Heb. text gave in nine places (cf. n. 175) to other passages (cf. p. 43 above). Thus in Isa. 42.19 the LXX rendered the singular of the Heb. text twice as a plural (עַבְדִּי = LXX οἱ παῖδές μου; עֶבֶד יהוה = LXX οἱ δοῦλοι τοῦ θεοῦ).²⁰⁸ Especially far-reaching in consequence was the fact that the LXX understood the phrase 'my servant' as collective also in Isa. 42.1, and expressed this sense by the addition of the word Ἰακώβ: Ἰακὼβ ὁ παῖς μου (Heb. only עַבְדִּי). Thus there arose a bifurcation in the understanding of Isa. 42.1ff.; following the LXX, Hellenistic Judaism refers the text to the people of Israel,²⁰⁹ and Palestinian Judaism understands it throughout as messianic (see pp. 60, 62 and n. 262; pp. 68, 72 and n. 306).

A further similar bifurcation is to be noted with regard to Isa. 53. Hellenistic Judaism, so far as we know, interprets the suffering servant in a generic or collective sense, as distinct from its messianic interpretation in Palestinian Judaism. The generic interpretation we find first in Wisd., which describes the just man, called παῖς κυρίου 'child of God' (2.13, cf. p. 46), and his fate in close connexion with Isa. 52.13ff. This applies above all to the final judgement scene where (Wisd. 4.20ff.) the sinners confess, trembling, that they have scorned and misesteemed the just and have departed from the way of truth. Here, in trait after

---

²⁰⁶ So the Qumran texts and the Syro-Hexaplarist translation. Theodoret of Cyrus maintained, however, that Theodotion translated Isa. 42.1 עֶבֶד by δοῦλος. It speaks for the correctness of the reading δοῦλος that Theodotion always appears to render עֶבֶד by δοῦλος and that παῖς (cf. Hatch and Redpath s.v.) simply does not occur in the fragments which have come down to us from him (except the v.l. on Isa. 42.1).
²⁰⁷ Preserved in Isa. 41.8, 9; 42.1, 19 (twice); 49.6; 52.13.
²⁰⁸ Cf. further Isa. 44.26 where LXX (A) translates עֲבָדָיו (of God) plurally by παίδων αὐτοῦ and Isa. 48.20 where LXX (A) renders עַבְדּוֹ יַעֲקֹב by τὸν λαὸν αὐτοῦ Ἰακώβ.
²⁰⁹ Justin, *Dial.* 123.8f.; cf. Dalman, I, 32 and Fischel, 59. This interpretation of Isa. 42.1ff. is also presupposed in *Dial.* 121.4.

The Servant of God in Late Judaism

trait, there is allusion to Isa. 52.13ff.; cf. Wisd. 4.18 with Isa. 53.3; Wisd. 4.20 and 5.3 with Isa. 52.15; Wisd. 5.1 (πόνοι) with Isa. 53.11; Wisd. 5.2 (ἐκστήσονται) with Isa. 52.14; Wisd. 5.3f. with Isa. 53.2–4; Wisd. 5.5 (κλῆρος) with Isa. 53.12 (κληρονομήσει); Wisd. 5.6f. with Isa. 53.6; Wisd. 5.15f. with Isa. 53.10–12; further, Wisd. 2.13 with Isa. 52.13; 53.11; Wisd. 2.19f. with Isa. 53.7f.[210] The παῖς θεοῦ of Isa. 52.13ff. is thus for Wisdom the type of the just man. Obviously then this writer was familiar with the generic interpretation of Isa. 53.[211] Of the collective interpretation we find an example in Origen, *Contr. Cels.* 1.55: he says that Jewish rabbis with whom he came into contact interpreted Isa. 53 'of the people considered as a person who had been scattered and tormented'. For Palestinian Judaism of the first millennium A.D. this collective application of the servant of Isa. 53 to Israel is completely unknown (it appears first in Rashi, died 1105).[212] We must therefore assume that the informants of Origen were Hellenistic Jews.

To sum up, Hellenistic Judaism is inclined to understand the παῖς θεοῦ of Deutero-Isaiah as 'child of God' and prefers the generic or collective interpretation.

(ii) *Palestinian Judaism*. In Palestinian Judaism of the first millennium three distinct interpretations of the Deutero-Isaiah servant are found. It is important to note that—with some exceptions—these three interpretations do not overlap but each of them is limited to certain of the nineteen passages (cf. p. 52) referring to the servant.

(*a*) *The collective interpretation* (Isa. 41.8f.; 42.19 [twice]; 44.1, 2, 21 [twice]; 45.4; 48.20; 49.3, 5f. [?]; 50.10). In the Heb. text the collective application of Deutero-Isaiah's servant of God to the people of Israel was present in nine of the nineteen passages (Isa. 41.8f.; 44.1, 2, 21 [twice]; 45.4; 48.20; 49.3). Thus was established[213] for the following centuries the application to Israel of these nine passages, as *Targ.* Isa. shows (see n. 176).

[210] Cf. Dalman, I, 32, n. 1.
[211] W. Staerk, 'Zur Exegese von Jes 53 im Diasporajudentum', *ZNW*, 35, 1936, 308.
[212] Dalman, I, 34f.; S.-B. I, 481.
[213] Applications of this text to Israel are to be found outside *Targ.* in the following places: Isa. 41.8f.: Luke 1.54; *Gen.R.* 44.3 on 15.1; Isa. 44.2: Bar. 3.36 (cf. n. 177); *Midr. Ps.* 111 §1; Isa. 49.3: *Siphre Deut.* §355 on 33.26 par. *Mekhilta Ex.* 15.2; *Lev.R.* 2 on 1.2; *Ex.R.* 21 on 14.15 (for further comments on Isa. 49.3 see Dalman, I, 97, n. 1).

The Servant of God

Under the influence of Isa. 49.3 ('My servant art thou, Israel') the *Targ.* appears, moreover, to see an allusion to Israel in the following verses (5, 6).[214] Other servant passages were not in the older rabbinic tradition, as distinct from the Hellenistic (cf. pp. 54f.), applied to Israel.[215] In particular, Isa. 53 in Palestinian rabbinic Judaism of the first millennium A.D. was nowhere referred to Israel (cf. p. 55); rather in rabbinic literature the collective application to Israel was strictly confined to those passages and their context where the Heb. text demanded it.[216]

As far as the application of individual servant passages to the just, the prophets and the scribes is concerned, the following points are to be noted: it is merely a question of *allusions* when in Ecclus. 11.13[217] a free quotation from Isa. 52.15 is applied to the suffering righteous (cf. G. Bertram, θαῦμα κτλ., *TWNT*, III, 30, n. 17) and in Dan. 12.3[218] a phrase from Isa. 53.11 is applied, in the plural, to the teachers of Israel. But we have *exegesis* when in *Targ.* Isa. 42.19 (twice) the servant is connected with penitent sinners,[219] and in 50.10 with the prophets.[220, 221] In B. Ber. 5a

---

[214] *Targ.* Isa. 49.5f. is usually thus understood; cf. Dalman, I, 97, n. 1; Humbert, 25, n. 5; S.-B., II, 330; Seidelin, 202. But it cannot be stated quite confidently, in view of the alteration of the number, of whom the *Targ.* was thinking in referring to the 'serving servant' (*Targ.* Isa. 49.5 *singular*) and the 'servants of God' (*Targ.* Isa. 49.6 *plural*). Fischel, 60, 74, rightly sets a question mark against the application of *Targ.* Isa. 49.5f. to Israel. (On the sentence construction and translation of *Targ.* Isa. 49.5f. cf. the notes of Humbert, 25, n. 5, which are worth consideration.) For the interpretation of Isa. 49.6 in rabbinic literature cf. n. 305.

[215] According to Fischel, 76, Isa. 42.19 was referred to Israel in rabbinic literature, but he gives no example. Presumably he is thinking of *Targ.* Isa. 42.19 where, however, it is a question of penitent sinners (cf. n. 219).

[216] The correct observation of Fischel, 65f., that 'in the tannaitic and amoraic periods, apart from the reports of Justin and Origen, applications to Israel of 42.1ff., 50.4ff. and ch. 53 are lacking', must be extended to include the points (1) that it should be made to cover all the servant passages of Deut. Isa. except those mentioned above; and (2) that for Palestinian rabbinic Judaism the reservation made with regard to Justin (cf. n. 209) and Origen (cf. p. 55), is to be expunged.

[217] ויתמהו עליו רבים ('and many will be astonished at him') is the earliest existing reference to Isa. 52.13ff.

[218] מַצְדִּיקֵי הָרַבִּים ('which have brought many to righteousness'). Cf. H. L. Ginsberg, 'The Oldest Interpretation of the Suffering Servant', *Vetus Testamentum*, 3, 1953, 400–4.

[219] *Targ.* Isa. 42.19: 'will not the wicked when they return be called "my servant" ' (Heb. עַבְדִּי, *Targ. Codd.* also; only the MS. British Museum, Or. 1474, has the plural עַבְדַּי)? If they return they will be called the "servants of God" ' (Heb. עֶבֶד יְהוָה; *Targ.* has the plural עבדיא דיהוה).

[220] Heb. עַבְדּוֹ is rendered by the *Targ.* with עבדוהי נבייא.

[221] On the other hand it is questionable whether *Targ.* Isa. 44.26 belongs here. In

The Servant of God in Late Judaism

(Rab Huna, died 297) and *Seder Eliahu* R. 7[222] Isa. 53.10 is applied to penitent sufferers; B. *Yoma* 86a applies Isa. 49.3 (Abbaye, died 338/9) and *Seder Eliahu* R. 14 and 25[223] applies Isa. 53.11 to upright teachers of the torah; but in these last-named five cases words are isolated from their context, so that inferences with regard to the interpretation of the latter are precluded.[224] Only in isolated instances has Palestinian Judaism applied Deut. Isa. servant passages to the just, the prophets and the scribes.[225]

In the Qumran texts there is no conclusive evidence of a collective application of the servant to the Essene community.[225a]

(b) *Application to the prophet Isaiah* (Isa. 49.5; 50.10). It must have seemed obvious to interpret some of the servant passages as self-expressions of the prophet; this is true especially of the description of suffering given in the first person in Isa. 50.4ff., which reaches its climax in the summons to hear the voice of the servant (v. 10). In point of fact the commentary of Jerome on Isaiah attests specifically, and with reference to v. 10, that the Jews explained this section as bearing on the prophet Isaiah himself.[226] Isa. 49.5,[227] which also has the 'I' form, is

---

this text the Heb. עַבְדִּי is indeed rendered by עבדוהי צדיקיא. But the *parallelismus membrorum* makes it probable that the form עבדו was intended as a plural עֲבָדָיו in the original text (thus BHK[2,3] ad loc.) and since the LXX (παίδων αὐτοῦ) has so understood the Heb. text, it must be asked whether the *Targ.* likewise has not so read the original text. In that case *Targ.* Isa. 44.26 would be an example not of the collective interpretation of the servant, but of the use of the plural to denote the pious. Cf. n. 169.

[222] S.-B., I, 484. At the earliest, second half of the fifth century; according to Strack, *Einl.*, 220: second half of the tenth century.

[223] S.-B., I, 484f.

[224] Cf. the warning of Moore, III, 166, n. 255.

[225] For medieval authors who represent this view, cf. Fischel, 61, 74–76.

[225a] Several passages have been adduced which seem to draw in terminology or substance upon the servant songs (M. Black, 'Servant of the Lord and Son of Man', *Scottish Journal of Theology*, 6, 1953, 4–8; W. H. Brownlee, 'The Servant of the Lord in the Qumran Scrolls', *Bulletin of the American Schools of Oriental Research*, 132, Dec. 1953, 8–15; 135, Oct. 1954, 33–38; F. F. Bruce, *Biblical Exegesis in the Qumran Texts*, Exegetica III, 1, 1959, 50–58), but they are at best allusions. Furthermore, the concept of *'ebed* is lacking in all instances.

[226] In Migne, PL, 24, 496. In *Lev.R.* 10.2 on 8.1 par. *Pesiqta* 125b (ed. S. Buber, 1868), R. Jehuda bar Simon (*circa* 330) explains Isa. 50.6 with reference to Isaiah. When *Targ.* Isa. 50.10 translates Heb. עַבְדּוֹ by 'his (God's) servants the prophets' (n. 220) here too a reference to Isaiah is implied. Isa. 50.4–10 was at no time interpreted messianically in Judaism, cf. Seidelin, 206, n. 28, and especially Fischel, 63, 74f.; p. 58 below.

[227] *Siphre Deut.* §27 on 3.24.

The Servant of God

at times referred to Isaiah.[228] The extension of this interpretation to Isa. 53.7f. in the question of the treasurer (Acts 8.34) has on the other hand no parallel in the history of the time.[229]

The recurring applications of individual servant passages to particular persons are without significance. For the linking of Isa. 41.8 with the patriarch Jacob (*Siphre Deut.* §27 on 3.24), of עַבְדִּי, Isa. 43.10, with David (*Midr. Ps.* 51 §3 on 51.6), of Isa. 44.26 with the angel with whom Jacob wrestled (*Gen. R.* 78.3 on 32.27f. by R. Levi, *circa* 300), of Isa. 49.8f. with Noah and his family[230] who left the ark with him, and of Isa. 50.10 with Abraham (*Gen. R.* 60 on 24.12);[231] as also the relating of Isa. 53.12 with Moses' eschatological reward (*Siphre Deut.* §355 on 33.21), with the jealous action of Phinehas (*Siphre Num.* §131 on 25.13) and with R. Akiba[232] or the men of the great synagogue (*J. Sheq.* 5.1 [48 c 48])[233]—all these are without exception references to single verses in isolation which give no clue as to how the rabbis concerned interpreted the respective contexts as a whole.[234] As regards the relating of Isa. 53.12 to Moses' act of intercession (*B. Sotah* 14a)[235] it has its source in R. Simlai (*circa* 250) who plays a part in Palestine tradition chiefly on account of his controversy with the Christians.[236] In applying Isa. 53.12 to Moses his object no doubt is to prevent Christian apologists from applying it to Jesus.[237] That is all the more likely as the same tendency with regard to Isa. 53.12 was already pre-

---

[228] Correspondingly Isa. 49.1 is referred to Isaiah: *Midr. Ps.* 9 §59 on 9.6, 43a; *Pesiqta* R. 129a.
[229] In particular there is to be found in the reports about the martyrdom of Isaiah no allusion to the '*ebed*, and this is pointed out by Fischel, 63.
[230] *Aggadat Bereshit* 7 (ed. A. Jellinek, *Bet ha-Midrasch* IV, 1857, 12).
[231] S.-B., II, 608.
[232] The author is R. Jona (*circa* 350).
[233] The last three texts in S.-B., I, 483f.
[234] Schlatter, Moore, Kuhn, cf. n. 198. Kuhn (loc. cit. in n. 198) rightly remarks with reference to the relation of Isa. 53.12 to the jealous deed of Phinehas (*Siphre Num.* §131 on 25.13): 'thus this explanation does not suggest that the prophecy of Isa. 53.12 relates to Phinehas'. But Fischel, 63, n. 51 referring to Ecclus. 48.10 (cf. p. 59) and Mark 9.13 sees in the relation of Isa. 53.12 to Phinehas more than an incidental homiletic allusion; but the equation of Phinehas and Elijah, which Fischel assumes for *Siphre Num.* §131, belongs only to the post-N.T. period (J. Jeremias, 'Ἠλ(ε)ίας, *TWNT*, II, 935, 21f.), and it is doubtful whether it is already present in *Siphre Num.* §131. Also K. G. Kuhn doubts it, as he has informed the author; otherwise S.-B., IV, 463.
[235] S.-B., I, 483.
[236] W.Bacher, *Die Agada der Palästinensischen Amoräer*, I, 1892, 555f.
[237] Moore, III, 166, n. 254.

The Servant of God in Late Judaism

sumably at work in Theodotion in the second century A.D. (cf. pp. 66f.).

(c) *Messianic exegesis* (Isa. 42.1; 43.10; 49.6; 52.13; 53.11). Messianic interpretations of certain Deut. Isa. servant passages can most probably be traced back to pre-Christian times (cf. p. 43).

(α) In Ecclus. 48.10 one of the three tasks of the returning Elijah (cf. J. Jeremias, *'Ηλ(ε)ίας*, *TWNT*, II, 933, 12ff.) is described as להכין שבטי ישראל; the expression comes from Isa. 49.6 where the *'ebed* receives the mission of לְהָקִים אֶת־שִׁבְטֵי יַעֲקֹב. The restoration of the twelve tribes is a messianic task and its assignment to Elijah must have marked the latter as the coming saviour.[238] But since the verse contains no more than a broad allusion to Isa. 49.6, conclusions about a messianic interpretation of Isa. 49.6 from Ecclus. 48.10 alone are not quite secure[239] (but cf. n. 305). In any case it is significant that Ecclus. explained the servant in Isa. 49.6 in an individual sense.[240]

(β) The next relevant source from the point of view of time is the so-called Visionary Discourses[244] of the *Ethiopian Enoch* (chs. 37–71) which are certainly pre-Christian.[245] Here the Messiah is

[238] Cf. J. Jeremias, *'Ηλ(ε)ίας*, *TWNT*, II, 933, 16ff. and n. 17, also Dalman, I, 28; S.-B., IV, 780.

[239] Similarly, most recently, North, 7. More confident is the judgement of Dalman, I, 28.

[240] The Qumran texts which follow chronologically after Ecclesiasticus are sometimes held to combine references to the Messiah and the servant, and to identify the Teacher of Righteousness with this (Messiah-)servant figure (thus especially A. Dupont-Sommer, 'Le livre des Hymnes découvert près de la Mer Morte', *Semitica*, 7, 1957, 64, n. 8, 10; *Les écrits esséniens découverts près de la Mer Morte*, 1959, 377). Both these hypotheses are unacceptable, however, for the following reasons: (*a*) The messianic passages contain no straightforward quotations of, nor allusions to, the servant texts of Deutero-Isaiah. (*b*) All that can be brought forward in favour of the identification of the Teacher of Righteousness with the servant are some uncertain and remote reminiscences of Deutero-Isaiah, the general description of the Teacher as a humble and humiliated person, and two quotations from Isa. 50.4 (1QH 7.10; 8.35f.). But there is no mention of vicarious suffering on the Teacher's part. The epithet of *'ebed* is used in connexion with him, but only by himself in the accepted sense of a humble self-description of the worshipper (cf. pp. 47f.); it is never applied to him by somebody else, and is never combined with references to the servant songs (cf. the detailed discussion by G. Jeremias, *Der Lehrer der Gerechtigkeit*, 299–307 [Lit.]).

[244] The translation 'Visionary Discourses' has established itself and is therefore retained, but it is not exact. Ethiopic *mesel* (pl.), Hebrew מָשָׁל, Greek παραβολή refers to three apocalyptic visions—*Eth. En.* 37.5; 38.1; 45.1; 57.3; 58.1; 68.1; 69.29. Thus the word has here the meaning 'instructive speech with secret meaning'.

[245] The dating of the Discourses is dependent on the fact that they (56.5–7) make allusion to the Parthian invasion of Palestine of 40 B.C. They will have been composed shortly afterwards and a little later fitted into the scheme of *Enoch*. The untenability of the view that the Discourses as a whole are Christian or have been

The Servant of God

depicted to a quite striking extent by means of traits drawn from Deut. Isa. Apart from the titles 'son of man' and 'Messiah'[246] he bears constantly the name 'the chosen one',[247] besides occasionally that of 'the righteous one'.[248] 'The chosen one' is, however, in Isa. 42.1 the title of the servant of God[249] and the same applies to 'the righteous one' in Isa. 53.11.[250] Thus we are led straight away to those two sections of Deut. Isa. which, also in the subsequent periods, are the ones interpreted messianically: Isa. 42.1ff., 52.13ff.[251]

In *En.* 48.4 the son of man is called 'the light of the peoples'; this is an exclusive attribute of God's servant (Isa. 42.6; 49.6). It is said further that his name was named before creation 'in the presence of the Lord of Spirits' (*En.* 48.3); this is an amplification of Isa. 49.1: 'my name he named when I was not yet born'. Then he was 'hidden before God' (*En.* 48.6, cf. 62.7) which is a reference to Isa. 49.2: 'He hid me in the shadow of his hand'.[252] Again, in the description of the revelation of the son of man the Visionary Discourses constantly depict the humiliation of kings and the mighty before him with a reminiscence of Isa. 49.7;

---

provided in part with Christian interpolations has recently been demonstrated by Sjöberg, *Der Menschensohn im äthiopischen Henochbuch*, 3-24. The main argument is the total lack of anything specifically Christian.

[246] 'The anointed': *En.* 48.10; 52.4.

[247] *En.* 39.6; 40.5; 45.3 v.l., 4; 49.2; 51.3, 5; 52.6, 9; 53.6; 55.4; 61.5, 8, 10; 62.1; cf. 46.3; 48.6; 49.4.

[248] *En.* 38.2 (v.l. 'righteousness', cf. Sjöberg, *Der Menschensohn im äthiopischen Henochbuch*, 96, n. 48); 53.6 ('the righteous and chosen one'). Cf. further 39.6: 'the elect of righteousness and faith'; 46.3: 'the son of man who has righteousness and with whom righteousness dwells'; 71.14.

[249] The allusion to Isa. 42.1 is generally recognized, and rightly. Cf. especially *En.* 49.4: 'He has been chosen before the Lord of Spirits as the latter has willed' (for translation see Sjöberg, 122, n. 33) with Isa. 42.1: 'my chosen in whom my soul delighteth'. Ps. 89.3, 19 where David is called 'my chosen' (v. 3) and 'a chosen one' (v. 19) does not apply as an O.T. prototype, since late Judaism always related both verses to the historical David, never to the Messiah.

[250] The Messiah is called 'righteous' also in Zech. 9.9 (cf. 'righteous branch' Jer. 23.5; 33.15). However, in view of the many allusions to Deut. Isa., as far as *Eth. En.* is concerned only Isa. 53.11 is in question as a prototype. Cf. S.-B., I, 481.

[251] S.-B., I, 481: 'The messianic exegesis (of Isa. 53) is first (but see pp. 43f., 59) met with in the Visionary Discourses of Enoch'; also cf. Wolff, 38f.; Fischel, 61; lastly H. Kosmala, 'Jom Kippur', *Judaica*, 6, 1950, 16.

[252] Cf. with Isa. 49.2: 'in the shadow of his hand', *En.* 39.7: 'I saw his dwelling under the pinions of the Lord of Spirits'. The idea of the hiddenness of the Messiah plays a great part in subsequent periods, also in the N.T. (cf. for example, Matt. 24.26; John 7.27; Rev. 12.5; further, Justin, *Dial.* 8, 110; Dalman, I, 34; Sjöberg, *Der verborgene Menschensohn*, 41-89).

The Servant of God in Late Judaism

52.15.[253] It is said that they will see him in his glory (*En.* 55.4; 62.1, 3), rise before him (*En.* 46.4; 62.3), and cast themselves down (48.10 v.l.; 62.9; cf. 48.5), thus with an allusion to Isa. 49.7: 'Princes and kings will see it and arise and cast themselves down'. It is said further that their countenance will be fallen (*En.* 46.6; 48.8) alluding to Isa. 52.15: 'Kings will shut their mouths before him'. In particular in *En.* 62.1ff. the conduct of kings, the mighty and those who possess the earth, is depicted in close connexion with Isa. 52.13ff.; thus *En.* 62.5f.: 'They will be afraid (cf. Isa. 52.14), they will lower their eyes (cf. Isa. 52.15), and pain will seize them when they see the Son of Man sitting on the throne of his glory; kings (cf. Isa. 52.15), the mighty and all who possess the earth will glorify, praise and exalt him who rules over all (cf. Isa. 52.13), who was hidden (cf. Isa. 52.15)'. That this passage takes up Isa. 52.13ff. is confirmed by the fact that it is understood, just as in contemporary exegesis (Wisd. 4.20ff.; '*A*; Θ; *Targ.*), as a final judgement scene. Again it is the passages Isa. 42.1ff.; 52.13ff. (cf. p. 60) which are messianically interpreted; together with 49.1f., 6f. Finally there are the following statements which have a loose connexion with Deut. Isa. The chosen has the spirit of righteousness (*En.* 62.1f.; cf. [besides Isa. 11.2, 4] 42.1: 'My chosen . . . I have laid my spirit upon him'). He executes judgement (*En.* 41.9; 45.3; 49.4; 55.4; 61.9; 62.2f.; 69.27; cf. Isa. 42.4 '*A*, Θ, *Targ.*). *En.* 48.4b: 'He will be the light of the peoples and the hope of the sad' combines Isa. 42.6 ('light of the peoples') with its context (42.7: salvation of the blind and wretched). The son of man of the Visionary Discourses is thus to a large extent[255] depicted with traits which are borrowed from servant passages of Deut. Isa. (42.1–7; 49.1f., 6f.; 52.13–15; 53.11).

This combination of traits describing the servant of God with the son of man, here brought about for the first time, although restricted to the traits exalting the servant's glory,[255a] was of decisive importance for Jesus' understanding of his mission.[256]

[253] Cf. Billerbeck, 108; Fischel, 61.
[255] Billerbeck, 107: 'almost exclusively'. Cf. Staerk, *Soter*, 72–77, 82f.
[255a] The suggestion that this combination in *Ethiopian Enoch* embraces the statements about the servant's humiliation as well (S.-B., II, 282, n.1; J. Jeremias, 'Erlöser und Erlösung', 106ff.; Staerk, *Soter*, 83, 86) is untenable.
[256] Buber, 112f. An echo of this combination of son of man and servant in *Ethiopian Enoch* is to be seen in the fact that in the *Heb. En.* the Meṭaṭron, who bears many

The Servant of God

(γ) The *Peshitta* explains Isa. 53—including the passages about suffering—in a messianic sense.[258] This is clear from the passages where the *Peshitta* discloses its understanding of Isa. 53 by deviations from the Heb. text. Thus the *Peshitta* saw in the servant a figure awaited in the future (52.14a) who shall 'cleanse' many peoples (52.15); this figure is denied (53.2) and slain (53.5) but exalted by God and (at the last judgement) will convey forgiveness (53.5: healing). These statements can only refer to the Messiah.[259] However, it is uncertain whether the *Peshitta* of Isaiah is of Jewish[259a] and/or of Christian origin.

(δ) In one place the N.T. too gives us a piece of evidence for the messianic exegesis of a servant passage in late Judaism. According to Luke 23.35 (which comes from Luke's special source[259b]) the ἄρχοντες mock the Crucified with the words: ἄλλους ἔσωσεν, σωσάτω ἑαυτόν, εἰ οὗτός ἐστιν ὁ χριστὸς τοῦ θεοῦ, ὁ ἐκλεκτός. For our purpose the point is that it is the Jewish ἄρχοντες who here describe the Messiah with the title ὁ ἐκλεκτός. Christian influence on this formulation is not probable, for as a christological formula ὁ ἐκλεκτός appears elsewhere in the N.T. only[260] in John 1.34.[261] But we are already acquainted with this title from the *Eth. En.* where, as we have seen, it appears as a pre-Christian Jewish messianic predicate derived from Isa. 42.1 (cf. p. 60).[262]

---

attributes of the son of man (Odeberg, 146) is called עֶבֶד (of God) or נַעַר; see n. 194.
Cf. J. Bowman, 'The Background of the Term "Son of Man" ', *ET*, 59, 1947–8, 288.
[258] Hegermann, 127.
[259] Hegermann, ibid.
[259a] P. Kahle, *The Cairo Genizah*², 1959, 265–73; also Hegermann, 22–27.
[259b] J. Jeremias, 'Perikopenumstellungen bei Lukas?', *New Testament Studies*, 4, 1957–8, 115–19.
[260] In Luke 9.35 we find the divergent form ὁ ἐκλελεγμένος as the (probably original) reading. In the Apostolic Fathers and the apologists ὁ ἐκλεκτός is never used for 'Christ'.
[261] The fact that the reading ὁ ἐκλεκτός in John 1.34 offered by the oldest MSS., in spite of the small number of attestations (P⁵ ℵ* 77 218 sy^sc a b e ff²), represents the correct text, has been convincingly demonstrated by A. v. Harnack, 'Zur Textkritik und Christologie der Schriften des Johannes', *SAB*, 1915, 552–6 = *Studien I* (Arbeiten zur Kirchengeschichte, 19), 1931, 127–32. For in all three linguistic zones of the early church, Greek, Syriac, and Latin, textual history begins unanimously with this reading. In the fourth century, in the struggle against adoptionist christology, it was replaced by ὁ υἱός.
[262] Otherwise as such it occurs plainly only in the *Apocalypse of Abraham* 31.1. On the other hand *Test. B.* 11.4: καὶ ἔσται ἐκλεκτὸς θεοῦ ἕως τοῦ αἰῶνος (cf. G. Schrenk, ἐκλεκτός, *TWNT*, IV, 190, 2f.) certainly belongs to a Christian interpolation, as the text itself shows (11.2b–5), and is related not to Christ but to the Benjamite Paul (R. H. Charles, *The Testaments of the Twelve Patriarchs translated*, 1908, 215f., note on ch. XI).

The Servant of God in Late Judaism

Thus in Luke 23.35 we have an echo of the messianic exegesis of Isa. 42.1 in late Judaism. Further let it be noted here, in confirmation of what we have been saying, that also in the N.T. the messianic interpretation of Deut. Isa. servant texts is limited to Isa. 42.1–4, 6; 49.6; 52.13–53.12 (cf. p. 94).

(ε) At the beginning of the second century A.D.[263] Aquila completed in Palestine a new translation of the O.T. into Greek, designed to replace the LXX, as the latter offered Christians too much scope for the production of christological proof-texts.[264] Aquila's interpretation of the servant in Isa. 53 is to be inferred, *inter alia*, from his exegesis of 53.8f. as referring to the judgement which the servant holds, which is in agreement with *Targ.*; messianism is implicit at this point.[266] Further, Aquila translates (according to Jerome) נָגוּעַ (Isa. 53.4) by ἀφημένον[267] ('leprous', cf. *Vulgate: quasi leprosum*), a translation

[263] The dating of the translation of the O.T. by Aquila is determined by the fact that he was a pupil, on the one hand, of R. Akiba (Jerome on Isa. 8.11ff. [Migne, *PL*, 24, 119 A]: '*Akibas quem magistrum Aquilae proselyti autumant*'; *J. Qid.* 1. 1 [59 a 9]), on the other hand of R. Eli'ezer ben Hyrcanos and of R. Jehoshua' ben Hananiah (*J. Meg.* 1. 11 [71c 9]); the activity of the two last named reached its zenith c. A.D. 90. But R. Jehoshua' had served in the Temple as a Levite (*B.'Ar.* 11b; *Sipbre Num.* §116 on 18.3; *T. Sbeq.* 2.14) and thus before the destruction of the Temple must have reached the canonical Levitical age of 20, and consequently must have been born before A.D. 50. R. Eli'ezer b. Hyrcanos was still older than R. Jehoshua', for he did not begin his studies until the age of 22 or 28 (*Pesiqta R. Eli'ezer* 1; *Gen. R.* 42.3 on 14.1; *Ab. R. Nat.* 6) and he pursued them many years under Rabban Jochanan b. Zakkai before A.D. 70. Thus he must have been born, say between A.D. 30 and A.D. 40 (J. Klausner, *Jesus von Nazareth*, 1930, 46; cf. R. T. Herford, *Christianity in Talmud and Midrash*, 1903, 142, n. 1; and according to Klausner, op. cit., 65, he was already at an advanced age c. A.D. 80). As far as the date of Eli'ezer's death is concerned, we know that he died before R. Akiba, hence before A.D. 135 (*B. Sanb.* 68a); for some time up to his death he was in banishment and was avoided by colleagues and pupils. Since Aquila read his translation both to him and to R. Jehoshua' (*J. Meg.* 1. 11 [71c 9]) it can hardly have been produced after A.D. 110, and more likely earlier.

[264] *Septuaginta*, ed. A. Rahlfs, 1935, I, vii f.

[266] Hegermann, 42, 112; see 122ff. for further observations, notably with regard to the agreement between Aquila and the *Targ.*

[267] Jerome (on Isa. 53.4 [Migne, *PL*, 24, 507 A]): '*Pro eo quod Symmachus transtulit, ἐν ἀφῇ ὄντα, hoc est in lepra, Aquila posuit ἀφημένον, id est leprosum; quod multi non intelligentes putant relictum (ἀφειμένον), et alii legunt καθήμενον, id est sedentem*'. According to Eusebius (cf. Ziegler, *Isaias*, ad loc.) Aquila translated נָגוּעַ by τετραυματισμένον.

But without question Jerome gives here the correct text (ἀφημένον); for the context of the reading, as conveyed by Eusebius, excludes its derivation from Aquila (cf. J. Ziegler, *Textkritische Notizen zu den jüngeren griechischen Übersetzungen des Buches Isaias*, NGG, Fachgruppe V, N.F. I, 4, 1939, 97f.); further Aquila consistently renders the Heb. root נגע by the Greek word group ἀφή/ἅπτεσθαι. The pass. ἀφᾶσθαι which is not elsewhere attested has been derived from ἀφή which in Jewish Greek had the specific connotation of 'plague', 'leprosy'. There is no reason to doubt Jerome's statement that the participle of perf. pass. ἀφημένος meant 'leprous'.

The Servant of God

which is explained by the fact that the passive participle of נגע in post-biblical Hebrew (Puʻal) and Aramaic (Paʻel) has the meaning 'leprous'. For our question this translation is very illuminating because the exegesis 'leper' for Isa. 53.4 is met with also in rabbinic literature and is here referred to the Messiah.[268]

We are thinking of two places in *B. Sanh*. 98 which alone in the *Talmud*, along with a late *Midrash* text,[269] have preserved the curious conception of a leprous Messiah.[270] One text is *B. Sanh*. 98b, from *circa* A.D. 200.[271] In an enumeration of messianic titles it is here said: 'And the teachers said "the leprous one" (חִוָּרָא), those of the House of Rabbi[272] said "the sick man" is his name, for it is written: "Surely he hath borne our griefs and carried our sorrows, but we thought him stricken with leprosy (נָגוּעַ), smitten and tormented by God" (Isa. 53.4)'.[273] The other text is *B. Sanh*. 98a (alleged experience of R. Jehoshuaʻ ben Levi, *circa* A.D. 250), where it is described how the Messiah sits outside the gates of Rome among the wretched people who 'bear pain' (cf. Isa. 53.4),[274] and alone among them unbinds and binds just one wound at a time, so that without delay he may fulfil the summons to save Israel.

---

[268] The supposition of Euler, 31f., that Aquila is thinking of a leprous priest is wrong. Euler's remarks on Aquila suffer throughout from the fact that he has not recognized the translation technique of Aquila (see pp. 53f. and Hegermann, 15f., 28–45).

[269] *Sepher Zerubbabel* (ed. A. Jellinek, *Bet ha-Midrasch*, II, 1853–4, 54, 19ff., cf. S.-B., II, 291). The comparison with *B. Sanh*. 98a shows that the 'wounds' from which men hide their faces are those of the leper.

[270] The essay of H. Gressmann, 'Der aussätzige Messias', *Die Christliche Welt*, 34, 1920, 663–8, contains nothing helpful to our investigation.

[271] This date results from the introductory formula רבנן אמרי, cf. Dalman, I, 37; same date in S.-B., II, 286.

[272] Rabbi is R. Jehuda, I (135–c. 217).

[273] Thus the text which Raymundus Martini read (*Pugio fidei*, after A.D. 1278, ed. D. J. de Voisin, 1651, 672), cf. Dalman, I, 36, n. 2; rightly (cf. n. 309) followed by E. B. Pusey in Driver-Neubauer, II, p. XXXIV, and by North, 14. The present text of *B. Sanh*. 98b reads: 'And the teachers said: "the leper of the House of Rabbi" is he called, for it is written: "Verily he . . ." (Isa. 53.4)'. Thus the text is interpreted messianically, but it is an obvious corruption; as a result of the omission of the word חָלְיָה ('the sick man') arose the senseless messianic name: 'the leper of the House of Rabbi'.

[274] Rashi explains these words as follows: 'who are smitten with leprosy, and he too is leprous, see Isa. 53.3, 4' (text, see Wünsche, 58, n. 2). Pointing to leprosy (so too Dalman, I, 39) are also the number of the wounds which must be bound up, but especially the sitting before the gates (see J. Jeremias, *Jerusalem zur Zeit Jesu*³, 1962, 132f., especially 133); the rule about walled towns being closed to lepers (S.-B., IV, 751–7) is transferred to Rome.

The Servant of God in Late Judaism

Aquila's translation of Isa. 53 permits us to trace back this reference of Isa. 53.4 to the leprous Messiah as far as A.D. 100.[275] But we must go back yet a step further; the messianic interpretation of Isa. 53.4 cannot have arisen first *circa* A.D. 100, for it is completely out of the question that the Jews should have begun to interpret messianically the passion texts of Isa. 53 only at a time when Christians were already using Isa. 53 as the decisive christological proof text.[276]

(ζ) The translation of Aquila was followed by that of Theodotion[277] in the second century A.D.[278] Theodotion too interpreted Isa. 53 in a messianic sense. This stands out most plainly from his translation of the concluding sentence of the chapter. Isa. 53 (M.T.) concludes with the words וְלַפֹּשְׁעִים יַפְגִּיעַ (53.12). The verb הִפְגִּיעַ/פָּגַע means 'to have to do with a person', either *in bonam partem*—'to intercede'—or *in malam partem*—'to attack someone'. The Heb. text certainly had intended the first meaning, to judge by the context: 'and he made intercession for the transgressors'. The following understand it correctly: the N.T. (Rom. 8.34; Heb. 7.25; I John 2.1f.), Justin,[280] the *Vulgate*,[281] *Targum*,[282] B. *Talmud*;[283] also the very free rendering of the LXX (καὶ διὰ τὰς ἁμαρτίας αὐτῶν παρεδόθη) alluding to martyrdom has understood הִפְגִּיעַ *in bonam partem*. For the first time the *Peshitta*

---

[275] That the leper exegesis of Isa. 53.4 attests the messianic understanding of the servant as early as the tannaitic period has been shown by H. J. Schoeps, 'Symmachusstudien III', *Biblica*, 29, 1948, 38f. = *Aus frühchristlicher Zeit*, 1950, 108f.

[276] Franz Delitzsch, *Der Messias als Versöhner*, 1885, 21; Schlatter, 50; Aytoun, 176; North, 11; cf. Riesenfeld, 84; Torrey, 'The Messiah Son of Ephraim', 257.

[277] Until 1939 research had at its disposal only the collection of hexaplarist material by F. Field, *Origenis Hexaplorum quae supersunt*, 1875. For Isaiah there has now appeared, in place of this work, the excellent hexaplarist apparatus which Ziegler, *Isaias*, offers. Ziegler was able on the basis of the MSS. to improve at many points the collection of Field, outstanding in its day, and, above all, to make use of the hexaplarist notices which are to be found (1) in the Isaiah commentary of Theodoret of Cyrus (ed. A. Möhle, 1933), (2) in an Isaiah commentary, supposedly of Chrysostom, which has come down to us in Armenian (pub. Venice, 1880) and (3) in the not yet edited Isaiah Commentary of Eusebius (preserved in the margin of the Florentine codex, Laurentianus Pluteus XI 4).

[278] According to Epiphanius (*De mensuris et ponderibus* 17) under Commodus (180-92).

[280] Justin, *Apol.* 50.2: καὶ τοῖς ἀνόμοις ἐξιλάσεται ('he will make atonement', F. Büchsel, ἱλάσκομαι, *TWNT*, III, 315, 38).

[281] *Et pro transgressoribus rogavit.*

[282] 'And for his sake the rebellious will be forgiven'.

[283] B. *Sotah* 14a: ' "He interceded for the transgressors" (Isa. 53.12): for he implored mercy for the transgressors of Israel that they might return in penitence; by this "intercession" is meant nothing other than prayer.'

The Servant of God

understands the verb *in malam partem*,[284] as also does Aquila who translated, according to Pseud. Chrys. (n. 277): *occurret irridentibus eum*, and Symmachus: καὶ τοῖς ἀθετοῦσιν (*contradicentibus* Pseud. Chrys.) ἀντέστη (Cod. 86) 'and he opposed those who rejected him'. In Theodotion this interpretation *in malam partem* continues; he translates: *et impios torquebit* (Pseud. Chrys.). Thus with him the chapter concludes with the quite monstrous image of the servant torturing the godless. If we refuse to accept a crude error on the part of the Pseud. Chrys. text, which has unfortunately only been preserved in Armenian, we shall have to take as our point of departure the fact that LXX, 'A, and Targ. agree to regard Isa. 53.9 as a description of the last judgement,[285] and so by 'torture' Theodotion is thinking of eternal damnation.[286] The fact that he saw in the servant the ultimate judge shows that he interpreted Isa. 53 messianically.[287]

Since, unlike Aquila and Symmachus, Theodotion did not prepare a new translation, but took the LXX, also in use among the Christians, as his basis and ever and again improved it by reference to the original, it is to be expected that in some of his corrections he was influenced by the intention of excluding christological interpretations which the LXX made possible. The text already discussed (Isa. 53.12 end) arouses this suspicion. That Theodotion replaced the LXX text καὶ διὰ τὰς ἁμαρτίας αὐτῶν παρεδόθη is not surprising, since here the LXX had translated very freely. But that Theodotion substituted for the statement of the LXX about the vicarious martyrdom of the servant a phrase which in its offensive harshness was not warranted by the Heb. text ('and he will torment the impious') might well be due to dislike of the Christian use of the LXX (cf. Rom. 4.25). Among the few fragments of the Theodotion translation of Isa. 53[287a] his rendering of Isa. 53.12d: וְאֶת־ פֹּשְׁעִים נִמְנָה 'and he was reckoned with the transgressors', is also very unusual. The LXX here translates: καὶ ἐν τοῖς ἀνόμοις ἐλογίσθη, but Theodotion: καὶ τῶν ἀσεβῶν ἀπέσχετο (Cod. 86) 'and

---

[284] Cf. Hegermann, 107f. on Isa. 53.12 *Peshitta*.
[285] Cf. Hegermann, 42, 86f., 123 on Isa. 53.9 *Targ*.
[286] Hegermann, 52 compares Isa. 66.24; Matt. 25.41, 46; Rev. 14.10f.
[287] Further observations in Hegermann, 113f. Symmachus also gives the messianic interpretation.
[287a] Careful analysis of the extant fragments by Hegermann, 45–52.

The Servant of God in Late Judaism

he kept aloof from the impious'. The striking feature here is that Theodotion has replaced a completely correct translation of the LXX by one which says exactly the opposite: the servant who is reckoned with the wicked (Heb., LXX, 'A, Σ) has become in Theodotion the servant who holds himself aloof from the wicked.[288] In the elimination of this reference to the servant's suffering anti-Christian prejudice may have again played a part. Indeed the LXX already exhibits a tendency to modify or eliminate the passion texts of Isa. 53,[288a] but it stops before 53.12. It is not by chance that Theodotion goes a big step further. The text Isa. 53.12d was especially important for Christians (cf. Luke 22.37) because it did not refer in merely general terms to the suffering of the servant, but asserted that vicariously (53.12e) he was numbered with the criminals. More plainly than elsewhere in Isa. 53 they could find here a prophecy of the scandal of the cross. By reversing the meaning of the text Theodotion most probably wished to make impossible the Christian interpretation.[288b]

(η) The Aramaic translation of Isaiah must be considered here from a chronological point of view, for, although the *Targ.* on Isaiah[289] in its present form is not older than the fifth century A.D., the text was fixed much earlier. The history of the oral tradition of translation, the result of which the *Targ.* represents,

---

[288] Hegermann, 51. R. Brinker-London put forward to the author the illuminating suggestion that Theodotion, instead of נִמְנָה ('he was counted'), read נִמְנַע ('he held himself aloof').
[288a] 53.5b: instead of 'he was bruised', μεμαλάκισται 'he was sickly'; 53.8c: instead of 'he was cut off', αἴρεται '(his life) was taken away', i.e. 'lifted up' (Fascher, 8); 53.9ab: reinterpreted to mean the verdict that is passed upon the wicked and the rich; 53.10a: 'to bruise' becomes 'to cleanse'; 53.10b: the Hebrew text is corrupt, but it is clear that it contains a statement about the servant which the LXX evades by changing the subject to the second pers. pl.
[288b] Note that Theodotion does not eliminate the servant's passion and death in general, but only his dying ignominiously (Hegermann, 114).
[289] Editions: P. de Lagarde, *Prophetae Chaldaice*, 1872, from the *Codex Reuchlini*; with apparatus: Stenning, 1949. The section Isa. 52.13–53.12 has been published by G. Dalman in *Aramäische Dialektproben*², 1927, 10f. The very meritorious work of Seidelin comes to debatable results because the distinction between the Jewish-Hellenistic and the Jewish-Palestinian exegesis of Isa. 42 and 53 is not recognized and in the evaluation of rabbinic material no distinction is made between allusions to and interpretations of Isa. 53. Besides that, the age of the rabbinic interpretations of Isa. 53.4 has not been realized, and the meaning of the anti-Christian polemic undervalued.

The Servant of God

goes back to pre-Christian times.[290] In particular it can be shown that the messianic exegesis of the servant texts Isa. 42.1 and Isa. 52.13 in the *Targ.* Isa. is old. Of the nineteen servant passages in the Heb. text (cf. p. 51) only three are messianically interpreted in the *Targ.* Isa.: 42.1; 43.10; 52.13;[291] in all three texts the Heb. עַבְדִּי is rendered עבדי משיחא by the *Targ.*[292] Our conclusions so far make it certain that the messianic interpretation of Isa. 42.1 and 52.13 rests upon ancient tradition (cf. pp. 59ff.).[293] The observation that the description of the Messiah

[290] A specially clear example of the great age of the tradition of translation preserved in the *Targ.* is furnished by Isa. 6.10. The Heb. text runs: וְרָפָא לוֹ and the LXX: καὶ ἰάσομαι αὐτούς, Σ: καὶ ἰαθῇ. Quite otherwise is the translation of *Targ.*: וְיִשְׁתְּבֵיק לְהוֹן 'and they shall be forgiven'. רָפָא ('to heal') is mistaken for רָפָה ('to remit'); see Schlatter, *Markus*, on 4.12. This understanding of the text is very ancient; for it is already to be found in syr[pal]: ונשתבק לה and Mark 4.12: καὶ ἀφεθῇ αὐτοῖς (cf. T. W. Manson, *The Teaching of Jesus*, 1948, 77 and J. Horst, οὖς, *TWNT*, V, 555, n. 116). With regard to Isa. 53 in particular, in many instances the age of the synagogue tradition of translation crystallized in the *Targ.* can be shown by means of the LXX, the *Peshitta*, 'A, Σ, and Θ. A few examples may be mentioned: (i) Isa. 52.13: for the age of the expression עבדי משיחא cf. p. 51. (ii) Isa. 53.3b is interpreted in the *Targ.* (otherwise in the Heb. text and the LXX) with reference to the turning away of the *shekhina*, as also in 'A. (iii) Isa. 53.4: for חֳלָיֵנוּ 'our infirmities' the *Targ.* says חוֹבָנָא; likewise the LXX ἁμαρτίας ἡμῶν. (iv) Isa. 53.5: מְחֹלָל is on the part of the LXX derived from חָלָל Po'al 'to pierce': ἐτραυματίσθη; the *Targ.* on the contrary derives it from חָלָל Pu'al 'to be dishonoured': אִיתְּחַל 'he was profaned' as also already in 'A: βεβηλωμένος. (v) Isa. 53.7: נִגַּשׂ is derived by the LXX and Itala from נָגַשׂ 'he was abused', but the *Targ.* derives it from נָגַשׁ 'he approached', as already in Σ and the *Vulgate.* (vi) Isa. 53.9: application to the judgement found in the *Targ.* is already in the LXX, 'A, and Θ (cf. p. 66). (vii) Isa. 53.10: the LXX translates דַּכְּאוֹ by καθαρίσαι, as does the *Targ.*: מְצָרָף (see Hegermann, 122–5).

[291] Of the remaining sixteen texts the *Targ.* refers (i) to Israel 41.8, 9; 44.1, 2, 21 (twice); 45.4; 48.20; 49.3; and probably also 49.5, 6 (see n. 214); (ii) to penitent sinners (see n. 219) 42.19 (twice); (iii) to the prophets (see n. 220) 50.10; (iv) 44.26 the Heb. text was perhaps read by the *Targ.* as a plural (see n. 221); (v) 53.11 (Heb. text עֲבָדִי) in the *Targ.* is an infinitive: 'in order to make servants of the law'.

[292] Textual uncertainty exists only with regard to *Targ.* Isa. 42.1: עבדי משיחא is read in the *Codex Reuchlini* (see n. 289), the Nüremberg MS. (see Stenning, XXIX) and the Wilna edition, 1893. But the MS. British Museum, Or. 2211, and others have simply עבדי. Yet the reading עבדי משיחא is supported by the fact that the whole Palestinian tradition—as distinct from the Hellenistic (see pp. 53f.)—from before the Christian era onwards, interprets Isa. 42.1ff. messianically (see p. 78).

[293] The messianic interpretation of Isa. 43.10, which perhaps is occasioned by Heb. עַבְדִי in the mouth of God, as in 42.1; 52.13 (Seidelin, 228), has on the contrary no parallel in other late Jewish literature; *Midr. Ps.* 51 §3 on 51.6 refers Isa. 43.10 to David. But Jerome says on Isa. 43.1–10 that the Jews had interpreted the section *de secundo Salvatoris adventu, quando post plenitudinem gentium omnis salvandus sit Israel* (cf. Seidelin, 222, n. 79).

The Servant of God in Late Judaism

as servant of God is to be found only in the pre-rabbinic layer of late Jewish literature (IV Ezra, *Syr. Bar.*, cf. p. 51) but nowhere in rabbinic literature outside the *Targ.* (cf. p. 52), points to the same conclusion. Above all, the ancient date of the messianic exegesis of Isa. 52.13 in the *Targ.* is clear from the fact that *Targ.* Isa. explains the whole context Isa. 52.13– 53.12 uniformly in a messianic sense; for the messianic interpretation of 53.1–12 cannot, as we saw (p. 65), have first arisen in the Christian era.

The *Targ.* Isa. 52.13–53.12 runs: (52.13) 'Behold my servant, the Messiah, will have success, will become exalted, great and strong.' (14) 'As the house of Israel have hoped in him many days when their appearance was overcast in the midst of the peoples and their brightness less than that of the sons of men;' (15) 'so will he scatter many peoples; for his sake kings will be silent, will lay their hand on their mouth; for they see what they had never been told and perceive what they had never heard of.' (53.1) 'Who hath believed this our message? and to whom hath the strength of the mighty arm of the Lord thus[294] been revealed?' (2) 'And the righteous[295] shall be great before him, yea, as sprouting branches and as a tree which sends out its roots beside water brooks, so will the holy generations increase in the land which was in need of him. His appearance is not like that of worldly things and the fear which he inspires is not an ordinary fear, but his brightness will be holy so that all who see him will gaze (fascinated) upon him.' (3) 'Then (he) will be despised and will (make to) cease[296] the glory of all kingdoms. They will become weak and pitiable—behold, like

---

[294] כדין; ed. Venice 1517: כדן ('now'), probably scribal error.

[295] צדיקיא (plural); on the other hand *Codex Reuchlini* (n. 289, *Biblia Hebraica Rabbinica*, ed. J. Buxtorf the elder, 1618–19) and the Arab. ed. of the *Targ. Yerushalmi* I (1196 A.D.; see Dalman, I, 48, n. 1) read the singular: צדיקא. The singular is supported by the striking singular of the immediately preceding verb: וְיִתְרַבָּא. It could refer to the Messiah (cf. the messianic explanation of our text by R. Berechiah [*circa* 340] which seems to have been removed from talmudic literature, n. 328a). Probably, however, a collective singular was intended, so that between the better attested plural and the singular reading there is no difference of meaning.

[296] The textual question to be discussed here is of great importance. There are two alternative readings, which though hardly distinguishable in writing are, in fact, very different. (1) The MS. British Museum, Or. 2211, and the bulk of the MSS., as also the Wilna edition (1893), read: יפסיק Aph'el: 'he will make to cease'. (2) But

The Servant of God

a man of sorrows and as one destined to ills and as if the *shekhina* had turned its face from us (who are) despised and disregarded'. (4) 'Then he will make intercession for our transgressions and for his sake our sins shall be forgiven, though we were accounted bruised, smitten by Yahweh and afflicted.' (5) 'But he will build up the sanctuary which was desecrated because of our transgressions and surrendered because of our iniquities, and by his teaching his peace²⁹⁷ will be richly upon us, and when we gather to listen to him our transgressions will be forgiven us.' (6) 'We were all scattered as sheep, each one had gone his own way into exile; but it was Yahweh's will to forgive the transgressions of us all for his sake.' (7) 'When he prays he receives an answer and hardly does he open his mouth, but he finds a hearing. He will deliver the strong from among the peoples to be slaughtered as a lamb, and as a ewe that is dumb before its shearers, and no one will (dare to) open his mouth and plead.' (8) 'He will bring our exiles home from their suffering and chastisement. Who can tell the wonders which will come upon us in his days? For he will remove the dominion²⁹⁸ of the peoples from the land of Israel; he will lay to their charge²⁹⁹ the sins of which my people were guilty.' (9) 'And he will deliver over to hell the godless and those who have enriched themselves by robbery unto the death of

---

MS. British Museum, Or. 1474, reads: יפסוק Qal: 'it will cease'. *Codex Reuchlini* יפסק is ambiguous on account of the missing *mater lectionis*. The two versions presuppose a different subject: in the first (reading: יַפְסִיק) the Messiah is the subject and the translation is: 'Then he (the Messiah) will be despised and will make to cease the glory of all kingdoms' (for this reading see Wünsche, 41; Humbert, 445, 38, n. 1; S.-B., I, 482; II, 284; Kittel, 179; Brierre-Narbonne, 99; North, 12). In the second case (reading: יִפָּסוּק) 'the honour of all kingdoms' is the subject, and the translation is: 'As a result the honour of all kingdoms will turn to shame and will cease' (for this reading see Dalman, op. cit. in n. 289, 10, n. 18; Seidelin, 207, 211f.). Without question the textual evidence points predominantly to the first reading (יַפְסִיק): the weakly attested second reading (יִפָּסוּק) stands moreover under the suspicion of wishing to set aside the suffering of the Messiah. Thus in *Targ.* Isa. 53.3, in the statement: 'then will he be despised', we have possibly a trace of the idea of messianic suffering.

²⁹⁷ שלמיה; *Codex Reuchlini* (see n. 289), the Nüremberg MS. (cf. n. 292) and the Venice edition (1517) read שלמא without suffix.

²⁹⁸ שולטן can also mean 'ruler'.

²⁹⁹ ימטי is to be read with Dalman, op. cit. in n. 289, 11, n. 6 as Aph'el = יַמְטֵי (MS. British Museum, Or. 2211: יְמָטֵי).

The Servant of God in Late Judaism

(eternal) destruction, so that they who commit sin may not be preserved and may no (longer) speak cunningly with their mouth.' (10) 'And it pleased Yahweh to refine and purify the remnant of his people in order to cleanse their soul from transgressions. They shall see the kingdom of their Messiah; they will have many sons and daughters;[300] they will live long, and those who fulfil the law of Yahweh will by his good pleasure have success.' (11) 'From subjugation by the peoples he will deliver their soul; they will see the punishment of them that hate them; they will be satiated by the plunder of their kings. By his wisdom he will acquit the innocent to make many servants of the law. And he will make intercession for their transgressions.' (12) 'Hereafter will I apportion to him the plunder of many peoples and he will distribute the property of strong towns as booty, because he surrendered[301] his soul to death and brought the rebels under the yoke of the law. And he will make intercession for many transgressions and for his sake the rebellious will be forgiven.'

It can be seen how, step by step, in *Targ*. Isa. 52.13–53.12 is depicted the glorious establishment of the messianic kingdom over Israel. The statements about the passion of the servant have been so radically and consistently refashioned by artificial contrivances to mean partly Israel, partly the gentiles, that faint traces remain only in two places.[302] Even allowing for the targumic translation technique, the section *Targ*. Isa. 52.13–53.12 stands out by the unusual freedom of its paraphrase in the context of *Targ*. Isa. 40–66,[303] which elsewhere keeps more closely to the Heb. text. Now we already noted an earlier tendency in the LXX to attenuate the passion texts of Isa. 53, but for this violent treatment of the

---

[300] יסגון is with Dalman, op. cit. in n. 289, 11, n. 9 to be read as Aph'el = יַסְגוּן (MS. British Museum, Or. 2211: יְסגוּן).

[301] As Dalman has shown, I, 48, n. 3, it is not necessarily implied that this statement relates to accomplished execution; involvement in the peril of death might also be meant (thus also S.-B., I, 482f.; Seidelin, 215, n. 62). The text does not state on what occasion he 'surrendered himself to death'. The allusion might be to the war which precedes the messianic time (thus Weber, 361; Seidelin, 215), or rather, according to the original text, to death (or danger of death) from ill-treatment (cf. Isa. 53.7f.).

[302] Two texts are in question: (i) *Targ*. Isa. 53.3: 'he will become despised', יהי לבסרן, see n. 296; (ii) *Targ*. Isa. 53.12: 'he surrendered his soul to death', מסר למותא נפשיה, see n. 301; and Humbert, 5; Bonsirven, 383; Fischel, 70.

[303] Cf. Aytoun, 172.

The Servant of God

chapter in the *Targ.*, a reinterpretation which consistently reverses its meaning, there is only one possible explanation: we have here a piece of anti-Christian polemic.[304] From the second century at the latest, Judaism was concerned in various ways to wrest Isa. 53 from its use by Christians as a christological scriptural proof text (cf. p. 76). The curious form of Isa. 53 in the *Targ.* shows to what extremes this attempt was carried through. The whole section was indeed messianically explained because the messianic interpretation of Isa. 52.13–53.12 was so firmly rooted that *Targ.* Isa. could not escape it, but the passages about suffering, in brusque contradiction to the original, are replaced by the current view of the Messiah. The fact that this thoroughgoing process of reinterpretation of Isa. 52.13–53.12 was applied to both the Greek (see pp. 66ff.) and the Aramaic texts of Isa. 53 shows how firmly rooted in Palestinian Judaism was the messianic exegesis.

(*θ*) On the part of the Rabbis, likewise, only two Deut. Isa. servant passages have been understood in a messianic sense: Isa. 42.1ff. and Isa. 52.13ff.[305] These are in fact the two passages which, so far, we have constantly found to be interpreted messianically. As for Isa. 42.1ff., it is essential to note that only the messianic interpretation[306] is found in rabbinic literature. The messianic interpretation of Isa. 52.13–53.12 by the Rabbis[307] concerns both the passages of exaltation and the passages about suffering.[308]

[304] This is generally admitted. Even Dalman, who had tried to escape this conclusion (I, 43–49), was forced to grant it later: G. Dalman, *Jesus-Jeshua*, 1929, 172. The tendentious overworking is plainly distinguishable against an older version of the text—Hegermann, 116–22. In the following period the Jewish exegesis of Isa. 53 remains understandably determined by the opposition to the Christian interpretation (see Fischel, 66f.).

[305] Whether Isa. 49.6 is to be quoted as a third instance is extremely doubtful. It is true that Raymundus Martini, op. cit. in n. 273, 645, read a messianic interpretation of Isa. 49.6 in *Gen. maior* on 41.44 (Dalman, I, 97, n. 1); further in the post-talmudic period, in *Pesiqt.* R. 31 (cf. Seidelin, 218; Fischel, 62) Isa. 49.8 is once given a messianic interpretation. In this occasional messianic exegesis of the servant of Isa. 49.6 there might, in view of Ecclus. 48.10 (see p. 59), the Visionary Discourses *Eth. En.* (p. 60) and of the N.T. (n. 403), be an echo of an older tradition. But that is not certain. In any case, the *Targ.* does not explain Isa. 49.6 messianically (see n. 214) and we have no other evidence for the rabbinic explanation of Isa. 49.6, apart from the two late texts mentioned.

[306] *Midr. Ps.* 2 §9 on 2.7 (S.-B., I, 483); 43 §1 on 43.3 (S.-B., I, 87); *Pesiqt. R.* 36 (S.-B., II, 288); *Yalqut Shim'oni*, II, 88d, 104d (Dalman, I, 97, n. 1); *Seder Gan 'Eden* (ed. A. Jellinek, *Bet ha-Midrasch*, III, 1885, 133,12). Also *Targ.* Isa. ad loc. (see p. 68).

[307] A choice of rabbinic texts in S.-B., I, 481–3; further see 50.

[308] Rabbinic applications to the Messiah of the exaltation passages of Isa. 52.13ff.: *Targ.* Isa. ad loc. (see p. 69); *Tanch.* תולדות §20 (70a, Buber); *Midr. Ps.* 2 §9 on 2.7. Further examples and parallels, cf. Wünsche, 76; Dalman, I, 84, n. 3; S.-B., I, 483. Cf. Moore, III, 166.

The Servant of God in Late Judaism

In particular the reference of the passages about suffering in Isa. 53 to the Messiah emerges early in the writings of the Rabbis. The earliest piece of evidence is textually uncertain. Raymundus Martini (*post* 1278),[309] who usually proves to be trustworthy,[310] read in *Siphra Lev.* a statement of R. Jose the Galilaean (*ante* A.D. 135) which explained Isa. 53.5f. as referring to the suffering and sorrowing King-Messiah who, through his passion, justifies all peoples. This statement, which seeks to give information about 'the merit of the King-Messiah and the recompense of the just', opens with a reference to the fact that the one transgression of Adam caused innumerable death-sentences and concludes from this by means of the axiom of God's two different measures:[311] If Adam's sin had already caused such punishment to fall upon him and his followers, though God punishes less than is deserved, 'how much more then will the King, the Messiah, who suffers and sorrows for the godless, justify all mankind, as it is written: "But he was wounded for our transgressions" (Isa. 53.5). The same is meant by Isa. 53.6: "But the Lord hath laid upon him the iniquity of us all".' In our *Siphra Lev.* texts there is a different form of this passage (*Siphra Lev.* 12.10 on 5.17).[312] Here, the subject is limited to the 'recompense of the just', not the 'merit of the Messiah', and the contrast with Adam's sin is not the passion of the Messiah but the fulfilment of certain commandments by the just. Which reading is the original one? In the light of the severity with which Judaism opposed the Christian interpretation of the passion texts of Isa. 53, we must reckon with the possibility of a textual excision, especially since the messianic interpretation of Isa. 53 seems elsewhere to have been suppressed (cf. n. 328a). In this particular instance, however, the

---

[309] Op. cit. in n. 273, 675, cf. Dalman, I, 79f.; 44, n. 2; for text cf. Wünsche, 65f.; Driver-Neubauer, II, 10f.

[310] About the credibility of Raymundus Martini cf. L. Zunz, *Die gottesdienstlichen Vorträge der Juden historisch entwickelt*², 1892, 301; H. L. Strack, article on 'Raimundus Martin', in *RE*³, 16, 414f. About the value of his traditions, which has been brilliantly confirmed by a textual discovery in Prague (see Dalman, II, 6), cf. n. 273; Driver-Neubauer, XXV–XXXV; Zunz, ibid., 300–5; Strack, *Einl.*, 223f. (Lit.).

[311] The axiom says that God's measure of goodness is greater than that of punitive justice, i.e., that he punishes less but rewards more than is deserved (in addition to the reference quoted above see *B. Yoma* 76a; *B. Sanh.* 100a; *T. Sotah* 4.1; *Midr. Qoh.* 4.1, and cf. *B. Sotah* 11a; *Mekh. Ex.* 12.12 par. 14.4).

[312] First edition, Venice, 1545, 15b; ed. Weiss, 1862, 27a.

The Servant of God

messianic form attested by Raymundus Martini is probably secondary. The idea of a Messiah who acquires merit by suffering for the 'godless' fits poorly into an assertion which focuses on the 'recompense of the just'; in fact, the whole context is concerned with those who fulfil or break the law.³¹³ The reading preserved in our present text of *Siphra Lev.*, which contrasts Adam and the just, the one who violated and the one who fulfils the commandments, appears to be original. Next comes a witness from the middle of the second century A.D. — Justin's *Dialogue with Tryphon*. Justin reports that Tryphon³¹⁴ several times granted him that the Messiah was παθητός (36.1; 39.7; 49.2; 76.6–77.1; 89.1f., cf. especially 90.1: παθεῖν μὲν γὰρ καὶ ὡς πρόβατον ἀχθήσεσθαι [= Isa. 53.7] οἴδαμεν), and that this was also the opinion of the Jewish teachers (διδάσκαλοι) in general (68.9). Certainly we must be on our guard against the statements of an apologist. On the other hand, they are not to be dismissed too lightly. The credibility of Justin's account of his dialogue with Tryphon is strengthened by his frank admission that it was a failure. Therefore, his report seems to be trustworthy that the final parting of ways occurred not over the preliminary question of whether the Messiah was παθητός, but the Christian doctrine that he had not only suffered, but died on the cross, a death upon which God had laid his curse.³¹⁵ Still, Justin's statements must not be pressed. It is to be noted that, according to him, Tryphon and the other Jewish rabbis whom Justin quotes do not advance the idea of the Messiah's passion as part of their case, but concede it as Justin confronts them with Isa. 53.

The first indubitable rabbinic quotation comes from *circa* A.D. 200 (cf. n. 271). It is the description of the Messiah as 'the leper' and 'the sick man', on the basis of Isa. 53.4, in *B. Sanh.* 98b (cf. p. 64). The idea that the servant is described as a leper, Isa. 53.4, we first met with in Aquila (cf. pp. 63f.). Aquila was a

---

³¹³ Thus Dalman, I, 43, 81; Sjöberg, *Der verborgene Menschensohn*, 262f.
³¹⁴ Tryphon has often been identified with R. Tarphon (the most detailed presentation of this view is by Th. Zahn, 'Studien zu Justinus Martyr', *Zeitschrift für Kirchengeschichte*, 8, 1885, 1–84, see 61–65). The evidence does not support this, as N. Hyldahl, 'Tryphon und Tarphon', *Studia Theologica*, 10, 1956, 77–88, has conclusively shown.
³¹⁵ *Dial.* 32.1; 89.2; 90.1. Sjöberg, *Der verborgene Menschensohn*, 247–54, overstates his case in saying that Justin's presentation at this point is just literary fiction.

The Servant of God in Late Judaism

pupil of R. Akiba (see n. 263). It can hardly have been an accident that R. Akiba himself taught a suffering of the Messiah[317] and that R. Dosa (*circa* A.D. 180), who for the first time in rabbinic literature explains Zech. 12.12 with reference to the slaying of the Messiah b. Joseph,[318] is known to have reported words of Akiba's pupil Jehuda b. El'ai.[319] R. Akiba, the most influential biblical scholar of the first two centuries A.D., lived *circa* A.D. 50–135.[320] It was his school which, above all, preserved the idea of the Messiah's suffering.

In the third century R. Jochanan (*circa* A.D. 200–279),[321] and in the fourth R. Acha (*circa* A.D. 320),[322] applied Isa. 53.5: 'He was wounded for our transgressions', to the sorrows of the Messiah. R. Berechiah (*circa* A.D. 340) follows with the messianic explanation of Isa. 53.2.[323] In the post-talmudic period examples multiply,[324] yet on the whole are not numerous. This fact is to be explained by the contradiction between such a conception of the Messiah and the customary one, but especially by the opposition to Christianity.

[317] S.-B., II, 284. Akiba concluded from the typology of Mosaic time and messianic time that the latter would involve a forty-year period of distress in the desert, and supported his point by reference to Job 30.4 (*Tanch.* עקב, ed. Vienna 1863, 7b; J. Jeremias, Μωυσῆς, *TWNT*, IV, 865, 3ff.).
[318] *B. Sukka* 52a. The casual way of mentioning Messiah b. Joseph and his death shows that we have here a well-known idea (Moore, II, 370). The messianic exegesis of Zech. 12.10ff. is old: John 19.37; Rev. 1.7, cf. Matt. 24.30; *Targ.* (S.-B., II, 583f.); *Midr.* (S.-B., II, 298f.). It is possible that it goes back to the original text (see G. Stählin, κοπετός κτλ., *TWNT*, III, 848, 16ff.; Torrey, 'The Messiah Son of Ephraim', 253–77).
[319] W. Bacher, *Die Agada der Tannaiten*, II, 1890, 389; Strack, *Einl.*, 131. It should further be mentioned that two of Akiba's pupils, R. Jehuda and R. Nechemiah (both *circa* A.D. 150) took part in the oldest rabbinic discussion about Messiah b. Joseph (*Gen. R.* 75 on 32.6).
[320] P. Benoit, 'Rabbi Aqiba ben Joseph, sage et héros du judaïsme', *RB*, 54, 1947, 56.
[321] *Ruth R.* 5 on 2.14 (H. L. Strack, 'Zur altjüdischen Theologie', *Theologisches Literaturblatt*, 2, 1881, 10f.; S.-B., I, 27; II, 285). As the name of the author we should read with *Yalqut Shim'oni* ad loc. 603 R. Jochanan instead of R. Jonathan (S.-B., I, 27; II, 285; Fischel, 62; the correct reading can be found already in Bacher, op. cit. in n. 236, 312).
[322] *Midr. Sam.* 19 §1 (S.-B., II, 287). Cf. Dalman, I, 52, n. 1 for the v.l. citing R. Idi (I, *circa* A.D. 250) as author.
[323] S.-B., I, 49f., cf. n. 328a.
[324] Dalman, I, 53–84; Dalman, II, 3–18 and the comprehensive collection of texts of Brierre-Narbonne, but from the point of view of material not going further than Dalman. We must draw attention to the great description of messianic suffering in *Pesiqt. R.* 34–37 which, according to B. J. Bamberger, 'A Messianic Document of the Seventh Century', *HUCA*, 15, 1940, 425–31, took shape in Palestine in the years 632–7 and was based upon considerably older material. Isa. 53, it is true, is explicitly quoted only in the form of the text to be found in *Gen. R. maior* of R. Moshe ha-darshan (see Wünsche, 79, n. 1 after Raymundus Martini, op. cit. in n. 273, 664), but

The Servant of God

(i) From the second century A.D. the history of Jewish exegesis of Isa. 53 is shaped increasingly by the opposition to Christianity.[325] This process begins by the avoidance of the description of the Messiah as 'servant of God' and 'the chosen', which the pseudepigraphic writers had used without embarrassment (cf. p. 52 and n. 262), and also of the title 'son of man',[326] and 'Jesus', which had become a *nomen odiosum* (cf. W. Foerster, 'Ἰησοῦς, *TWNT*, III, 287, 20ff.). From the end of the second century the apologetic method of changing the text[327] and of tendentious interpretation was seized upon in translating Isa. 53, in order to dispose of passages which were of use to Christians in their text proofs. This polemical method is used especially in *Targ*. Isa. 53 (cf. pp. 67ff.). A similar mode of apologetic is used by R. Simlai (*circa* A.D. 250), who applies Isa. 53.12 to Moses (see n. 329). As far as possible, however, Isa. 42.1ff. and 53 are not used at all.[328] Indeed, it seems that messianic interpretations of Isa. 53 were at times excised; in several instances there is at least a suspicion of this sort.[328a] These observations are very important for our judge-

---

the statements about the vicarious punishment of the Messiah in *Pesiqt*. R. 34–37 rest upon the ideas expressed in Isa. 53 (cf. Dalman, I, 67) as is shown especially by the allusion to Isa. 53.11 in *Pesiqt*. R. 37 (Moore, I, 552, n. 1). *Pesiqt*. R. 34–37 tells how the Messiah, before he gloriously defeats Israel's enemies, is imprisoned and threatened with death until God comes to his rescue. Christian influence is out of the question; it is excluded, *inter alia*, by the fact that the Messiah is merely threatened with death, not killed (Fascher, 30f.).

[325] The rich material concerning the anti-Christian apologetic and polemic of Judaism in the first centuries has not yet been exhaustively dealt with.

[326] As distinct from *Eth. En.* it is lacking in *Slav.* and *Heb. En.* and in the whole of rabbinic literature (S.-B., I, 959; there also the apparent exception *J. Ta'an.* 2. 1 [65 b 60]).

[327] For an example of the change of the Greek text see p. 66 and for an example of the change of the Aramaic text see n. 296.

[328] Fischel, 66, n. 67: 'Probably the not very frequent use of 42.1ff.; 50.4ff., and 52.13ff. in the *Midrash* is occasioned by the great significance of these texts in Christian exegesis.'

[328a] Justin already reproaches the Judaic teachers with the fact that they completely eliminated from the LXX many texts (πολλὰς γραφὰς τέλεον περιεῖλον) which pointed to the Crucified (*Dial*. 71.2); of the four examples which he names (72.1–73.6, cf. 120.5) three are obviously Christian interpolations. In any case the quick replacement of the LXX by the translation of Aquila shows that in fact already in the second century A.D. the removal of undesired texts was one of the weapons of Jewish anti-Christian polemic. As regards Isa. 53, in particular, 'the single application in *Sanh*. 98b of Isa. 53 to the suffering Messiah' proves that we have to reckon with textual abbreviations (Strack, *Einl.*, 79). This conclusion is supported by the report of medieval sources (Ibn Ezra, died 1167 or 1168; according to Dalman, I, 40, n. 2, also מלחמת מצוה, composed 1240) that the section beginning with Isa. 52.13 in *Sotah* 1 was referred to the Messiah. In our texts of B. *Sotah* this exegesis is not found. Rashi too (died 1105) did not find the messianic exegesis of Isa. 52.13ff. (apart from

The Servant of God in Late Judaism

ment of late Jewish exegesis of Isa. 53. The widespread conclusion, that the relative infrequency of messianic interpretations of Isa. 53 in late Judaism shows that the latter was not acquainted with the idea of the suffering Messiah, does not do justice to the sources; for it ignores the great part which—very understandably—the debate with Christianity played in this question.

The slender amount of evidence is counterbalanced by the fact that there is not to be found a definitely non-messianic exegesis of Isa. 53 in the rabbinic literature of the first millennium A.D.[329] This is especially striking when we examine the rabbinic statements about the atoning power of death.[329a] This idea gains ground extraordinarily in late Judaism. The execution has atoning effect if the criminal has made the expiatory vow ('May my death expiate all my sins', see n. 475); every dying person is entreated to say this expiatory vow. Furthermore, late Judaism from pre-Christian times realizes the vicarious expiatory power inherent in the death of the high priest, of the martyrs, of the righteous, of the patriarchs, of the innocent children. It is astonishing that in this rich material there is no reference to Isa. 53.[330] Of this there is only one possible explanation: the connexion of Isa. 53 with the Messiah was from pre-Christian days so firmly and exclusively held by Palestinian

---

53.4, cf. n. 274) in the *Talmud*, rather, as he expressly says, he only knew of it from hearsay (*Commentary on Isa. 53*, text in Wünsche, 94). Further, it is striking that a messianic exegesis of Isa. 53.2 on the part of R. Berechiah, living *circa* A.D. 340 (S.-B., I, 49f.), has been preserved only through the Christian Raymundus Martini writing about one thousand years later, after A.D. 1278 (op. cit. in n. 273, 594), while in the older sources no trace of it is to be found. The trustworthiness of the information that R. Berechiah explained Isa. 53.2 messianically is supported by the fact that this scholar expounded the doctrine of the suffering of the Messiah (S.-B., II, 285f.; cf. I, 86f.). Finally a messianic exegesis of Isa. 53.3, reported by Moshe ha-darshan (in the first half of the eleventh century) in his work *Gen. R. maior* on 24.67 (text, Dalman, II, 6f. after A. Epstein; Wünsche, 69 after Raymundus Martini, op. cit. in n. 273, 671; cf. Dalman, I, 79) is the only citation of Raymundus from *Gen. R. maior*, for which the source is not to be found in the older literature (Dalman, I, 80f.).

[329] It is very questionable whether in Palestinian Judaism of the first millennium there existed any other exegesis of Isa. 53 except the messianic one (unlike Hellenistic Judaism; cf. p. 54), if one leaves out of account B. *Sotah* 14a, where Isa. 53.12 is referred by R. Simlai (*circa* 250) to Moses' intercession; for here it is a question of a distortion for apologetic motives (see pp. 58f.). The passages collected by S.-B. in 'Isa. 53 in the Older Jewish Literature' (I, 481-5), under the heading 'B. References to the Righteous' (I, 483-485), are references to isolated texts torn from their context (see pp. 55f., 58). The one *Midrash* text quoted by S.-B. under 'C. References to the people of Israel' (I, 485), *Num. R.* 13 on 13.2 (anonymous), comes from a *Midrash* composed in the twelfth century.

[329a] Lohse, 104-9; J. Jeremias, *Eucharistic Words*, 151f.

[330] The sole exception, R. Simlai (*circa* A.D. 250), is apparent only; see n. 329.

The Servant of God

Judaism that the application of this chapter to the expiatory death of the righteous was automatically excluded from consideration.[331] To sum up: (1) messianic interpretation of the Deutero-Isaianic servant in Palestinian Judaism was limited to Isa. 42.1ff.,[332] 43.10,[333] 49.1f., 6f.,[334] and 52.13ff.;[335] with this the New Testament data agree.[336] (2) For Isa. 42.1ff. and 52.13–15 messianic interpretation is constant from pre-Christian times. Isa. 52.13–15 is in this connexion regarded as a last judgement scene.[337] (3) As far as the messianic interpretation of the passages about suffering in Isa. 53.1–12 is concerned, this can be traced back not with equal

---

[331] I owe this important observation to E. Lohse.—In passing we must deal with two objections to our conclusion. First: is it not implied by the repeated remark of the evangelists that the disciples did not understand the predictions of the passion that the conception of a suffering Messiah was completely unknown to them (cf. Rowley, 80–84)? Now Mark mentions the failure of the disciples to understand solely after the second account of the prediction of the passion (9.32: οἱ δὲ ἠγνόουν τὸ ῥῆμα, καὶ ἐφοβοῦντο αὐτὸν ἐπερωτῆσαι). This remark concerning the disciples' lack of understanding, however, is but a secondary variant of the objection of Peter to Jesus' suffering (8.32, in connexion with the first prediction of the passion), the antiquity of which is assured by the sharpness of the rebuke of Jesus denouncing Peter as Satan. Moreover, the disciples' failure to understand is by no means, in Mark, related solely to the passion of Jesus, but runs like a motif through the whole of Mark's Gospel (4.13, 40f.; 6.52; 7.18; 8.16–21; 9.32; 10.38); cf. W. Wrede, *Das Messiasgeheimnis in den Evangelien*, 1901, 93–114. In Mark 6.52 the disciples' lack of understanding occurs in a remark of the evangelist; 8.16–21 is, quite plainly, by its reference to the doublet of the feeding miracle, recognizable as a piece of literary composition. This confirms the conclusion reached above that the only passage where Mark reports the disciples' failure to understand Jesus' announcement of his passion is part of the redaction of Mark's gospel. In Luke the motif is still more distinct (cf. 9.45 with Mark 9.32): in 18.34 he has added it without a Marcan parallel. Finally, the Gospel of John broadens the motif into a constant misunderstanding of the most far-reaching extent. Parallels in comparative religion make it probable that we have here an epiphany motif (H. J. Ebeling, 'Das Messiasgeheimnis und die Botschaft des Marcus-Evangelisten', *ZNW*, Beiheft 19, 1939, 167f., 170). If that is correct then historical deductions are illegitimate. But even apart from that the misunderstanding (ἀγνοεῖν, Mark 9.32, can also mean 'fail to acknowledge') would be intelligible, for the passion and death of the Messiah completely contradicted popular expectations. Second: is it not implied in the offence which the Jews found in the preaching of the cross (I Cor. 1.23) that the conception of a suffering Messiah was alien to them? In fact the messianic interpretation of Isa. 53 must have been foreign to Hellenistic Judaism (cf. p. 54). So much more must the manner of the death of Jesus have been offensive to them; even for Palestinian Judaism this was the real scandal: death on the cross is accursed (Gal. 3.13; Justin, *Dial*. 90).

[332] Cf. p. 54.
[333] Only in the *Targ*. ad loc. See p. 68 and n. 293.
[334] Cf. pp. 6of. and n. 305 and p. 58, also p. 59.
[335] Cf. pp. 59–78.
[336] Cf. p. 94. Only the messianic exegesis of Isa. 43.10 is not to be found in the N.T.
[337] Hellenistic and Palestinian Judaism agree in relating Isa. 52.13ff. to the last judgement (Wisd. 4.20ff.; *Eth. En.* 46.4f.; 48.8; 55.4; 62.1–9; 63.1–11; A; Θ; *Targ*. (cf. J. Jeremias, 'Lösegeld', 263f.).

The Servant of God in Late Judaism

certainty, but with some probability[337a] to pre-Christian times.[338] Here the suffering of the Messiah is thought of without exception up to the talmudic period as taking place before the final victorious establishment of his rule.[339] When the meaning of messianic suffering is considered, the answer is that the Messiah suffers vicariously to expiate the sins of Israel.[340]

[337a] Cf. especially p. 65.
[338] This interpretation is to be found in the *Peshitta* (see p. 62), in Aquila (p. 63), in Theodotion (n. 288b) and in rabbinic texts (see p. 75) and traces of it probably in *Targ.* Isa. 53 (see p. 71). Against the idea that the messianic interpretation of Isa. 53 in Judaism belongs only to the second century A.D. Buber has expressed himself with decision (see Buber, 105, n. 1).
[339] S.-B., II, 291.
[340] B. *Sanh.* 98b, and B. *Sanh.* 98a, see p. 64 (cf. S.-B., II, 286); *Ruth R.* 5 on 2.14, see n. 321; *Midr. Sam.* 19 §1, see n. 322; *Pesiqt. R.* 31 (S.-B., II, 287); *Pesiqt. R.* 36 (S.-B., II, 288); *Midr. Konen* (S.-B., II, 290). Cf. S.-B., II, 291f. But note that only according to the *Peshitta* the Messiah suffers for the sins of many peoples (see Hegermann, 96f. on Isa. 52.15). The article by Rese (cf. p. 109) who takes exception to my argumentation on pp. 55–79, is widely based on secondary sources (this is especially clear in his inadequate treatment of *Targ.* Isa. 53), and adduces no new evidence. Nevertheless this article has drawn welcome attention to certain points at which my argument needed clarification.

IV

Παῖς (Θεοῦ) IN THE NEW TESTAMENT

The expression παῖς (of God)[341] occurs only rarely in the N.T. as in late Judaism (cf. p. 45): Matt. 12.18; Luke 1.54, 69; Acts 3.13, 26; 4.25, 27, 30. Of these eight texts one refers to Israel (Luke 1.54), two to David (Luke 1.69; Acts 4.25), the remaining five to Jesus.[342] The phrase in the Magnificat: ἀντελάβετο Ἰσραὴλ παιδὸς αὐτοῦ (Luke 1.54) is a reference to LXX Isa. 41.8f.: σὺ δέ, Ἰσραήλ, παῖς μου Ἰακώβ, ὃν ἐξελεξάμην, σπέρμα Ἀβραάμ, ὃν ἠγάπησα, οὗ ἀντελαβόμην. The collective use of the expression corresponds to what we find in the O.T. (cf. n. 175) and in late Judaism (cf. nn. 177, 213). As in *Ps. Sol.* 12.6 the pious nucleus of Israel is thought of. The liturgical style is also common to Luke 1.54 and *Ps. Sol.* 12.6; 17.21. The description of David as servant (of God) likewise is late Jewish in character. As there (see n. 184) so too in primitive Christianity we find the use of it occurring exclusively in prayers: in the Benedictus, Luke 1.69: ἐν οἴκῳ Δαυὶδ παιδὸς αὐτοῦ; in the prayer of the primitive community after the release of the apostles, Acts 4.25: ὁ τοῦ πατρὸς ἡμῶν διὰ πνεύματος ἁγίου στόματος Δαυὶδ παιδός σου εἰπών;[343] and in the eucharistic prayer said over the chalice, *Did.* 9.2: εὐχαριστοῦμέν σοι, πάτερ ἡμῶν, ὑπὲρ τῆς ἁγίας ἀμπέλου Δαυὶδ τοῦ παιδός σου 'of whom David thy servant speaks' (i.e., in Ps. 80.8ff.).[344] 'David thy servant' is therefore a liturgical prayer formula of late Judaism which primitive Christianity took over.

---

[341] Throughout the N.T. with the possessive pronoun: ὁ παῖς μου (Matt. 12.18), σου (Acts 4.25, 27, 30), αὐτοῦ (Luke 1.54, 69; Acts 3.13, 26), i.e., of God.
[342] Christians on the other hand are called δοῦλοι θεοῦ, never παῖδες θεοῦ.
[343] The text is overcharged. Presumably the two words πνεύματος ἁγίου are quite an old gloss.
[344] R. Eisler, 'Das letzte Abendmahl', *ZNW*, 25, 1926, 6f., has demonstrated convincingly that this is the meaning of the apparently puzzling expression ἡ ἁγία ἄμπελος Δαυίδ.

The Servant of God in the New Testament

It is likewise a question of O.T. and late Jewish usage when in I *Cl.* 39.4 (= Job 4.18) the angels, in IV Ezra 1.32; 2.1 (second century A.D.) the prophets and in 2.18 Isaiah and Jeremiah are called the servants (of God) (cf. n. 174 [angels] and n. 167 [prophets]).

1. Παῖς (Θεοῦ) AS A PREDICATION OF JESUS

(i) *The origin of the predication.* The N.T. calls Jesus παῖς (θεοῦ) strikingly seldom, viz. only in one quotation in Matt. (12.18 = Isa. 42.1), and in four places in Acts (3.13, 26; 4.27, 30). In all five instances we have to do with an ancient tradition.

For Matt. 12.18 this is clear from the mixed character of the quotation. Behind Matt. 12.18-20 (= Isa. 42.1-3) there lies the Heb. text,[345] but in the last verse of the quotation (Matt. 12.21 = Isa. 42.4d) suddenly we find that the LXX is cited.[346] Thus two hands are visible,[347] which allows us to infer a previous history of the text. That the first hand uses the Heb. text points back to the area of Semitic linguistic usage. As regards the four passages in the Acts, the parallel use of παῖς σου in the prayer of Acts 4.24-30 as a designation of David (4.25) as well as of Jesus (4.27-30) shows that Luke is using archaic expressions which he has borrowed from the language of liturgical prayer (cf. p. 84).[348] The fact that he does not employ the formula except in his description of the primitive community of Jerusalem as given in Acts 3 and 4 makes it clear that he was aware of its archaic character.[348a]

But it may be presumed that the description of Jesus as παῖς (θεοῦ) lies behind yet other N.T. passages. We must note here chiefly the voice of the baptism (Mark 1.11 par.) and the voice at the transfiguration (Mark 9.7 par.).

---

[345] The wording of the text in Matthew deviates much from the LXX, whose collective interpretation of παῖς in Isa. 42.1 (see p. 54) would not have made possible the application of the passage to Jesus. (Against the hypothesis of Kahle, op. cit. in n. 259a, 251, that Matthew used an older lost Greek translation of Isa., cf. P. Katz, 'Das Problem des Urtextes der Septuaginta', *TZ*, 5, 1949, 18.)

[346] LXX has for לְתוֹרָתוֹ (Isa. 42.4) ἐπὶ τῷ ὀνόματι αὐτοῦ which must be a scribal error for ἐπὶ τῷ νόμῳ αὐτοῦ (Ziegler, *Isaias*, ad loc.). In Matt. τῷ ὀνόματι αὐτοῦ the scribal error of LXX recurs.

[347] A. Schlatter, *Der Evangelist Matthäus*, 1929, 402. Matthew himself seems to be quoting from LXX.

[348] J. C. O'Neill, *The Theology of Acts in its Historical Setting*, 1961, 135 (following M. J. Wilcox).

[348a] O'Neill, op. cit., 139.

The Servant of God

The comparison of:

Mark 1.11 = Luke 3.22[349] with	Isa. 42.1 (as quoted in
par. Matt. 3.17	Matt. 12.18)
σὺ εἶ (οὗτός ἐστιν Matt.) ὁ υἱός μου	ἰδοὺ ὁ παῖς μου ὃν ᾑρέτισα,
ὁ ἀγαπητός,	ὁ ἀγαπητός μου
ἐν σοὶ (ᾧ Matt.) εὐδόκησα	ὃν εὐδόκησεν ἡ ψυχή μου·
(cf. Mark 1.10 par.: τὸ πνεῦμα	θήσω τὸ πνεῦμά μου ἐπ' αὐτόν
... καταβαῖνον εἰς αὐτόν)	

has long since suggested the question whether the υἱός μου of the voice at the baptism and the transfiguration does not go back to παῖς μου (so LXX Isa. 42.1). In that case Mark 1.11 par. and 9.7 par. would not be a combined quotation from Ps. 2.7 and Isa. 42.1, but originally only Isa. 42.1 (Heb. text) would have been quoted and the ambiguous παῖς μου (1: 'my servant'; 2: 'my child') would before Mark have been interpreted as υἱός μου on Hellenistic territory where the description of Jesus as παῖς (θεοῦ) was early avoided.[350]

The hypothesis that the voice at the baptism was originally purely an echo of Isa. 42.1 is supported by several considerations. First, the heavenly voice, Mark 1.11, is obviously meant to explain the impartation of the Spirit (Mark 1.10) as a fulfilment of scripture.[351] As so often in O.T. quotations, e.g., in rabbinic literature, the continuation of the passage (Isa. 42.1 in Matt. 12.18c) is implied but not actually quoted: θήσω[352] τὸ πνεῦμά μου ἐπ' αὐτόν. Thus the heavenly voice affirms that the promise given in Isa. 42.1 about the gift of the Spirit has just been fulfilled. Second, when the text of the divine declaration at the baptism and the transfiguration wavers between ἀγαπητός (Mark 1.11 par.; 9.7 par. Matt. 17.5 and Luke 9.35 v.l.; II Peter 1.17) and ἐκλελεγμένος (Luke 9.35), we presumably have varia-

---

[349] The Western reading of Luke 3.22: υἱός μου εἶ σύ, ἐγὼ σήμερον γεγέννηκά σε (= LXX Ps. 2.7) is nothing except one of those assimilations of N.T. quotations to the O.T. original (in this case supposed) which the Western text has undertaken in numerous instances and which are highly characteristic of it, e.g., Mark 15.34 par. Matt. 27.46, where the Western text has replaced the Aramaic quotation of Ps. 22.2 by the Heb. text.

[350] Dalman, *WJ*, 277; Bousset, 57, n. 2; Lohmeyer, *Gottesknecht*, 9; Cullmann, *Baptism in the New Testament*, 16–18. A similar process occurs with regard to the text of John 1.34 where the original ὁ ἐκλεκτός becomes ὁ υἱός (see n. 261); here again it is a question of Isa. 42.1.

[351] Dalman, *WJ*, 277.

[352] The perfect of the Heb. text is translated as future in Matt. 12.18.

The Servant of God in the New Testament

tions in the translation of בְּחִיר Isa. 42.1, which is sometimes rendered by ἐκλεκτός (LXX, Σ and Θ), and sometimes by ἀγαπητός (Matt. 12.18). Third, in John 1.34 the heavenly voice at the baptism,[353] according to the supposedly oldest text (see n. 261), is given in the words: οὗτός ἐστιν ὁ ἐκλεκτὸς τοῦ θεοῦ. But 'the chosen of God' is a messianic designation coming from Isa. 42.1 (cf. pp. 59ff.). John 1.34 shows very plainly that the baptismal declaration originally must have been a consistent quotation from Isa. 42.1. If that is correct then it would be confirmed (cf. p. 81) that the designation of Jesus as παῖς (θεοῦ) belongs to a very old (pre-Marcan) layer of the tradition.[354]

Further indirect evidence of the παῖς (θεοῦ) predication and its great antiquity is possibly furnished by the Johannine literature.

First, we have John 1.29, 36: ἴδε ὁ ἀμνὸς τοῦ θεοῦ (+ v. 29: ὁ αἴρων τὴν ἁμαρτίαν τοῦ κόσμου). It has already been shown (J. Jeremias, ἀμνός κτλ., *TWNT*, I, 342f., cf. 185,19ff.) that the expression ὁ ἀμνὸς τοῦ θεοῦ conceals both a factual and a linguistic difficulty. (1) The description of the Saviour as a lamb is unknown to late Judaism. (2) The expression is an unparalleled genitive combination. Both difficulties are solved if we refer to the Aramaic where טַלְיָא means (a) the lamb, (b) the boy, the servant.[355] Probably behind the phrase ὁ ἀμνὸς τοῦ θεοῦ lies an Aramaic טַלְיָא דַּאלָהָא in the sense of עֶבֶד יהוה (cf. nn. 164, 176);[356] this supposition is also supported by the reference of John 1.

---

[353] Cullmann, *Baptism*, 16ff., also *Early Christian Worship*, 64f.

[354] The consequences which result from this are extraordinarily far-reaching. It means not merely that the voice at baptism has nothing to do with kingly enthronement, adoption, etc., but that there arises above all the question whether the παῖς θεοῦ predication (along with scriptural texts like Ps. 2.7; II Sam. 7.14) does not play an essential part in the emergence of the messianic title ὁ υἱὸς τοῦ θεοῦ which was unknown to late Judaism.

[355] Examples of טַלְיָא = 'servant' in the west Aramaic dialects (Palestinian *Midrash* and *Talmud*, the *Targums*, and Christian Palestinian dialect) may be found in J. Jeremias, "'Ἀμνὸς τοῦ θεοῦ'", 116f.

[356] C. J. Ball, 'Had the Fourth Gospel an Aramaic Archetype?', *ET*, 21, 1909–10, 92f.; Burney, 107f.; E. Lohmeyer, *Die Offenbarung des Johannes* (HNT, 16)², 1953, 52; J. Jeremias, "'Ἀμνὸς τοῦ θεοῦ'", 115–23; Zolli, 228–33; W. F. Howard, *Christianity According to St John*, 1943, 100f.; G. S. Duncan, *Jesus, Son of Man*, 1947, 91, n. 4; Cullmann, *Baptism*, 21, n. 1; *Early Christian Worship*, 65f.; *Christology*, 71f. In regard to the doubts expressed by C. H. Dodd (in his discussion of the *TWNT* article ἀμνός) in *JTS*, 34, 1933, 285, that *Targ.* Isa. renders עֶבֶד יהוה by עַבְדָּא (not by טַלְיָא), we must recall what was said on pp. 53f.: from about A.D. 100, Greek-speaking Judaism brusquely changes from παῖς θεοῦ to δοῦλος θεοῦ; we may assume that Aramaic-

The Servant of God

29b ὁ αἴρων τὴν ἁμαρτίαν τοῦ κόσμου to the *'ebed* phrase Isa. 53.12 (וְהוּא חֵטְא רַבִּים נָשָׂא, cf. J. Jeremias, αἴρω, ἐπαίρω, *TWNT*, I, 185, 25ff.). Also the description of Jesus in Rev. (28 times) as ἀρνίον³⁵⁷ must, on account of the lack of an analogy in late Judaism, go back to the same ambiguous טַלְיָא.³⁵⁸ If this hypothesis is correct, then the predication παῖς (θεοῦ) of Jesus must spring from the Aramaic-speaking primitive church.

A surprising confirmation of the great antiquity of the predication is furnished, finally, by its history in the ancient church.³⁵⁹ Apart from three quotations³⁶⁰ and from Acts, the description of Jesus as παῖς (θεοῦ) in gentile Christian literature is met with up to 170 only at eleven places and only in three writings.

It is found in the *Didache* in the old prayers of the agape³⁶¹ (celebrated before the eucharist) to be said before and after the meal (9.2, 3; 10.2, 3) and in the prayer for unction (10.7 Copt.);³⁶² in all five places we have the stereotyped formula: διὰ Ἰησοῦ τοῦ παιδός σου;³⁶³ also in the great Roman church prayer I *Cl*. 59.2–4,³⁶⁴ in Polycarp's prayer joined³⁶⁵ to the eucharistic prayer of Smyrna, *Mart. Pol*. 14.1–3,³⁶⁶ and in the concluding doxology of the *Mart. Pol*. 20.2.³⁶⁷ Thus in all eleven places we have to do with prayers and (with the exception of the doxological formulae I *Cl*. 59.4, see n. 364; *Mart. Pol*. 14.1, see n. 366) always with the liturgical formula: διὰ Ἰησοῦ τοῦ παιδός σου.

---

speaking Judaism made a similar change from טַלְיָא to עַבְדָּא. Besides, a text which uses טַלְיָא for the servant of God has now been found in Isa. 52.13 syrᵖᵃˡ (n. 156).

³⁵⁷ Probably (owing to the lacking τοῦ θεοῦ) circuitously through ἀμνὸς τοῦ θεοῦ (a point made by K. G. Kuhn).
³⁵⁸ J. Jeremias, ἀμνός κτλ., *TWNT*, I, 343, 15–19; Lohmeyer, *Offenbarung*, 52.
³⁵⁹ By the brilliant investigation of A. v. Harnack, 'Die Bezeichnung Jesu als "Knecht Gottes" und ihre Geschichte in der alten Kirche', this has been illuminated in exemplary fashion.
³⁶⁰ Matt. 12.18; further *Barn*. where παῖς κυρίου (6.1) and παῖς μου (9.2) are inserted in O.T. quotations.
³⁶¹ Cf. J. Jeremias, *Eucharistic Words*, 84f.
³⁶² Ed. C. Schmidt, 'Das koptische Didache-Fragment des British Museum', *ZNW*, 24, 1925, 84f., cf. 94.
³⁶³ *Did*. 10.3: read Ἰησοῦ with the Coptic translation.
³⁶⁴ I *Cl*. 59.2: διὰ τοῦ ἠγαπημένου παιδός αὐτοῦ Ἰησοῦ Χριστοῦ; 59.3: διὰ Ἰησοῦ Χριστοῦ τοῦ ἠγαπημένου παιδός σου; 59.4: σὺ εἶ ὁ θεὸς μόνος καὶ Ἰησοῦς Χριστὸς ὁ παῖς σου.
³⁶⁵ See v. Harnack, 221, cf. Bousset, 56.
³⁶⁶ *Mart. Pol*. 14.1: ὁ τοῦ ἀγαπητοῦ καὶ εὐλογητοῦ παιδός σου Ἰησοῦ Χριστοῦ πατήρ, δι' οὗ . . .; 14.3: διὰ . . . Ἰησοῦ Χριστοῦ, ἀγαπητοῦ σου παιδός.
³⁶⁷ 20.2: διὰ τοῦ παιδὸς αὐτοῦ τοῦ μονογενοῦς Ἰησοῦ Χριστοῦ.

The Servant of God in the New Testament

This plain prayer formula is very old.[368] So much is already clear from the absence of Χριστός in the oldest examples of the formula (Acts 4.30; *Did.* 9.2, 3; 10.2, 3, 7)[369] but especially from the observation that in διὰ Δαυὶδ τοῦ παιδός σου (Acts 4.25) it has an old Palestinian[370] parallel. Further, of the four examples in Acts, two stand in a prayer (4.27, 30), and one of these likewise offers the formula διὰ . . . τοῦ . . . παιδός σου Ἰησοῦ (4.30). Surveying the examples of the designation of Jesus as παῖς (θεοῦ) we may conclude (1) that the predication παῖς (θεοῦ) was at no time on gentile Christian territory an accepted designation of the Messiah (it is not found in Paul); the titles κύριος, Χριστός, υἱὸς τοῦ θεοῦ were there preferred. (2) In the gentile churches the predication lived on rather as a liturgical formula which became fixed at an early date and which was anchored in the eucharistic prayer, in the doxology and in the confession.[371]

Later times confirm these views.[372] παῖς (θεοῦ) remains infrequent. The designation persists in prayers and doxologies, otherwise almost solely in solemn sacral speech. It does not influence the phraseology of dogmatics but remains confined to liturgy and exalted speech. From the fifth century παῖς disappears altogether as a designation of Christ.[373]

If our examination so far has, step by step, pointed to the ancient date of the title and its origin in Palestine, the information given by Epiphanius that the Ebionites ἕνα θεὸν καταγγέλλουσι καὶ τὸν τούτου παῖδα Ἰησοῦν Χριστόν[374] gains in significance. Above all, the disappearance in Palestinian Judaism of 'God's servant' as a description of the Messiah (cf. p. 51) is indirect evidence of the fact that the designation of Jesus as servant (of God) was alive in Palestinian Christianity. Thus we must seek the home and origin

---

[368] v. Harnack, 235, n. 3 considers the question whether the frequent Pauline formula διὰ Ἰησοῦ Χριστοῦ is an imitation of διὰ Ἰησοῦ τοῦ παιδός σου.
[369] v. Harnack, 219f.
[370] Cf. II Sam. 3.18: בְּיַד דָּוִד עַבְדִּי = LXX: ἐν χειρὶ τοῦ δούλου μου Δαυίδ; I Macc. 4.30: ἐν χειρὶ τοῦ δούλου σου Δαυίδ (with διά cum acc. Isa. 37.35: διὰ Δαυὶδ τὸν παῖδά μου; with δοῦλος: III Βασ. 11.13, 32, 34; IV Βασ. 8.19; 19.34; 20.6; with ἕνεκεν: ψ 131.10).
[371] I Cl. 59.4: σὺ εἶ ὁ θεὸς μόνος καὶ Ἰησοῦς Χριστὸς ὁ παῖς σου is a formula of confession.
[372] Collection of material in v. Harnack, 224–33.
[373] v. Harnack, 236–8.
[374] Epiphanius, *Haer.* 29.7.3. Cf. Bousset, 56f., especially cf. 56, n. 2.

The Servant of God

of the predication in the first Palestinian community.[375] From the first it was offensive to the Hellenistic church because it did not seem to bring out the full significance of the majesty of the glorified Lord;[376] παῖς (θεοῦ) was therefore replaced by υἱὸς θεοῦ already in the Hellenistic Jewish Christian church (Rom. 1.3) (cf. n. 354).

(ii) *The meaning of the predication.* The fact that as a designation of Jesus παῖς (θεοῦ) means originally 'servant of God' (not 'child of God'), is implied by the striking reserve shown by the gentile church towards this predication—a reserve which can only be due to the offence caused by its lowly character. But it is also implied by the application of παῖς in neighbouring passages to David and Jesus in Acts (David: 4.25; Jesus: 4.27, 30) and in the *Didache* (David: 9.2; Jesus: 9.2, 3): for it is certain that David is here called servant of God.[377] This juxtaposition of David and Jesus as 'servants' which Acts seems to find inadequate[378] shows that παῖς is here a title of honour as it is applied to eminent men of God elsewhere (cf. pp. 50f.) in late Judaism.[379] Still, when speaking of Jesus as παῖς (θεοῦ) one had to remember the servant passages of Deutero-Isaiah sooner or later. This is demonstrated by the quotations Matt. 12.18 cf. Mark 1.11 (see pp. 81f.) as well as by the reference to Isa. 52.13ff. in Acts 3.13ff.[380]

(iii) *The semantic change from 'servant of God' to 'child of God'.* In the gentile churches παῖς (θεοῦ) as a description of Jesus has acquired at latest by the second century the meaning 'child (of God)'.

This change of meaning is certainly present in *Mart. Pol.* 14. 1: κύριε ὁ θεὸς ὁ παντοκράτωρ, ὁ τοῦ ἀγαπητοῦ καὶ εὐλογητοῦ παιδός σου Ἰησοῦ Χριστοῦ πατήρ (as the combination παῖς/πατήρ shows)

---

[375] Rightly observed by Bousset, 57. See further, pp. 95ff. below.
[376] Maurer, 38; Hooker, 109.
[377] Cf. n. 370. παῖς θεοῦ in the meaning 'child of God' is besides extraordinarily infrequent in Hellenistic Judaism (cf. p. 45).
[378] The fact that only in Acts 4.27, 30 (not in 3.13, 26) is the adjective ἅγιος found in connexion with Jesus (ὁ ἅγιος παῖς σου Ἰησοῦς) could be caused by the intention to make a difference between the παῖς Jesus and the παῖς David (4.25).
[379] Thus especially Cadbury, 367; E. Haenchen, *Die Apostelgeschichte* (Meyer, 3)[13], 1961, on Acts 3.13; Hooker, 109f.
[380] Acts 3.13: ὁ θεὸς . . . ἐδόξασεν τὸν παῖδα αὐτοῦ Ἰησοῦν (cf. Isa. 52.13: ὁ παῖς μου . . . δοξασθήσεται), ὃν ὑμεῖς μὲν παρεδώκατε καὶ ἠρνήσασθε (cf. Isa. 53.2 Peshitta; *Eth. En.* 48.10); 3.14: τὸν ἅγιον καὶ δίκαιον (cf. Isa. 53.11: δίκαιον, cf. p. 60) ἠρνήσασθε; 3.18: (God) προκατήγγειλεν διὰ στόματος πάντων τῶν προφητῶν, παθεῖν τὸν χριστὸν αὐτοῦ. The reference of Acts 3.13 to Isa. 52.13 also appears in the fact that Acts 3.13 is the only text in the synoptics and Acts in which δοξάζειν has the meaning 'transfigure'.

The Servant of God in the New Testament

and 20.2: διὰ τοῦ παιδὸς αὐτοῦ τοῦ μονογενοῦς 'Ιησοῦ Χριστοῦ (as the association with μονογενής shows).³⁸² It is probable³⁸³ that the understanding of παῖς (θεοῦ) as 'child (of God)' is already present in I *Cl.* 59.2f. where Jesus Christ is called ὁ ἠγαπημένος παῖς; also the formula σὺ εἶ ὁ θεὸς μόνος καὶ 'Ιησοῦς Χριστὸς ὁ παῖς σου (59.4) points to the sense 'child of God'.³⁸⁴ On the other hand it is unlikely that Luke used παῖς (θεοῦ) Acts 3.13, 26; 4.27, 30 as a solemn expression for 'Son (of God)',³⁸⁴ᵃ considering that he undoubtedly understood it in the sense of 'servant' in Acts 4.25. It is certain that the semantic change from servant to child of God was a gradual one and that it did not take place everywhere at the same time.³⁸⁵ The meaning 'servant of God', as the *Didache* shows (cf. p. 86), persisted most obstinately in liturgical formulae.

How obvious for Hellenistic feeling the understanding of παῖς (θεοῦ) as 'child of God' must have been is clear from contemporary literature; for Hellenistic Judaism cf. pp. 46, 53, for Hellenistic paganism cf. *Corp. Herm.* XIII, 2³⁸⁷: ὁ γεννώμενος θεοῦ θεὸς παῖς; XIII, 4: ὁ τοῦ θεοῦ παῖς, ἄνθρωπος εἷς effects the new birth; XIII, 14: θεὸς πέφυκας καὶ τοῦ ἑνὸς παῖς. In addition the word παῖς had something archaic and distinguished about it,³⁸⁸ so that, for example, the emperor's son could be described as Καίσαρος παῖς.³⁸⁹ At the same time it must not be forgotten that in παῖς the more lowly associations are always

---

³⁸² Cf. the ecstatic exclamation of the prophets mentioned by Celsus: ἐγὼ ὁ θεός εἰμι ἢ θεοῦ παῖς ἢ πνεῦμα (Origen, *Cels.* 7.9). The exclamation is modelled upon the trinitarian formula which shows that θεοῦ παῖς means 'son of God'.

³⁸³ Dalman, *WJ*, 278: 'unmistakable'.

³⁸⁴ We are taken back to a still earlier period if the supposition is correct that a παῖς μου lay behind the υἱός μου of the story of the baptism and transfiguration (cf. pp. 81f.), and that the title ὁ υἱὸς τοῦ θεοῦ grew out of ὁ παῖς τοῦ θεοῦ (see n. 354).

³⁸⁴ᵃ Thus Haenchen, op. cit. in n. 379, on Acts 3.13.

³⁸⁵ The Old Latin codices of Acts 3.13, 26 and 4.27, 30 give us a glimpse into the process: in all four texts an original *puer* is gradually supplanted by *filius* (v. Harnack, 218). In this matter the codices are to some extent fluctuating; the *Vulgate* still has *filius* in Acts 3.13, 26; 4.30, but *puer* in 4.27 (under the influence of 4.25). The repugnance to *puer* is, in the western church, 'almost as old as the translation itself' (v. Harnack, 218); already the Bible text of Tertullian read, 4.27, *filius* (Tertullian, *Bapt.* 7; *Adversus Praxean*, 28). The Syr. has בר in all four places: Acts 3.13, 26; 4.27, 30. Quite similar is the fluctuation of the Christian translators of IV Ezra in the rendering of the messianic designation παῖς μου (see n. 196).

³⁸⁷ *Corp. Herm.*, ed. A. D. Nock-A. J. Festugière, I, II (Collection des Universités de France), 1945.

³⁸⁸ v. Harnack, 225; on p. 237 he compares the German word '*Weib*'.

³⁸⁹ Justin, *Epit.* 2.16; cf. Melito in Eusebius, *Hist. Eccl.* IV 26.7; Athenagoras, *Suppl.* 37.1.

The Servant of God

present as well; for this reason παῖς (θεοῦ), in spite of the semantic change from 'servant' to 'child (of God)', was unable to take root in the area of gentile Christianity (cf. pp. 85f.).

2. CHRISTOLOGICAL INTERPRETATIONS OF THE SERVANT TEXTS OF DEUTERO-ISAIAH IN THE NEW TESTAMENT

It became clear on investigating παῖς (θεοῦ) in late Judaism (pp. 45ff.) that mere linguistic inquiry, however indispensable as a basis, did not lead us to the heart of the problem of the servant of God. In order to grapple with this the question of the interpretation of Deut. Isa. servant passages in late Judaism had to be approached (cf. pp. 52ff.). Exactly the same applies to the N.T. We broach the decisive question only when we ask: (i) where in the N.T. do we find christological interpretations of the servant passages of Deut. Isa.? (ii) What is their historical setting in the life of the early church?

(i) *The evidence*. There are strikingly few N.T. passages where in specific quotation a word relating to the servant of Deut. Isa. is applied to Jesus: Matt. 8.17 (Isa. 53.4); 12.18–21 (Isa. 42.1–4); Luke 22.37 (Isa. 53.12); John 12.38 (Isa. 53.1); Acts 8.32f. (Isa. 53.7f.);[390] Rom. 15.21 (Isa. 52.15).[391] But the limitation to express quotations would give a false picture,[392] and in our problem especially would involve a serious error of method such as has not always been avoided.[392a] If we add to the quotations direct or indirect allusions then we have the following picture of the N.T. evidence of the christological interpretations of the Deut. Isa. servant:

(*a*) Pre-Pauline stock of tradition and formulae. Here must first be mentioned the archaic confession of I Cor. 15.3–5 which contains Semitic features,[393] and of which the κατὰ τὰς γραφάς

---

[390] In Acts 13.47: τέθεικά σε εἰς φῶς ἐθνῶν τοῦ εἶναί σε εἰς σωτηρίαν ἕως ἐσχάτου τῆς γῆς (= Isa. 49.6 LXX) it cannot safely be said whether the twofold σε is related to Jesus or to the apostles. But the introduction (οὕτως γὰρ ἐντέταλται ἡμῖν ὁ κύριος) and the comparison with Acts 26.18 says more for the second possibility.

[391] The christological feature lies in περὶ αὐτοῦ.

[392] Rightly emphasized by Wolff³, 69, 79, 85, 102, 106, etc. Also the usual limitation to Isa. 53, and omission of the other servant passages of Deut. Isa., prejudices the picture.

[392a] E.g., by restricting the scope of her study to explicit quotations and to the idea of vicarious suffering as expressed in Isa. 53, Miss Hooker is led to the conclusion that neither Jesus nor the early church attached any particular christological significance to the servant texts of Deutero-Isaiah. Cf. against this view Lohse², 220–4.

[393] J. Jeremias, *Eucharistic Words*, 129ff.

The Servant of God in the New Testament

('according to the scripture') of v. 3, because of the ὑπὲρ τῶν ἁμαρτιῶν ἡμῶν, must be an allusion to Isa. 53.[394] Further, to this pre-Pauline stock of tradition belong the liturgically formulated[395] eucharistic words of I Cor. 11.23-25,[396] the christological formula of Rom. 4.25[397] built up in synthetic *parallelismus membrorum*, the Christ hymn in Phil. 2.6-11,[398] the confessional formula of Rom. 8.34,[399] the word about ransom in I Tim. 2.6 (see n. 401), the ancient ὑπέρ formula, very frequent in Paul, with its variants (see n. 435), and finally the expression *(παρ)έδωκεν ἑαυτόν* which is in all instances connected with the ὑπέρ formula (Gal. 1.4; 2.20; Eph. 5.2, 25; I Tim. 2.6; Titus 2.14).[399a] The references to Isa. 53.12 and 11 contained in Rom. 5.16 *(πολλοί)*, 19 *(οἱ πολλοί)* most probably are traditional, too, as suggested by the fact that the Hebrew text is in the background.[399b] That the use of Isa. 53.1 (LXX) as quoted in Rom. 10.16 is pre-Pauline is confirmed by John 12.38.[399c] Whether Rom. 8.32 is traditional cannot be determined with certainty, because Paul refers to LXX.[399d] The only reference to a servant passage which is undoubtedly due to Paul himself is Rom. 15.21 where he grounds his missionary activity in Isa. 52.15 LXX (see below, p. 93). This means that all Pauline allusions to the '*ebed*-Yahweh texts of Deut. Isa. apart from Rom. 15.21 make use of an ancient stock of tradition.

---

[394] Cf. Lohmeyer, *Gottesknecht*, 39; Cullmann, *Christology*, 76.
[395] Jeremias, *Eucharistic Words*, 128ff.
[396] For the allusion to Isa. 53 see p. 96 below (a ὑπέρ formula).
[397] παρεδόθη διὰ τὰ παραπτώματα ἡμῶν Rom. 4.25a corresponds exactly to Isa. 53.5b Targ. אִתְמְסַר בַּעֲוָיָתָנָא; by contrast, Isa. 53.12 LXX (διὰ τὰς ἁμαρτίας αὐτῶν παρεδόθη) differs from Rom. 4.25 in its vocabulary (ἁμαρτίας) as well as by the personal pronoun (αὐτῶν). For the pre-Pauline character of the formula cf. H. Lietzmann, *An die Römer*⁴, 1933, ad loc.; E. Stauffer, *New Testament Theology*, 1955, 132, 136; R. Bultmann, *Theology of the New Testament*, I, 1953, 31.
[398] For the allusion to Isa. 53 Heb. text see pp. 97f. below. Lohmeyer, *Kyrios Jesus*, has demonstrated the pre-Pauline character of Phil. 2.6-11.
[399] Rom. 8.34 ὅς καὶ ἐντυγχάνει ὑπὲρ ἡμῶν takes up the end of Isa. 53.12 Heb. text (p. 95 below); LXX is different. Cf. C. H. Dodd, *According to the Scriptures*, 1952, 94.
[399a] The pre-Pauline age of the formula resorts from the translation variants (see p. 96 below).
[399b] J. Jeremias, πολλοί, *TWNT*, VI, 543, 545. Cf. S. Mowinckel, 'Die Vorstellungen des Spätjudentums vom heiligen Geist als Fürsprecher und der johanneische Paraklet', *ZNW*, 32, 1933, 121, n. 82; Cullmann, *Christology*, 77.
[399c] See p. 93 below.
[399d] Rom. 8.32 ὑπὲρ ἡμῶν πάντων παρέδωκεν αὐτόν refers to Isa. 53.6 LXX καὶ κύριος παρέδωκεν αὐτὸν ταῖς ἁμαρτίαις ἡμῶν (see p. 96 below).

The Servant of God

(*b*) Pre-synoptic stock of tradition and formulae. In the synoptics, too, most of the allusions to the '*ebed*-Yahweh texts of Deut.-Isa. can be shown to be based on ancient tradition. This is the case for the ancient eucharistic formula (Mark 14.24 par.)[400] and the λύτρον saying (Mark 10.45 par. Matt. 20.28)[401] with certainty on account of the linguistic characteristics; for the voice at the baptism (Mark 1.11 par. = Isa. 42.1) on account of its independence of LXX;[402] for Luke 2.32 on account of the whole stylistic and linguistic character of the hymn (2.29–32);[403] for Matt. 12.18–21 (= Isa. 42.1–4) on account of the mixed character of the text (cf. p. 81); for Luke 22.37 (= Isa. 53.12)[404] and for Matt. 8.17 (= Isa. 53.4 Heb. text) on account of the connexion with the Heb. text (cf. n. 424). That the numerous general references to scripture which are met with in all three synoptics in connexion with Jesus' words about his passion[405] are also—probably even primarily—allusions to Isa. 53, is shown by the ancient saying of Mark 9.12 (ἐξουδενηθῇ cf. ἐξουδενωμένος Isa. 53.3 'Α, Σ, Θ = נִבְזֶה)[406] and by Luke 22.37 (see p. 105), perhaps also by the frequent use of παραδίδοσθαι

---

[400] Allusion to Isa. 53: J. Jeremias, *Eucharistic Words*, 147ff., 123–5. For Palestinian character of the language: ibid. 118–26. Independence of LXX: ὑπέρ is missing in LXX Isa. 53, see n. 434.

[401] Allusions to Isa. 53.10–12 (Heb. text): J. Jeremias, 'Lösegeld', 262–4, also *Eucharistic Words*, 125; for Palestinian character of the language, cf. Jeremias, 'Lösegeld', 260–2, also *Eucharistic Words*, 123–5.

[402] Cf. furthermore what was said on pp. 83f. above about the great age of Mark 1.11 par. and 9.7 par.

[403] The expression in Luke 2.32: φῶς εἰς ἀποκάλυψιν ἐθνῶν is a reminiscence of a servant text which is literally the same in Isa. 42.6 and 49.6 (לְאוֹר גּוֹיִם); but the juxtaposition of heathen and Israel (Luke 2.32 a b) shows that Isa. 49.6 is the closer.

[404] Luke 22.37: καὶ μετὰ ἀνόμων ἐλογίσθη cf. Isa. 53.12: וְאֶת־פֹּשְׁעִים נִמְנָה; on the other hand LXX Isa. 53.12: καὶ ἐν τοῖς ἀνόμοις ἐλογίσθη (i.e., with article and ἐν). The words ἄνομοι and λογίζεσθαι are drawn from the LXX; the preposition μετά and the missing article, on the other hand, betray the influence of the Hebrew text.

[405] Mark 8.31 par. (δεῖ); 9.12 par.; 14.21 par. (γέγραπται); 14.49 par. (ἵνα πληρωθῶσιν αἱ γραφαί); Luke 18.31 (τελεσθήσεται πάντα τὰ γεγραμμένα διὰ τῶν προφητῶν), cf. Mark 10.32 par. (μέλλειν, so also Matt. 17.12, 22; Luke 9.44); peculiar to Matt., 26.54 (πῶς οὖν πληρωθῶσιν αἱ γραφαί . . . δεῖ); peculiar to Luke, 13.33; 17.25; 24.7, 25–27, 44–46 (δεῖ); 9.31 (ἤμελλεν πληροῦν); 22.22 (κατὰ τὸ ὡρισμένον); 24.32 (διήνοιγεν . . . τὰς γραφάς); 24.44 (δεῖ πληρωθῆναι πάντα τὰ γεγραμμένα), 46 (γέγραπται).

[406] Cf. Otto, 197–9; Michaelis, 8f. The antiquity of this is clear from the indefinite character of the announcement of the passion and from the observation that the four-part statement in Mark 8.31 is obviously a more recent expansion of the two-part statement of 9.12. H. Tödt, *The Son of Man in the Synoptic Tradition*, 1965, 164 ff., finds in Mark 9.12 an allusion to Ps. 118.22 because this verse is quoted in Acts 4.11

The Servant of God in the New Testament

(see below, p. 105);[407] it is clear from I Cor. 15.3 that the greater part of these scriptural allusions is pre-synoptic (cf. pp. 88f.). Quite astonishing is the almost complete non-appearance of the LXX in the synoptic texts: while many of them reveal the influence of the Heb. text,[408] that of the LXX is only visible in the *addendum* Matt. 12.21 (cf. p. 81) and Luke 22.37 (cf. n. 404). The result is similar to that in regard to Paul: almost all allusions to the Deut. Isa. '*ebed*-Yahweh texts to be found in the first three gospels come from an ancient stock of tradition and formulae.

(*c*) Stock of tradition and formulae in Acts. In Acts we find 8.32f. a citation from Isa. 53.7f. LXX in application to Jesus; it occurs in the fragment of tradition dealing with Philip, 8.5-40,[410] the antiquity of which is especially evident from the way baptism is described in 8.12ff., 36, 38f.[411] Also the designation of Jesus as παῖς,[412] the occurrence of which is limited to Acts 3 and 4, belongs to a very ancient stratum of the tradition. Further, Jesus is called ὁ δίκαιος three times in Acts (3.14; 7.52; 22.14, cf. p. 92). Since in all three passages there is an article but no noun, we are here faced by a title, most probably the messianic title 'the righteous one' known from the *Eth. En.* (cf. p. 60), and alluding in the latter to Isa. 53.11. A comparison of Acts 22.13f. with 9.17 *(ὁ δίκαιος/ὁ κύριος)* shows that ὁ δίκαιος is the older title of dignity.[413] Finally, in the discourses of Acts the scriptural allusions in passages about the suffering and death of Jesus occur so regularly[414] that we must see in them an integral part of the primitive *kerygma*.[415]

as ὁ λίθος ὁ ἐξουθενηθείς. But this form of Ps. 118.22 is not otherwise attested. It is probably due to Luke who has also changed the following word οἰκοδομοῦντες (Ps. 117 [118].22 LXX) to οἰκοδόμοι. Luke likes to trim his scriptural quotations to shape. In addition, he employs ἐξουθενέω in Luke 18.9; 23.11.
[407] Cf. also Luke 18.31: τὰ γεγραμμένα διὰ τῶν προφητῶν.
[408] Mark 1.11 par. (cf. 9.7 par.); 9.12; 10.45; 14.24; Matt. 8.17; 12. 18-20; Luke 22.37.
[410] J. Jeremias, 'Untersuchungen zum Quellenproblem der Apostelgeschichte', *ZNW*, 36, 1937, 215f.
[411] 8.12ff.: baptism without reception of the Spirit; 36, 38f.: baptism without catechumenate.
[412] For the reference of Acts 3.13f. to Isa. 53 see n. 380.
[413] F. J. F. Jackson and K. Lake, *Beginnings of Christianity*, I, 4, 1933, conclude from the comparison of Acts 9.17 with 22.14 that ὁ δίκαιος = צַדִּיק was perhaps 'the oldest title given to Jesus'.
[414] 2.23 (τῇ ὡρισμένῃ βουλῇ καὶ προγνώσει τοῦ θεοῦ, cf. Isa. 53.10); 3.18, cf. 7.52 (προκαταγγέλλειν); 13.27; 26.22f. (οἱ προφῆται); 3.18, cf. 10.43 (plerophorically πάντες οἱ προφῆται); 4.28 (προορίζειν); 13.29 (πάντα τὰ ... γεγραμμένα); 17.2 (γραφαί), 3 (ἔδει).
[415] M. Dibelius, *Die Formgeschichte des Evangeliums*⁴, 1961, 15.

The Servant of God

(*d*) Ancient formulae in I Peter and Hebrews. In I Peter 2.21–25 are to be found a whole series of free quotations from Isa. 53 LXX (v. 22: Isa. 53.9; v. 24a: Isa. 53.12, cf. 4, 11; v. 24b: Isa. 53.5; v. 25: Isa. 53.6), which were used in part as formulae (cf. p. 97); further, in I Peter 3.18 περὶ ἁμαρτιῶν is probably an allusion to Isa. 53.10; δίκαιος to 53.11. Both in I Peter 2.21–25 and in 3.18 the old ὑπέρ formula is met with (2.21; 3.18; cf. pp. 95f.). Both passages use traditional liturgical material, the first a hymn to Christ, the second christological formulae.[416] In I Peter 1.11 we find again the general allusion to scripture in connexion with the passion of Christ, familiar to us already from the archaic creed (cf. p. 88), the synoptics (cf. p. 90) and Acts (cf. p. 91). The epistle to the Hebrews makes use of LXX Isa. 53.12 in 9.28 (εἰς τὸ πολλῶν ἀνενεγκεῖν ἁμαρτίας). The expression has a formal character (cf. p. 97). This is also shown by the fact that the whole paragraph 9.27f. 'makes use of older catechetical material'.[416a] On Christ's intercession, 7.25, also 2.18; 9.24, cf. below, p. 95. 'The writer to the Hebrews does not actually quote from Isa. 53, but he takes it for granted and builds his own work upon it.'[417]

(*e*) Ancient formulae in the Johannine writings. Here again allusions to the '*ebed* of Deut. Isa. belong without exception to an old stratum of tradition. We first refer to what has already been discussed: on John 1.29 (ὁ ἀμνὸς τοῦ θεοῦ ὁ αἴρων τὴν ἁμαρτίαν τοῦ κόσμου) and 1.36 see p. 83; on 1.34 (ὁ ἐκλεκτός) see p. 83; on 3.14; 12.34 (δεῖ) see n. 405. On I John 2.1, 29; 3.7 (δίκαιος) see p. 91; on 2.2; 4.10 (ἱλασμός) see n. 431; on 3.5 (τὰς ἁμαρτίας αἴρειν) see p. 97; on 3.5 (ἁμαρτία ἐν αὐτῷ οὐκ ἔστιν) see p. 97; on ἀρνίον in Rev. see p. 84.[418] Further the expression τιθέναι τὴν ψυχήν (John 10.11, 15, 17, 18) is to be mentioned; it is reminiscent of Isa. 53.10 (Heb.), 53.12 (Aram.) and as the comparison with Mark 10.45 par. (διδόναι τὴν ψυχήν) and the ὑπέρ formula (pp. 95f.) show, it is traditional.[419] John 16.32 (σκορπισθῆτε ἕκαστος εἰς τὰ ἴδια), as ἕκαστος εἰς τὰ ἴδια shows,

---
[416] R. Bultmann, 'Bekenntnis- und Liedfragmente im ersten Petrusbrief', *Coniectanea Neotestamentica*, 11, 1947, 1–14.
[416a] O. Michel, *Der Brief an die Hebräer* (Meyer, 13)¹¹, 1960, on Heb. 9.27f. with detailed proof.
[417] B. Lindars, *New Testament Apologetic*, 1961, 83.
[418] On ὑψοῦν and δοξάζειν in John see n. 441.
[419] Cf. p. 96 below. The ὑπέρ formula also elsewhere in John, see n. 435.

The Servant of God in the New Testament

is an allusion to Isa. 53.6; moreover the Palestinian exegesis of אתבדרנא (= 'we were scattered'), preserved in the *Targ.*, is used.[420] Finally, with regard to the quotation John 12.38 (= Isa. 53.1 LXX), what is striking is the fact that the quotation immediately following in v. 40 (= Isa. 6.10) follows a different technique of translation;[421] even the introductory formulae are different. Since the introduction to the second quotation (John 12.40) reveals a typically Johannine style,[422] the first (12.38) may be traditional in form and content.[423] In fact Rom. 10.16 confirms the traditional character of the quotation from Isa. 53.1.

(*f*) Paul; Matthew. In Paul, apart from the richly extant traditional material (cf. pp. 88f.), there is to be found only one christologically interpreted '*ebed* quotation—Rom. 15.21 (= Isa. 52.15 LXX). But it is characteristic that here the emphasis lies not on the christological interpretation (περὶ αὐτοῦ) but on his particular missionary task to preach the gospel where it had not yet been heard, which Paul finds prophesied in this passage from Isa. The position is quite similar in the synoptic gospels. Apart from the rich traditional material which is to be found in them too (pp. 90f.) and with the exception of the supplement Matt. 12.21 (p. 81), we may attribute with certainty to one of the synoptic evangelists personally only the general scriptural allusion, Matt. 26.54, which is stamped by the characteristic style of Matt.[424]

The absence of allusions to the '*ebed* in James, II and III John, in Jude, II Peter, and Rev.[425] as well as their remarkable scarcity

---

[420] Hegermann, 81f.
[421] John 12.38 follows LXX, against the Hebrew text (as the addition of κύριε shows). 12.40, on the other hand, departs completely from LXX.
[422] διὰ τοῦτο ... ὅτι cf. Bultmann, *Das Evangelium des Johannes* (Meyer, 2), 1941, 346, n. 4; 177, n. 5.
[423] Cf. Bultmann, op. cit. in n. 422, 346, who attributes John 12.37f. to the 'σημεῖα source' used by this evangelist. We have intentionally formulated the matter in more general terms.
[424] πῶς in direct rhetorical question with following subjunctive in the N.T. only in Matt. (23.33; 26.54); πληροῦν (of scripture) is a favourite word of Matt. (twelve times, Mark once, Luke twice, John eight times; cf. E. Klostermann, *Das Matthäusevangelium* [HNT, 4]², 1927, on 1.22). On the other hand Matt. 8.17 can hardly be attributed with A. Schlatter, *Der Evangelist Matthäus*, ad loc., to the evangelist himself, because here Isa. 53.4 is translated from the Heb. text whereas Matt. in his own scriptural quotations follows LXX.
[425] Rev. 1.16; 19.15 (sword out of the mouth) is not to be counted among the allusions to the '*ebed*; for here the allusion is to Isa. 11.4 (with a suggestion of Isa. 49.2 and Ps. 149.6, see Schlatter, *Das Alte Testament in der johanneischen Apokalypse*, 37).

The Servant of God

in Paul, Hebrews, and the Gospel of John and, finally, the circumstance that the very numerous references are to be found almost without exception in the stock of old tradition and formulae—all this leads to the same conclusion: the christological interpretation of the Deutero-Isaiah servant belongs to the earliest period of the Christian community and at a very early stage became fixed in form. This result is confirmed and made precise by a further observation. A survey of all the Isaiah texts so far mentioned yields the conclusion that of the *'ebed* texts of Deut. Isa. only Isa. 42.1–4, 6; 49.6 and 52.13ff. were interpreted messianically in the N.T. But those are the precise texts which Palestinian Judaism—as opposed to Hellenistic (pp. 54f.)—interpreted messianically (pp. 78f.). Hence it is confirmed that the christological interpretation of these passages flows from the Palestinian pre-Hellenistic stage of the early church.[426]

(ii) *The historical setting in the life of the early church.* The result thus reached finds further confirmation and gains concrete form when we inquire into the historical setting of the christological interpretation of the *'ebed* in the early church.

(a) The fundamental setting of this exegesis in the early church —if we set aside for the moment the transmission of the words of Jesus (see pp. 99–106)—is proof from scripture. The situation after the death of Jesus compelled the Christian community from the very first to supply a demonstration from scripture that the death on the cross was divinely ordained and possessed vicarious efficacy. That scripture proof for the death on the cross belonged to the most primitive *kerygma* and that it was carried out with the help of Isa. 53, is shown conclusively by I Cor. 15.3 (cf. pp. 88f.). Its importance may be measured by the great number of instances and the variety of the formulae (cf. nn. 405, 414). Whereas in the majority of cases Isa. 53 is presumed to be so well known that a general reference to scripture suffices,[427] Acts 8.32f. adduces a literal quotation of Isa. 53.7b–8a (LXX). Furthermore, the primitive (pp. 81, 90) tradition finds in Isa. 42 and 53 a prophecy of

---

[426] C. H. Dodd, *According to the Scriptures*, 1952, 94 with reference to the 'ubiquity' of the christological interpretation of Isa. 53 in the N.T.; Cullmann, *Christology*, 79: the *'ebed*-Yahweh christology is 'one of the oldest and most important Christologies'.
[427] J. Dupont, *Les problèmes du Livre des Actes d'après les travaux récents*, 1950, 110.

The Servant of God in the New Testament

individual traits in the life of Jesus (Matt. 8.17 = Isa. 53.4 Heb. text: healings of the sick; Matt. 12.18-20 = Isa. 42.1-3 Heb. text: the avoidance of public notice). In Isa. 53.1 is seen a prophecy of the unbelief of Israel (note the independent agreement of Paul and the fourth gospel: Rom. 10.16; John 12.38, see p. 93). Finally, in Isa. 52.15 Paul found prophesied his special missionary task of preaching Christ where as yet no one had heard of him (Rom. 15.21).[428]

(*b*) Secondly the '*ebed* of Deutero-Isaiah influenced very strongly the development of the christology of the early church. This is shown by the great number of christological predicates and formal turns of phrase which are connected with Isa. 42.1ff. and 52.13ff.

The following christological predicates should be mentioned: ὁ παῖς (of God) (pp. 81f., 86f.) and perhaps connected with it: ὁ υἱὸς τοῦ θεοῦ (p. 82), ὁ ἀμνὸς τοῦ θεοῦ (p. 83), and τὸ ἀρνίον (p. 84); further ὁ ἐκλεκτός (John 1.34, see n. 261), ὁ ἐκλελεγμένος (Luke 9.35) with its alternative ὁ ἀγαπητός;[429] finally, ὁ δίκαιος, although occurring not seldom in late Jewish literature (cf. G. Schrenk, δίκαιος, *TWNT*, II, 188, 23ff.) as a messianic attribute, should, as a predicate of Jesus, be connected in the first instance with Isa. 53.11 (see pp. 91f.).[430] Further, the description of Jesus as ἱλασμὸς περὶ τῶν ἁμαρτιῶν ἡμῶν (I John 2.2; 4.10)[431] rests presumably upon Isa. 53.10; his description as intercessor (I John 2.1: παράκλητος; Rom. 8.34 and Heb. 7.25: ἐντυγχάνειν) corresponds to Isa. 53.12 Heb. text;[432] on φῶς εἰς ἀποκάλυψιν ἐθνῶν, see n. 403.

Among christological formulae connected with Isa. 53 the ὑπέρ formula stands first by reason of its numerical preponderance. Its origin in Isa. 53 is suggested by the link with the word πολλοί (*ὑπὲρ πολλῶν* Mark 14.24; *περὶ πολλῶν* Matt. 26.28; *ἀντὶ πολλῶν* Mark 10.45; Matt. 20.28) which is a veritable keyword in Isa. 53, and by I Cor. 15.3 (*κατὰ τὰς γραφάς*). The great age

---
[428] Cf. further the similar reference to Isa. 42.7, 16 in Acts 26.18.
[429] Mark 1.11 par.; 9.7 par.; Matt. 12.18; Luke 9.35 v.l.; II Peter 1.17. Cf. Eph. 1.6: ὁ ἠγαπημένος.
[430] H. Dechent, 'Der "Gerechte"—eine Bezeichnung für den Messias', *TSK*, 100, 1927-8, 439-43.
[431] ἱλασμός = אָשָׁם Isa. 53.10 (?); on περὶ τῶν ἁμαρτιῶν ἡμῶν cf. Isa. 53.4-6; Wolff, 104f.
[432] Mowinckel, op. cit. in n. 399b, 120f. It should be noticed that Jesus, in I John 2.1, is called δίκαιος (cf. Isa. 53.11).

The Servant of God

of the ὑπέρ formula is shown by its use in the primitive confession (I Cor. 15.3) and in the eucharistic words (Mark 14.24 par.),[433] also by its independence of the LXX[434] and by the marked variation in the prepositions[435] arising from the varied translations of the Semitic text which lay behind it.[436] A second key-word, besides ὑπέρ, which in many places carries a reference to Isa. 53, is (παρα-)διδόναι. Two different stages of association with Isa. 53 may be distinguished, depending on whether the verb is construed in the active, or in the active with a reflexive object, or in the passive. The reflexive use leads us back into Semitic-speaking circles. This follows from the fact that παραδιδόναι ἑαυτόν (Gal. 2.20; Eph. 5.2, 25) alternates with the simple διδόναι ἑαυτόν (Gal. 1.4; I Tim. 2.6; Titus 2.14), the latter being a grecianized form of διδόναι τὴν ψυχήν (cf. Mark 10.45; Matt. 20.28) which, on its part, is paralleled by the synonymous τιθέναι τὴν ψυχήν (John 10.11, 15, 17f.; 15.13; I John 3.16). All forms are most probably mere translation variants of שִׂים נַפְשׁוֹ (Isa. 53.10 Heb. text) or מְסַר נַפְשֵׁהּ (Isa. 53.12 Targ.). Likewise, we are led back into a Semitic-speaking environment by the passive παραδίδοσθαι (the passive being used to circumscribe God's action). For in Rom. 4.25, παρεδόθη διὰ τὰ παραπτώματα ἡμῶν is an exact rendering of Isa. 53.5b Targ.: אִתְמְסַר בַּעֲוָיָתָנָא (cf. n. 397). On the other hand, the active παραδιδόναι having God for its subject, which is used in Rom. 8.32 ὑπὲρ ἡμῶν πάντων παρέδωκεν αὐτόν, points to a Hellenistic background, for here Isa. 53.6c LXX (καὶ κύριος παρέδωκεν αὐτόν) is referred to. In all

---

[433] With regard to the Semitic linguistic character of both sections see J. Jeremias, *Eucharistic Words*, 118ff. ὑπὲρ τῶν ἁμαρτιῶν ἡμῶν (I Cor. 15.3 = Isa. 53.5 a b Heb. text) is recognizable as pre-Pauline by the un-Pauline plural (ibid. 129f.).
[434] ὑπέρ is lacking in the LXX of Isa. 52.13-53.12; there διά with accusative (53.5 [twice], 12) and περί with genitive (53.4, cf. 10) are used.
[435] The following prepositions alternate in the statements about the death of Jesus: ἀντί: Mark 10.45; Matt. 20.28; ὑπέρ with genitive: Mark 14.24; Luke 22.19, 20; John 6.51; 10.11, 15; 11.51f.; 15.13; 17.19; 18.14; Rom. 5.6, 8; 8.32; 14.15; I Cor. 1.13; 5.7 v.l.; 11.24; 15.3; II Cor. 5.14, 15 (twice), 21; Gal. 1.4; 2.20; 3.13; Eph. 5.2, 25; I Thess. 5.10 v.l.; I Tim. 2.6; Titus 2.14; Heb. 2.9; 7.27; 10.12 (cf. 26); I Peter 2.21; 3.18; 4.1 v.l.; I John 3.16; περί with genitive: Matt. 26.28; Rom. 8.3; I Cor. 1.13 v.l.; Gal. 1.4 v.l.; I Thess. 5.10; I Peter 3.18; I John 2.2; 4.10; διά with accusative: Rom. 3.25; 4.25; I Cor. 8.11. It is not a matter of chance that in many of these passages the use of formal data can be recognized also by other indications. Also, the preponderance of ὑπέρ as over against περί, which is more frequent in Hellenistic Greek, indicates age (Lohse, 131, n. 4).
[436] A specially clear example of variants in the translation is furnished by Mark 10.45 par. (ἀντὶ πολλῶν) compared with I Tim. 2.6 (ὑπὲρ πάντων).

96

The Servant of God in the New Testament

instances just quoted (παρα-)διδόναι is linked with the ὑπέρ formula and its variants. Finally, the expression taken from Isa. 53.12 αἴρειν τὴν ἁμαρτίαν (John 1.29; plural I John 3.5) or ἀναφέρειν ἁμαρτίας (Heb. 9.28; I Peter 2.24),[440] probably also the phrase ἁμαρτίαν οὐκ ἐποίησεν (I Peter 2.22) or ἁμαρτία ἐν αὐτῷ οὐκ ἔστιν (I John 3.5), echoing Isa. 53.9b,[441] are of a formal character. The variety of the attempts to render in Greek the Hebrew אָשָׁם (Isa. 53.10) confirms the early and strong influence of Isa. 53 upon the christology of the early church.[442]

(c) Further, liturgy is to be taken into account. In the celebration of the eucharist, the πολλῶν of the liturgical words of the Last Supper (Mark 14.24 par. Matt. 26.28) pointed to the servant (cf. n. 400), and the old liturgical prayer formula διὰ 'Ιησοῦ τοῦ παιδός σου lives on with great persistence in the eucharistic prayer and in the doxology (pp. 85f.).[443] From pre-Pauline times (see n. 398 on Phil. 2.6–11) Jesus is also extolled in psalms as the servant of God (Phil. 2.6–11; I Peter 2.22–25; Luke 2.32, cf. Rom. 4.25).

The connexion of Phil. 2.6–11 with Isa. 53[444] becomes plain

---

[440] John 1.29; I John 3.5 follow Isa. 53.12 Heb. text, on the other hand Heb. 9.28; I Peter 2.24 use Isa. 53.12 LXX; this accounts for the alternation of αἴρειν and ἀναφέρειν.

[441] Cf. further τὸν μὴ γνόντα ἁμαρτίαν II Cor. 5.21. It cannot be said with certainty whether the formal use of the verbs ὑψοῦν, Acts 2.33; 5.31; John 3.14; 8.28; 12.32, 34 and δοξάζειν, Acts 3.13; John 7.39; 12.16, 23; 17.1, 5 and elsewhere, is connected with Isa. 52.13 LXX (thus O. Michel, 'Probleme der neutestamentlichen Theologie', DT, 9, 1942, 29; Wolff, 85; Cerfaux, 123, n. 1).

[442] λύτρον: Mark 10.45; Matt. 20.28 (Dalman, op. cit. in n. 304, 110; cf. Wolff, 61; J. Jeremias, 'Lösegeld', 262), hellenized as ἀντίλυτρον in I Tim. 2.6; περὶ ἁμαρτίας (= LXX Isa. 53.10) Rom. 8.3; for ἱλασμός see n. 431; perhaps also ἱλαστήριον Rom. 3.25.

[443] Cf. further the eucharistic epiclesis of the church order of Hippolytus (v. Harnack, 227f.; H. Lietzmann, *Messe und Herrenmahl*, 1926, 8of.) and the eucharistic liturgy of a Berlin papyrus not yet edited, in which it is said 'may the eucharist serve εἰς φάρμακον ἀθανασίας ... διὰ τοῦ ἠγαπημένου σου παιδός', H. Lietzmann, ibid., 257, n. 2.

[444] Affirmed by, among others, Lohmeyer, *Kyrios Jesus*, 32f., 35ff., 40–42, and H. Windisch in his review of Lohmeyer, *TLZ*, 54, 1929, 247; G. Kittel, ὑπακοή, ὑπήκοος, *TWNT*, I, 225, 34–37; Euler, 45, 47f., 101, 103, 118; H. Wheeler Robinson, loc. cit. in n. 445; G. Stählin, ἴσος κτλ., *TWNT*, III, 354; Cerfaux, 117–24; G. S. Duncan, *Jesus, Son of Man*, 1947, 193f.; Davies, *Paul and Rabbinic Judaism*, 274; Cullmann, *Christology*, 76f.; Schelkle, 95. The contesting of this connexion of Phil. 2.6ff. with Isa. 53, in K. H. Rengstorf, δοῦλος κτλ., *TWNT*, II, 281f. and Gewiess, 56, n. 149, turns upon the word δοῦλος, Phil. 2.7, in place of which, it is argued, παῖς would be expected. The connexion has been most recently disputed by E. Käsemann, 'Kritische Analyse von Phil. 2, 5–11', *ZTK*, 47, 1950, 313–60, reprinted in E. Käsemann, *Exegetische Versuche und Besinnungen*, I, 1960, 51–95.

The Servant of God

as soon as it is recognized that, whereas the hymn itself follows LXX in 2.10f., it makes use in 2.6–9 of a christological terminology which is drawn from Isa. 53 Heb. text; even the use of δοῦλος (instead of παῖς) loses its strangeness (see n. 444) when it goes back to the Hebrew עֶבֶד (Isa. 52.13). The decisive proof of our contention that the christology of Phil. 2.6–9 is rooted in Isa. 53 Heb. text lies in the fact that the expression ἑαυτὸν ἐκένωσεν (Phil. 2.7), attested nowhere else in the Greek and grammatically extremely harsh, is an exact rendering of הֶעֱרָה נַפְשׁוֹ .... (Isa. 53.12).[445] Apart from other verbal echoes,[446] allusion to Isa. 53 is to be seen further in the antithesis of

---

[445] Recognized by H. Wheeler Robinson, 'The Cross of the Servant', in *The Cross in the Old Testament*, 1955, pp. 57, 104f.; also, C. H. Dodd, *JTS*, 39, 1938, 292; *According to the Scriptures*, 1952, 93; J. A. T. Robinson, *The Body* (Studies in Biblical Theology, 5), 1952, 14, n. 1. The verb עָרָה means either 'to lay bare, to expose' or 'to pour out'. In the latter sense, the LXX and the Hexaplaric versions usually render it by ἐκκενοῦν (LXX Gen. 24.20; II Chron. 24.11; Ps. 136 [137]. 7; 'A' Ps. 141.8; cf. Σ Jer. 51 [28]. 58; cf. Dodd, *JTS*, 39, 1938, 292). In three instances, LXX prefers a free rendering, viz. Isa. 32.15 and in the two places which mention a 'pouring out of life', Isa. 53.12 παρεδόθη εἰς θάνατον ἡ ψυχὴ αὐτοῦ, and Ps. 140 [141].8 μὴ ἀντανέλῃς τὴν ψυχήν μου. It is to be noted, however, that 'A in this last instance has ἐκκενοῦν, thus confirming that this usual equivalent of עָרָה could also be used in this idiom. The use of Isa. 53.12 shows that the expression ἑαυτὸν ἐκένωσεν implies the surrender of life, not the *kenosis* of the incarnation. G. Bornkamm, 'Zum Verständnis des Christus-Hymnus Phil. 2, 6–11', in: *Studien zu Antike und Urchristentum*, 1959 = ²1963, 180, objects to the idea of ἑαυτὸν ἐκένωσεν being a rendering of Isa. 53.12 הֶעֱרָה לַמָּוֶת נַפְשׁוֹ, 1. that לַמָּוֶת is lacking, 2. that נַפְשׁוֹ, too, was left untranslated, and 3. that Jesus' death is not referred to until v. 8b. I have tried to show in 'Zu Phil ii 7: Ἑαυτὸν ἐκένωσεν', *Novum Testamentum*, 6, 1963, 182–8, that these objections are unfounded. 1. Ps. 141.8 ('pour not my life out', i.e., 'kill me not') proves that the idiom was used with (as in Isa. 53.12) or without (as in Phil. 2.7) לַמָּוֶת, the latter being no indispensable part of it. 2. That נַפְשׁוֹ was not translated is a mistaken assumption. It is represented, quite accurately, by the reflexive pronoun ἑαυτόν which often serves to translate נֶפֶשׁ when it holds the place of the reflexive pronoun lacking in Semitic. 3. To say that ἑαυτὸν ἐκένωσεν cannot take up Isa. 53.12 because Phil. 2.7a does not yet speak of Jesus' death is begging the question. It can in fact be shown that the hymn consists of three four-line stanzas (vv. 6–7a, 7b–8, 9–11), the first two of which run parallel in form and substance. Thus far from precluding our interpretation of Phil. 2.7a, the very structure of the hymn suggests that this clause refers to Jesus' death as well as v. 8b.

[446] With μορφή (Phil. 2.6, 7) is perhaps to be compared the rendering of תֹּאַר (Isa. 52.14; 53.2) by μορφή in 'A (see J. Behm, μορφή κτλ., *TWNT*, IV, 759, n. 53); with ἐταπείνωσεν ἑαυτόν (Phil. 2.8) cf. the rendering of מֻכֶּה (Isa. 53.4) by ταπεινοῦν in Σ and Θ; regarding ὑπήκοος (Phil. 2.8) cf. the rendering of נַעֲנֶה (Isa. 53.7) with ὑπήκουσεν by Σ (according to Eusebius); with διό (Phil. 2.9) cf. לָכֵן (Isa. 53.12); with ὑπερύψωσεν (Phil. 2.9) cf. יָרוּם וְנִשָּׂא וְגָבַהּ מְאֹד (Isa. 52.13).

The Servant of God in the New Testament

extreme meekness and exaltation, in the willingness to be humbled and in the mention of obedience and of death.[447]

The hymn to Christ (I Peter 2.22-25) (p. 92) is much like a short summary of Isa. 53; it shows how Jesus is regarded wholly from the point of view of the suffering servant. The song of praise of Simeon (Luke 2.29-32) takes up Isa. 49.6 (cf. n. 403) and refers this servant passage to Jesus.

(d) Finally, Isa. 53 plays a great part in primitive Christian paraenesis and the literature of martyrdom. Jesus as the suffering servant of God is put forward, as the contexts show, as the prototype of service (Mark 10.45 par.), of selflessness (Phil. 2.5-11), of willing innocent suffering (I Peter 2.21-25) and of humility (I Cl. 16.1-17). In particular, the martyr is the perfect imitator of the servant (Ignatius, *Eph.* 10.3; Eusebius, *Hist. Eccl.* V 1.23; V 2.2).[448]

The result is that there is no area of the primitive Christian life of faith which was not stamped and moulded by the *'ebed* christology. Its impact, to be observed equally throughout all areas in formal phrases, enables us to appreciate the antiquity and the deep roots of the *'ebed* christology and explains the infrequency of express quotations (pp. 88, 95). But if the christological interpretation of Isa. 42.1ff.; 49.6, and especially 52.13ff. belongs to the oldest Palestinian stage of the early church, the question then arises:

3. CAN JESUS HAVE REFERRED THE SERVANT PASSAGES OF DEUTERO-ISAIAH TO HIMSELF?

The gospels say so. In the following places they make Jesus apply to himself the Deut. Isa. servant passages:

Mark 9.12: ἐξουδενηθῇ, cf. Isa. 53.3: נִבְזֶה ('Α, Σ, Θ ἐξουδενωμένος) (see p. 90 above).[448a]—Mark 9.31 par.; 10.33 par.; 14.21 par., 41 par.; Matt. 26.2; Luke 24.7: παραδίδοται/παραδοθήσεται/ παραδίδοσθαι/παραδοθῆναι, cf. Isa. 53.5b *Targ.*: אִתְמְסַר.—Mark 10.45 par. Matt. 20.28: διακονῆσαι καὶ δοῦναι τὴν ψυχὴν αὐτοῦ λύτρον ἀντὶ

---

[447] Cf. further Cerfaux, 117-24.
[448] Cerfaux, 128f. With regard to the wide use of Isa. 53 in post-N.T. literature, especially in Justin, see Wolff[3], 108-42, further G. Bertram, καλός F, *TWNT*, III, 553ff.
[448a] Tödt has objected that Mark 9.12 refers rather to Ps. 118.22. Against this cf. n. 406.

The Servant of God

πολλῶν, cf. Isa. 53.10 Heb. text: אָשָׁם נַפְשׁוֹ אִם־תָּשִׂים; 53.11, 12: רַבִּים; διακονῆσαι is an allusion to the servant; λύτρον must be a free translation of אָשָׁם (in the common[451] meaning of 'compensation').[452]—Mark 14.8: Jesus expects to be buried as a criminal, without anointing, cf. Isa. 53.9.—Mark 14.24 par.: ἐκχυννόμενον ὑπὲρ πολλῶν, cf. Isa. 53.12 Heb. text: הֶעֱרָה רַבִּים...[453]—Mark 14.61 par. Matt. 26.63: Jesus is silent before the Sanhedrin; Mark 15.5 par. Matt. 27.12 and 14; John 19.9: before Pilate; Luke 23.9: before Herod Antipas, cf. Isa. 53.7 וְנֶאֱלָמָה.[454]—Luke 11.22: καὶ τὰ σκῦλα αὐτοῦ διαδίδωσιν, cf. Isa. 53.12 יְחַלֵּק שָׁלָל (LXX μεριεῖ σκῦλα) (?).[454a]—Luke 22.37: δεῖ τελεσθῆναι ἐν ἐμοί, τό· καὶ μετὰ ἀνόμων ἐλογίσθη = Isa. 53.12: וְאֶת־פֹּשְׁעִים נִמְנָה (LXX: καὶ ἐν τοῖς ἀνόμοις ἐλογίσθη).—Luke 23.34: Jesus makes intercession, cf. Isa. 53.12 Heb. text.[455]—John 10.11, 15, 17f.: τιθέναι τὴν ψυχήν, cf. Isa. 53.10 Heb. text: תָּשִׂים ... נַפְשׁוֹ.—Finally must be mentioned the many references to scripture which Jesus makes (see n. 405); concerning their connexion with Isa. 53 see pp. 90f.

Many of these passages are wholly or in part the work of the church; with regard to the silence of Jesus before his judges (Sanhedrin, Pilate, Herod) what strikes one is the fact that this detail is repeatedly reported (see above);[458] further, the predictions of the passion reveal, on comparison, a secondary tendency to assume concrete features and to become assimilated to the actual

---

[451] Cf. K. G. Kuhn, 'Die Abendmahlsworte', TLZ, 75, 1950, 406, n. 2.
[452] For the reference to Isa. 53 cf. Dalman, op. cit. in n. 304, 110; Wolff,³ 61; J. Jeremias, 'Lösegeld', 262; πολλοί, TWNT, VI, 536-45.
[453] J. Jeremias, Eucharistic Words, 148ff.; πολλοί, ibid. For Jesus' own comparison of himself with the paschal lamb (ibid., 144) cf. Isa. 53.7.
[454] H. W. Surkau, Martyrien in jüdischer und frühchristlicher Zeit, 1938, 87; J. Schniewind, Markus (N. T. Deutsch) on 14.61. On Mark 14.62 par. Matt. 26.64 ὄψεσθε cf. further Isa. 52.15.
[454a] W. Grundmann, ἰσχύω κτλ., TWNT, III, 403, 25ff. Yet it remains possible that in Luke 11.21f. par. there is present an image which is independent of the O.T. (thus W. Bieder, Die Vorstellung von der Höllenfahrt Jesu Christi, 1949, 35).
[455] This intercession is for unwitting sinners, cf. Isa. 53.10: אָשָׁם is the sacrifice for unwitting sins. (Luke 23.34a is missing in one part of the manuscripts and might well be a very early addition resting upon old tradition.)
[458] Cf. Wolff³, 76, n. 316 (folllwing J. Schniewind). On the other hand it could be argued that if the silence of Jesus is derived merely from Isa. 53.7, we would expect a scripture reference. In addition, Miss Hooker, 87-89, points out that Jesus merely refused to answer the *false* accusations.

The Servant of God in the New Testament

course of history.[459] Some observations on the texts forbid us, however, to declare spurious the whole of the references of Jesus himself to the 'ebed.[460]

The assertion of the Gospels that Jesus reckoned with the possibility of a violent death has the strongest historical probability behind it. First, the whole situation compelled him to recognize it. The reproach of βλασφημία (Mark 2.7 par.; John 10.33–36, cf. 5.18) meant the threat of stoning[461] with subsequent hanging of the body on the cross.[462] The same punishment (without subsequent hanging) was incurred by sabbath-breaking;[462a] of the two sabbath stories in Mark 2.23–3.7a the first reports the warning,[463] as a result of which any repetition of the transgression would be proved to be intentional and punishable; in 3.1ff. therefore Jesus is risking his life (cf. 3.6) and has to save himself by flight (3.7a: ἀνεχώρησεν).[464] If Mark 3.22b par.; Matt. 9.34 implies the reproach that Jesus used sorcery,[464a] he is again accused of a crime which entailed stoning.[464b] Finally, also the false prophet (cf. Luke 13.33) was threatened with capital punishment.[464c] The reports that Jesus

---

[459] Thus Mark has μετὰ τρεῖς ἡμέρας (8.31; 9.31; 10.34) while Matthew and Luke in the par. texts have changed, independently of each other and *ex eventu*, to τῇ τρίτῃ ἡμέρᾳ (or τῇ ἡμέρᾳ τῇ τρίτῃ). Or compare Mark 10.34, ἀποκτενοῦσιν, with the par. Matt. 20.19, σταυρῶσαι. Especially the so-called third prediction of the passion (more correctly, the third version of the announcement of the passion) in Mark 10.33f. par. might well have been touched up *ex eventu* (as a comparison with the first two versions in 8.31 and 9.31 leads one to suppose); yet at the same time it should not be overlooked that Mark 10.33f. contains no feature which could not normally be expected in capital proceedings against Jesus when we take into account the state of the law, and execution customs. This constitutes a warning to be cautious with a judgement of '*ex eventu*'.

[460] Thus Luke 11.22 is older than the dogmatics of the early church because the victory of Jesus over the satanic, demonic powers is associated not with the cross and resurrection but with the temptation of Jesus, cf. W. Grundmann, ἰσχύω κτλ., TWNT, III, 404, 28ff.; but the connexion of the text with Isa. 53 is not certain (see n. 454a).

[461] Sanh. 7.4; Siphre Lev. 24.11ff. (53a, 31ff. Venice ed., 1545); John 10.31, 33.

[462] Sanh. 6.4: 'All who are stoned are hanged'—words of R. Eli'ezer (b. Hyrcanos, circa A.D. 90, the representative of the older tradition). According to the halakha (ibid.) this applies only to the blasphemer and idolator.

[462a] Sanh. 7.4, 8.

[463] With regard to the warning in late Jewish law and in the N.T. cf. K. Bornhäuser, 'Zur Perikope vom Bruch des Sabbats', NKZ, 33, 1922, 325–34; J. Jeremias, op. cit. in n. 410, 208–13. οὐκ ἔξεστιν Mark 2.24 is a formula of warning, cf. John 5.10.

[464] Mark 3.7a has a par. in Matt. 15.21 and might originally have been the end of the pericope, Mark 3.1–6.

[464a] S.-B., I, 631. Cf. B. Sanh. 107b: 'Jeshu has practised sorcery'.

[464b] Sanh. 7.4, 11.

[464c] Sanh. 11.1.

The Servant of God

repeatedly stood in immediate danger of stoning,[465] especially in view of Mark 2.23-3.7a, are wholly within the sphere of the possible. Second, the history of Israel must have compelled Jesus to reckon with the possibility of death by violence. Jesus, in words which represent particularly authentic tradition,[466] classed himself among the prophets,[467] and expected the fate of the prophets, viz., martyrdom (Luke 13.33; Matt. 23.34-36 par., 37 par.).[468] We know from the N.T.,[469] from Jewish legend about the prophets,[470] and from the increasing custom of honouring the prophets' tombs by expiatory monuments[470a] to what a large extent, even by the time of Jesus, martyrdom was considered to be an integral part of the prophetic calling.[471] Jesus himself found in sacred history an uninterrupted succession of martyrdoms of the just from Abel to Zechariah (Matt. 23.35 par.). In particular, recent history, the fate of John the Baptist, the last prophet, foreshadowed to Jesus his own destiny (Mark 9.12f. par.; cf. 6.16; Luke 13.31).

A third observation may be added as an indication of the historical value of the suggestions that Jesus reckoned with the possibility of a violent death. Jesus' predictions of his passion contain a number of features which did not materialize. Jesus at times seems to have thought it possible, presumably on the basis of concrete experiences (cf. p. 101), that he would be stoned (Matt. 23.37 par.) by the Jews as a false prophet (Luke

---

[465] Luke 4.29; John 8.59; 10.31-36; 11.8; *Unknown Gospel* (British Museum, Egerton Papyrus 2), fragment 1 *recto*, lines 23f., cf. Matt. 23.37 par.
[466] R. Bernheimer, 'Vitae Prophetarum', *JAOS*, 55, 1935, 202f.
[467] Likewise Jesus places his disciples among the prophets: Matt. 5.12 par.
[468] The authenticity of these words is suggested above all by the fact that the early church only occasionally placed Jesus among the prophets.
[469] References in N.T. to the killing of prophets: Matt. 21.35f.; 22.6; 23.30-32 par., 34-36 par., 37 par.; Luke 13.33; Acts 7.51f.; Rom. 11.3; I Thess. 2.15; Heb. 11.35-38; Rev. 11.7; 16.6; 18.24; cf. Jas. 5.10.
[470] *Prophetarum vitae fabulosae*, ed. T. Schermann, 1907; *The Lives of the Prophets*, ed. C. C. Torrey (*JBL* Monograph Series, 1), 1946; M. R. James, *The Lost Apocrypha of the Old Testament* (Translations of Early Documents, Series I, 14), 1920; Josephus, *Ant.* 10.38; Origen, *Commentariorum series* 28, on Matt. 23.37-39 (*GCS*, 38, 50) and Catena fragment 457 II on Matt. 23.29-35 (*GCS*, 41, 190); Tertullian, *Scorpiace* 8 (Migne, *PL*, 2, 137 B); *Asc. Isa.* 2.16; 5.1-14; *Paral. Jer.* 9.21-32; S.-B., I, 940-2; III, 747; H. Vincent and F. M. Abel, *Jérusalem*, II, 1926, 855-74.
[470a] J. Jeremias, op. cit. in n. 471, *passim*.
[471] A. Schlatter, *Der Märtyrer in den Anfängen der Kirche* (BFT, 19.3), 1915, 18-22; O. Michel, *Prophet und Märtyrer* (BFT, 37.2), 1932; H. J. Schoeps, *Die jüdischen Prophetenmorde* (Symbolae Biblicae Upsalienses, 2), 1943; H. A. Fischel, 'Prophet and Martyr', *JQR*, 37, 1946-7, 265-80, 363-86, especially 279, 382; J. Jeremias, *Heiligengräber in Jesu Umwelt*, 1958, 61ff., 67ff., 82ff., 121f.

The Servant of God in the New Testament

13.33). This expectation, like that of burial as a criminal (Mark 14.8 par.), was not fulfilled. The same applies to the expectation that some of his disciples would have to share his fate (Mark 10.32-40 par.; Luke 14.25-33) or at least be in danger of death through his execution (22.36f.); curiously enough the Jewish authorities were content with the execution of Jesus and left the disciples undisturbed.[472]

But if Jesus reckoned with his violent death, then he must have had thoughts about the meaning of that death, especially in view of the extraordinary significance which the doctrine of the expiatory efficacy of death possessed for late Judaism.[473] The assertion of the sources that Jesus found in Isa. 53 the clue to the necessity and meaning of his passion can also claim strong historical probability. In general terms it may be pointed out here that Isa. 40ff. possessed great significance for Jesus' consciousness of his mission (cf. Matt. 11.5 par.; 5.3f.; Mark 11.17; Luke 4.18ff. See G. Friedrich, εὐαγγελίζομαι κτλ., *TWNT*, II, 706, 10ff.; 715, 8 ff.); the allusions to Isa. 53 thus fit into the framework of his preaching and use of scripture. If now we examine the passages quoted on pp. 99f. in detail, several observations speak for their ancient date. First, we are here in the presence of pre-Hellenistic tradition; for none of these texts, except Luke 22.37 (but see n. 404), shows the unequivocal influence of the LXX, which on the contrary is impossible for Mark 9.12; 10.45; 14.8, 24; Luke 23.34; John 10.11, 15, 17f. Thus, an older stratum of tradition emerges which is characterized by its use of the Hebrew text of Isa. 53.3, 9, 10-12.[473a] Further observations confirm this view. Mark 9.31 gives an Aramaic word-play: בַּר נָשָׁא/בְּנֵי נָשָׁא; the non-Greek expression εἰς χεῖρας is a rendering of the Aramaic preposition

---

[472] C. H. Dodd, *The Parables of the Kingdom*², 1936, 59. The Good Friday despair of the disciples is thus no compelling objection to the historicity of the predictions of the passion, because it was essentially rooted in the fact that the course of events contradicted the expectations which the disciples entertained as a result of the preaching of Jesus as a whole. They clearly expected indeed suffering and martyrdom both for Jesus and themselves (Mark 10.39 par.; 14.29 par., 31), but immediately following it a 'corporate triumph' (Luke 24.21; Acts 1.6, cf. T. W. Manson, 'The New Testament Basis of the Doctrine of the Church', *JEH*, I, 1950, 6, and n. 3). As regards the lack of understanding on the part of the disciples, see n. 331.
[473] Lohse, 9-110; J. Jeremias, *Eucharistic Words*, 151f.
[473a] Cf. R. H. Fuller, *The Mission and Achievement of Jesus* (Studies in Biblical Theology, 12), 1954, 55-59.

The Servant of God

לִידִי. The religious use of λύτρον (Mark 10.45 par.) is Jewish;[474] the expression δοῦναι τὴν ψυχήν (par. τιθέναι τὴν ψυχήν John 10.11, 15, 17f.) points to a Semitic-speaking environment (see p. 96 above). Luke 23.34 also presupposes Palestinian circumstances; for late Judaism the expiatory vow of the criminal is a formal part of the execution ('May my death expiate all my sins'),[475] which Jesus, like the Maccabaean martyrs,[476] reverses, but so as to transfer the expiatory virtue of his death to his tormentors (see n. 455). Secondly, several of the predictions of the passion could not well have been produced *ex eventu*: invention *ex eventu* is excluded with certainty in all those cases where announcements of what would happen were not borne out by the subsequent events. That applies not only to quite a few predictions of the passion (see pp. 102f. above), but also to several predictions of the glorification. For repeatedly 'the third day' is used to designate the moment, not of the resurrection, but of the 'fulfilment' (Luke 13.32, cf. John 16.16) or of the appearance of the New Temple (Mark 14.58 par.). We are entitled to conclude from this that Jesus talked in varying terms about God's triumph which was to occur 'within three days' or 'on the third day', i.e., 'immediately', and that only secondary interpretation referred these three days to the period between crucifixion and resurrection.[476a] This means: the core not only of the predictions of the passion, but also of the predictions of the glorification which interpret the passion is pre-Easter tradition, not yet coloured by the historic course of events. Thirdly, some of the words are so firmly anchored in the context that they cannot be detached from it. This is particularly true of the *logion* Mark 8.31, which is indissolubly bound up with the sharp rebuke to Peter (8.33); this description of Peter as Satan cannot have been subsequently put into the mouth of Jesus. The expectation, too, of a criminal's burial without anointing (Mark 14.8, cf. Isa. 53.9) is firmly rooted in the context; this becomes plain as soon as we recognize that in the pericope Mark 14.3–9 almsgiving (צְדָקָה 14.5) and the work of love (גְּמִילוּת חֲסָדִים

---

[474] J. Jeremias, 'Lösegeld', 249–58. In contrast to the Palestinian character of the language in Mark 10.42–45, the par. Luke 22.24–27 shows strong Hellenistic influence, ibid., 258–62.
[475] *Sanh.* 6.2; *T. Sanh.* 9.5; *B. Sanh.* 44b; *J. Sanh.* 6.4 (23 b 47), cf. A. Büchler, *Studies in Sin and Atonement*, 1928, 170, n. 4; K. G. Kuhn, 'Rm 6.7', *ZNW*, 30, 1931, 306.
[476] IV Macc. 6.29; II Macc. 7.37f.
[476a] C. H. Dodd, *The Parables of the Kingdom*², 1936, 98–101.

The Servant of God in the New Testament

14.6)[479], which counts more, are contrasted with each other, and that only the information given in 14.8 as to which of the offices of love the anointing woman has unconsciously performed for Jesus (viz., the burial of the dead) provides us with the clue to the pericope.[480] Similarly fixed to the context is Luke 22.37. This word, which is influenced by the Heb. text of Isa. 53.12 (see n. 404), stands between the two quite obviously ancient words about the swords (vv. 36, 38) of which the first, v. 36, announces the imminent outbreak of the eschatological time of distress and to this extent is an unfulfilled prophecy (cf. p. 103). The reason given in v. 37 for this announcement—that, because Jesus will be driven out of the community of Israel as an ἄνομος, so his disciples, too, will be treated as ἄνομοι and refused food and their lives threatened[481]— is indispensable to the whole context. Mark 9.12b is also to be mentioned here. If, as is probable (cf. J. Jeremias, 'Ηλ(ε)ίας, TWNT, II, 939, 22ff.), the disciples in Mark 9.11 cite the Elijah prophecy (Mal. 4.5f.) as an objection to Jesus' prediction of his passion—the restoration of all things which Elijah is to accomplish three days before the end makes messianic suffering superfluous—then the word about suffering (Mark 9.12b) is here, too, essential to the context. Fourthly, in Mark 9.31, a prediction of the passion which has a very archaic ring because of its conciseness, its enigmatic character and the word-play employed (see p. 103 above), the passive is used periphrastically to describe God's action: ὁ υἱὸς τοῦ ἀνθρώπου παραδίδοται εἰς χεῖρας ἀνθρώπων, 'God will deliver the man to the men'. The same παραδίδοσθαι, which is an allusion to Isa. 53.5b Targ. (see p. 99 above), recurs in Mark 10.33; 14.21, 41 and Matt. 26.2; Luke 24.7. Hence it is firmly rooted in the tradition. Representing God's action through the passive is a late Jewish manner of speaking; but it is nowhere even remotely as frequent as in the words of Jesus, and must therefore be considered as a token of his personal style.[481a] Fifthly, it is of decisive importance that at one point of the oldest and most reliable stratum of tradition we come upon Isa. 53: in the eucharistic

---

[479] Concerning alms and the works of love cf. S.-B., IV, 536–610.
[480] J. Jeremias, 'Die Salbungsgeschichte Mc 14.3–9', ZNW, 35, 1936, 75–82. The genuineness of Mark 14.8 is supported also by the fact that we have here an unfulfilled prophecy (cf. p. 100). Jesus was spared a dishonourable burial (Mark 15.45f.; John 19.38ff.).
[481] A. Schlatter, *Das Evangelium des Lukas aus seinen Quellen erklärt*, 1931, 428.
[481a] J. Jeremias, *Die Abendmahlsworte Jesu*³, 1960, 194f.

The Servant of God

words of Jesus (Mark 14.24 par.: ὑπὲρ πολλῶν). Paul received his version of the eucharistic words which he passed on to the Corinthians (I Cor. 11.23-25) in A.D. 49-50, in a Hellenistic environment,[482] probably after 40 in Antioch.[483] Since the synoptic versions prove themselves older than the linguistically Hellenized Pauline one on account, among other things, of their numerous Semitic features,[484] they take us back to the thirties. Here, therefore, we strike the bedrock of the tradition.

The fact that the number of texts in which Jesus relates Isa. 53 to himself is not great, and that they are altogether absent in the *ligia* common to Matt. and Luke, must be connected with the fact that Jesus only allowed himself to be known as the servant in his esoteric and not in his public preaching.[485] Only to his disciples did he unveil the mystery that he viewed the fulfilment of Isa. 53 as his God-appointed task,[486] and to them alone did he interpret his death as a vicarious dying for the countless multitude (see article πολλοί, *TWNT*, VI, 536-45) of those who lay under the judgement of God (Mark 10.45; 14.24). Because he goes to his death innocently, voluntarily, patiently and in accordance with the will of God (Isa. 53) his dying has boundless atoning virtue. It is life flowing from God, and life in God[487] which he outpours.

---

[482] J. Jeremias, *Eucharistic Words*, 127.

[483] Antioch is suggested by the relationship between the Pauline and the Lucan representation (Luke 22.19b-20a agrees almost literally with I Cor. 11.24f.; see J. Jeremias, *Eucharistic Words*, 131).

[484] For Semitisms in Mark 14.22-25 see J. Jeremias, *Eucharistic Words*, 118ff. In addition literary considerations, ibid., 106ff. As regards the ὑπέρ phrase in particular, the Pauline ὑπὲρ ὑμῶν (I Cor. 11.24) is certainly secondary as compared with the ὑπὲρ πολλῶν of Mark 14.24; for in Paul, the Semitic πολλοί is avoided (see article πολλοί, *TWNT*, VI, 536-45), and under the influence of liturgical custom the theological statement (in the third person) has become a distribution formula (in the second person). Besides this the Pauline association of the ὑπέρ phrase with the bread is likely to be secondary as opposed to the Marcan association with the cup (J. Jeremias, *Eucharistic Words*, 110, 128).

[485] Cf. Buber, 107; Taylor, *Life and Ministry*, 145.

[486] Cf. Buber, 107: 'If we view the connexion rightly, Jesus understood himself, under the influence of the conception of Deutero-Isaiah, to be a bearer of the Messianic hiddenness.' Ibid., 113: 'The idea of the "servant", modified by the Apocalypses [through the combination with the Son of man],' has entered 'into the actual life-story' of Jesus.

[487] Schniewind, *Markus* (N.T. Deutsch) on 10.45.

BIBLIOGRAPHY

CHAPTER I

W. W. Baudissin, 'Zur Entwicklung des Gebrauchs von '*ebed* in religiösem Sinne', in *Festschrift K. Budde* (*ZAW*, Beiheft 34), 1920, 1–9

W. W. Baudissin, *Kyrios als Gottesname*, III, 1929, 176–242, 524–55

J. Begrich, 'Das priesterliche Heilsorakel', *ZAW*, 52, 1934, 81–92

J. Begrich, *Studien zu Deuterojesaja* (*BWANT*, 4.25), 1938, esp. 131–51

A. Bentzen, *King and Messiah*, 1955

P. A. H. de Boer, *Second-Isaiah's Message* (*OTS*, 11), 1956, esp. 102–17

K. Budde, *Die sogennanten Ebed-Jahve-Lieder und die Bedeutung des Knechtes Jahves in Js 40–55*, 1900

K. Budde, *Das Buch Jesaia Kap. 40–66* (in Kautzsch, *HSAT*[4]), 1922

E. Burrows, 'The Servant of Yahweh in Isaiah', in *The Gospel of the Infancy and other Biblical Essays*, 1940

B. Duhm, *Das Buch Jesaia*[4], 1922

L. Dürr, *Ursprung und Ausbau der isr.-jüdischen Heilandserwartung*, 1925, 125–52

O. Eissfeldt, 'The Ebed-Jahwe in Isaiah xl–lv in the Light of the Israelite conceptions of the Community and the Individual, the Ideal and the Real', *ET* 44, 1932–3, 261–68

K. Elliger, *Deutero-Jesaja in seinem Verhältnis zu Trito-Jesaja* (*BWANT*, 4.11), 1933

I. Engnell, 'The 'Ebed-Yahweh Songs and the Suffering Messiah in "Deutero-Isaiah" ', *BJRL*, 31, 1948, 54–93

F. Giesebrecht, *Der Knecht Jahves des Deutero-Jesaja*, 1902

H. Gressmann, 'Die literarische Analyse Deutero-Jesajas', *ZAW*, 34, 1914, 254–97

H. Gressmann, *Der Ursprung der isr.-jüdischen Eschatologie*, 1905, 301–33

H. Gressmann, *Der Messias*, 1929, 287–339; index s.v. '*Ebed Jahveh*

J. Hempel, 'Vom irrenden Glauben', *ZST*, 7, 1930, 631–60

O. Kaiser, *Der königliche Knecht* (*FRL*, 70), 1959

L. Köhler, *Deutero-Jesaja stilkritisch untersucht* (*ZAW*, Beiheft 37), 1937

J. Lindblom, *The Servant Songs in Deutero-Isaiah* (Lunds Universitets Årsskrift, N.F. Avd. 1, 47.5), 1951

C. Lindhagen, *The Servant Motif in the O.T.*, 1950

S. Mowinckel, *Der Knecht Jahwäs*, 1921

S. Mowinckel, 'Die Komposition des deutero-jesajanischen Buches', *ZAW*, 49, 1931, 87–112, 242–60

S. Mowinckel, *He That Cometh*, 1956, esp. 187–257

Bibliography

C. R. North, *The Suffering Servant in Deutero-Isaiah*, 1948
H. Wheeler Robinson, 'The Hebrew Conception of Corporate Personality', in *Werden und Wesen des AT*, ed. J. Hempel (ZAW, Beiheft 66), 1936, 49–62. See *The Cross in the O.T.*, 1955, 65–80
H. H. Rowley, *The Servant of the Lord and Other Essays on the Old Testament*, 1952
W. Rudolph, 'Der exilische Messias', ZAW, 43, 1925, 90–114
E. Sellin, *Serubbabel*, 1898
E. Sellin, *Mose und seine Bedeutung für die isr.-jüdische Religionsgeschichte*, 1922, 77–113
E. Sellin, 'Die Lösung des deuterojesajanischen Gottesknechtsrätsels', ZAW, 55, 1937, 177–217
N. H. Snaith, 'The Servant of the Lord in Deutero-Isaiah', *Studies in O.T. Prophecy, Festschrift T. H. Robinson*, 1950, 187–200
J. J. Stamm, *Das Leiden des Unschuldigen in Babylon und Israel*, 1946
P. Volz, *Jesaia II* (Kommentar zum AT, IX, 2), 1932
H. W. Wolff, *Jesaja 53 im Urchristentum*[2], 1950,[3] 1952
J. Ziegler, *Untersuchungen zur LXX des Buches Isaias*, 1934

CHAPTER 2

K. F. Euler, *Die Verkündigung vom leidenden Gottesknecht* (BWANT, 4.14), 1934
J. Ziegler, *Isaias* (Septuaginta, XIV), 1939

CHAPTER 3

R. A. Aytoun, 'The Servant of the Lord in the Targum', *JTS*, 23, 1922, 172–80
P. Billerbeck, 'Hat die alte Synagoge einen präexistenten Messias gekannt?', *Nathanael*, 21, 1905, 89–150
J. Bonsirven, *Le Judaïsme palestinien au temps de Jésus-Christ*, I, 1934, 380–5
J.-J. Brierre-Narbonne, *Le Messie souffrant dans la littérature rabbinique*, 1940
M. Buber, 'Jesus und der "Knecht"', in *Pro regno, pro sanctuario* (Festschrift G. van der Leeuw), 1950, 71–78; reprinted in *Two Types of Faith*, 1951, 102–13
R. Bultmann, 'Reich Gottes und Menschensohn', TR, 9, 1937, 26–30
G. Dalman, *Der leidende und der sterbende Messias der Synagoge im ersten nachchristlichen Jahrtausend* (Schriften des Institutum Judaicum Berlin, 4), 1888; quoted as: Dalman, I

Bibliography

G. Dalman, *Jesaja 53, das Prophetenwort vom Sühnleiden des Gottesknechtes*[2] (Schriften des Institutum Judaicum Berlin, 13), 1914; quoted as: Dalman, II

W. D. Davies, *Paul and Rabbinic Judaism*, 1948, [2]1955, 274–84

S. R. Driver and A. Neubauer, *The Fifty-Third Chapter of Isaiah according to the Jewish Interpreters*, I, II, 1876–7

H. A. Fischel, 'Die deuterojesajanischen Gottesknechtlieder in der jüdischen Auslegung', *HUCA*, 18, 1943–4, 53–76

H. Hegermann, *Jesaja 53 in Hexapla, Targum und Peschitta* (BFT, 2nd Series, 56), 1954

P. Humbert, 'Le Messie dans le Targum des prophètes', *RTP*, 43, 1910, 420–47; 44, 1911, 5–46

S. Hurwitz, *Die Gestalt des sterbenden Messias. Religionspsychologische Aspekte der jüdischen Apokalyptik* (Studien aus dem C. G. Jung-Institut Zürich, 8), 1958

G. Jeremias, *Der Lehrer der Gerechtigkeit* (Studien zur Umwelt des Neuen Testaments, 2), 1963

J. Jeremias, 'Erlöser und Erlösung im Spätjudentum und Urchristentum', *DT*, II, 1929, 106–19

J. Jeremias, "Ἀμνὸς τοῦ θεοῦ-παῖς θεοῦ", *ZNW*, 34, 1935, 115–23

N. Johansson, *Parakletoi*, 1940, 96–119

G. Kittel, 'Menschensohn', *RGG*[2], III, 1929, 2118–21

I. [H.] Leisegang, *Indices ad Philonis Alexandrini opera* (L. Cohn-P. Wendland edd., *Philonis Alexandrini opera*, VII), 1926–30

W. Manson, *Jesus the Messiah*, 1943, 99, 171ff.

G. F. Moore, *Judaism*, I, 1927, 229, 549–51; III, 1930, 63, 166

H. Odeberg, *3 Enoch or the Hebrew Book of Enoch*, 1928

R. Otto, *The Kingdom of God and the Son of Man*[2], 1943

M. Rese, 'Überprüfung einiger Thesen von Joachim Jeremias zum Thema des Gottesknechtes im Judentum', *ZTK*, 60, 1963, 21–41

H. Riesenfeld, *Jésus transfiguré* (Acta Seminarii Neotestamentici Upsaliensis, 16), 1947, 81–96, 307–17

H. H. Rowley, 'The Suffering Servant and the Davidic Messiah', *OTS*, VIII, 1950, 100–36; reprinted in H. H. Rowley, *The Servant of the Lord and other Essays on the Old Testament*, 1952, 59–88

A. Schlatter, *Das Alte Testament in der johanneischen Apokalypse* (BFT, 16.6), 1912, 50f.

A. Schlatter, *Die Theologie des Judentums nach dem Bericht des Josefus* (BFT, 2nd Series, 26), 1932; quoted as: Schl. Theol. d. Judt.

A. Schlatter, *Markus. Der Evangelist für die Griechen*, 1935

H. J. Schoeps, 'Symmachusstudien III. Symmachus und der Midrasch', *Biblica*, 29, 1948, 31–51, esp. 38f. ('V. Der aussätzige Messias')

Bibliography

P. Seidelin, 'Der 'Ebed Jahwe und die Messiasgestalt im Jesajatargum', *ZNW*, 35, 1936, 194–231

E. Sjöberg, *Der Menschensohn im äthiopischen Henochbuch* (Acta Regiae Societatis Humaniorum Litterarum Lundensis, 41), 1946, 116–39

W. Staerk, *Soter* (BFT, 2nd Series, 31), 1933, 72–84

W. Staerk, *Die Erlösererwartung in den östlichen Religionen*, 1938, 406–8

J. F. Stenning, *The Targum of Isaiah*, 1949

H. L. Strack, *Einleitung in Talmud und Midrasch*[5], 1921

C. C. Torrey, 'The Messiah Son of Ephraim', *JBL*, 66, 1947, 253–77

F. Weber, *Jüdische Theologie auf Grund des Talmud und verwandter Schriften*[2], 1897

A. Wünsche, יִסּוּרֵי הַמָּשִׁיחַ *oder die Leiden des Messias*, 1870

CHAPTER 4

O. Bauernfeind, *Die Apostelgeschichte*, 1939, on 3.13, 26 and 4.27

W. Bousset, *Kyrios Christos*[2] (FRL, 21), 1921, 56f., 69–74

R. Bultmann, *Theology of the New Testament*, I, II, 1953, 1955

F. C. Burkitt, *Christian Beginnings*, 1924, 35–41

C. F. Burney, *The Aramaic Origin of the Fourth Gospel*, 1922, 104–8

H. J. Cadbury, 'The Titles of Jesus in Acts', in F. J. F. Jackson and K. Lake, *Beginnings of Christianity*, I, 5, 1933, 364–70

L. L. Carpenter, *Primitive Christian Application of the Doctrine of the Servant*, 1929

L. Cerfaux, 'L'hymne au Christ-Serviteur de Dieu (Phil. II, 6–11 = Is., LII, 13–LIII, 12)', in *Miscellanea historica in honorem Alberti de Meyer* (Université de Louvain, Recueil de Travaux d'Histoire et de Philologie, 3e série, 22e fascicule), 1946, 117–30

O. Cullmann, *Baptism in the New Testament* (SBT, 1), 1953

O. Cullmann, *Early Christian Worship* (SBT, 10), 1953

O. Cullmann, *Christology of the New Testament*, 1959, [2]1963, 60–82

G. Dalman, *The Words of Jesus*, 1902; cited as: Dalman, *WJ*

E. Fascher, *Jesaja 53 in christlicher und jüdischer Sicht* (Aufsätze und Vorträge zur Theologie und Religionswissenschaft, 4), 1958

J. Gewiess, *Die urapostolische Heilsverkündigung nach der Apostelgeschichte* (Breslauer Studien zur historischen Theologie, N.F. 5), 1939, 38–57, 75–81

L. Goppelt, *Typos* (BFT, 2nd Series, 43), 1939, 113–16, 120–7

A. v. Harnack, 'Die Bezeichnung Jesu als "Knecht Gottes" und ihre Geschichte in der alten Kirche', *SAB*, 28, 1926, 212–38

M. D. Hooker, *Jesus and the Servant*, 1959

J. Jeremias, 'Das Lösegeld für Viele', *Judaica*, 3, 1947–8, 249–64

Bibliography

J. Jeremias, 'Zu Phil ii 7: *'Εαυτὸν ἐκένωσεν'*, *Novum Testamentum*, 6, 1963, 182–8 = in *Χάρις καὶ Σοφία*. *Festschrift Karl Heinrich Rengstorf anlässlich seines 60. Geburtstags*, 1964, 182–8

J. Jeremias, *The Eucharistic Words of Jesus*, 1955

G. Kittel, 'Jesu Worte über sein Sterben', *DT*, III, 1936, 166–89

E. Lohmeyer, 'Kyrios Jesus', SAH 1927–8, No. 4; reprinted separately, 1961, 33–36, 42, 49, n. 4, 69

E. Lohmeyer, *Gottesknecht und Davidsohn* (Symbolae Biblicae Upsalienses, 5), 1945

E. Lohse, *Märtyrer und Gottesknecht*[2] (FRL, 64), 1963

C. Maurer, 'Knecht Gottes und Sohn Gottes im Passionsbericht des Markusevangeliums', *ZTK*, 50, 1953, 1–38

W. Michaelis, *Herkunft und Bedeutung des Ausdrucks 'Leiden und Sterben Jesu Christi'*, 1945

O. Procksch, 'Jesus der Gottesknecht', in *In piam memoriam Alexander von Bulmerincq* (Abhandlungen der Herder-Gesellschaft zu Riga, VI, 3), 1938, 146–65

J. H. Ropes, 'The Influence of Second Isaiah on the Epistles', *JBL*, 48, 1929, 37–39

G. Sass, 'Zur Bedeutung von δοῦλος bei Paulus', *ZNW*, 40, 1941, 24–33

K. H. Schelkle, *Die Passion Jesu in der Verkündigung des N.T.*, 1949, 60–194

E. Sjöberg, *Der verborgene Menschensohn in den Evangelien* (Acta Regiae Societatis Humaniorum Litterarum Lundensis, 53), 1955, esp. 247ff.

V. Taylor, *Jesus and His Sacrifice*, 1937

V. Taylor, *The Atonement in N.T. Teaching*[2], 1945

V. Taylor, *The Life and Ministry of Jesus*, 1954, 142–5

C. C. Torrey, 'The Influence of Second Isaiah in the Gospels and Acts', *JBL*, 48, 1929, 24–36

G. Wiencke, *Paulus über Jesu Tod* (BFT, 2nd Series, 42), 1939, 161–4

I. Zolli, *Il Nazareno*, 1938, 228–33, 331–55

INDEX OF AUTHORS

Abel, F.-M., 102
Alt, A., 12, 18
Augusti, J. W. C., 27
Aytoun, R. A., 65, 71, 108

Bacher, W., 58, 75
Ball, C. J., 83
Bamberger, B. J., 75
Barr, J., 40
Barth, C., 35
Baudissin, W. W., 15, 18, 25, 107
Bauernfeind, O., 110
Baumgärtel, F., 37
Begrich, J., 19, 26, 31–33, 35, 107
Behm, J., 98
Benoit, P., 75
Bentzen, A., 27f., 34, 49, 107
Bernheimer, R., 102
Bertram, G., 56, 99
Bewer, J. A., 27
Bieder, W., 100
Billerbeck, P., 46, 57–61, 64, 70–72, 75–77, 79, 101, 103, 108
Black, M., 57
de Boer, P. A. H., 107
Bonsirven, J., 71, 108
Bornhäuser, K., 101
Bornkamm, G., 98
Bousset, W., 46, 82, 84–86
Bowman, J., 62
Brierre-Narbonne, J.-J., 70, 75, 108
Brinker, R., 67
Brownlee, W. H., 57
Bruce, F. F., 57
Brüll, A., 48
Buber, M., 51, 61, 79, 106, 108
Buber, S., 57, 72

Büchler, A., 104
Büchsel, F., 65
Budde, K., 26f., 30, 107
Bultmann, R., 89, 92f., 108, 110
Bunsen, C. J., 28
Burkitt, F. C., 110
Burney, C. F., 83, 110
Burrows, E., 107
Burrows, M., 27
Buxtorf Sr., J., 69

Cadbury, H. J., 86, 110
Carpenter, L. L., 110
Cerfaux, L., 97, 99, 110
Charles, R. H., 62
Cullmann, O., 82f., 89, 94, 97, 110

Dalman, G., 46, 54–56, 59f., 64, 67, 69, 70–77, 82, 87, 97, 100, 108–110
Davies, W. D., 97, 109
Dechent, H., 95
Delitzsch, F., 11, 65
Dibelius, M., 91
Dietze, K., 27
Diringer, D., 13
Dittenberger, W., 40
Dodd, C. H., 83, 89, 94, 98, 103f.
Driver, S. R., 64, 73, 109
Drummond, J., 51
Duhm, B., 26, 33, 107
Duncan, G. S., 83, 97
Dupont, J., 94
Dupont-Sommer, A., 59
Dürr, L., 28, 107

Ebeling, H. J., 78
Eisler, R., 80
Eissfeldt, O., 26f., 107

Index of Authors

Elliger, K., 26, 33, 107
Engnell, I., 28, 107
Epstein, A., 77
Euler, K. F., 43f., 53, 64, 97, 108
Ewald, G. H. A., 51

Fahlgren, K., 30
Fascher, E., 67, 76, 110
Feldmann, F., 46
Fichtner, J., 46
Field, F., 65
Fischel, H. A., 52, 54, 56–58, 60f., 71f., 75f., 102, 109
Fischer, J., 27
Foerster, W., 76
Friedrich, G., 103
Fritzsche, O. F., 46
Fuller, R. H., 103

v. Gall, A., 51
Galling, K., 13
Gerber, W. J., 11
Gese, H., 22
Gewiess, J., 97, 110
Giesebrecht, F., 26f., 107
Gildemeister, J., 51
Ginsberg, H. L., 56
Goppelt, L., 110
Gressmann, H., 26–28, 64, 107
Grundmann, W., 100f.
Gunkel, H., 19

Haenchen, E., 86f.
v. Harnack, A., 51, 62, 84f., 87, 97, 110
Hatch, E., 54
Hegermann, H., 44, 53, 62–64, 66–68, 72, 79, 93, 109
Heidenheim, W., 50
Heinisch, P., 46
Hempel, J., 31, 107
Herford, R. T., 63
Herrmann, J., 37
Hertzberg, W., 30
Hirsch, S. R., 50f.
Hooker, M. D., 86, 88, 100, 110
Horst, J., 58
Howard, W. F., 83

Humbert, P., 56, 70f., 109
Hurwitz, S., 109
Hyldahl, N., 74

Itkonen, L., 27

Jackson, F. J. F., 91
James, M. R., 102
Jellinek, A., 58, 64, 72
Jeremias, G., 59, 109
Johansson, N., 109
Junge, E., 12

Kahle, P., 62, 81
Kaiser, O., 27, 107
Käsemann, E., 97
Katz, P., 40, 50, 81
Kautzsch, E., 27, 30, 46
Kittel, G., 70, 109, 111
Klausner, J., 63
Klostermann, E., 93
Köhler, L., 14, 26, 107
Kosmala, H., 60
Knudtzon, J. A., 14
Krätzschmar, R., 28
Kraus, H. J., 22
Kuhn, K. G., 52, 58, 84, 100, 104
Kutsch, E., 29

de Lagarde, P., 67
Lake, K., 91
Lande, I., 14
Leisegang, I. [H.], 45, 47, 109
Lietzmann, H., 48, 89, 97
Lindars, B., 92
Lindblom, J., 27, 107
Lindhagen, C., 11, 13f., 18–20, 48f., 107
Lohmeyer, E., 82–84, 89, 97, 111
Lohse, E., 77f., 88, 96, 103, 111

Manson, W., 109
Manson, T. W., 68, 103
Maurer, C., 86, 111
Michaelis, W., 90, 111
Michel, O., 45, 92, 97, 102
Milik, J. T., 50
Möhle, A., 65

Index of Authors

Moore, G. F., 52, 57f., 72, 76, 109
Mowinckel, S., 26, 28, 89, 95, 107

Neubauer, A., 64, 73, 109
Nock, A.D. and Festugière, A. J., 87
Nöldeke, T., 11
North, C. R., 26, 28, 59, 64f., 70, 108
Noth, M., 14, 18, 24, 40
Nyberg, H. S., 34

Odeberg, H., 51, 62, 109
O'Neill, J. C., 81
Otto, R., 90, 109

Pedersen, J., 13, 30
Pinckert, J., 16
Procksch, O., 25, 111
Pusey, E. B., 64

v. Rad, G., 24, 28, 33
Rahlfs, A., 37, 40, 53, 63
Redpath, H. A., 54
Rengstorf, K. H., 97
Rese, M., 79, 109
Riesenfeld, H., 65, 109
Robinson, H. W., 27, 97f., 108
Robinson, J. A. T., 98
Ropes, J. H., 111
Rowley, H. H., 26f., 78, 108f.
Rudolph, W., 42, 108

Sass, G., 49, 111
Schelkle, K. H., 97, 111
Schermann, T., 102
Schlatter, A., 45f., 48, 52, 58, 65, 68, 81, 93, 102f., 109
Schmidt, C., 84
Schniewind, J., 100, 106
Schoeps, H. J., 65, 102, 109
Schottroff, W., 29
Schrank, W., 16

Schrenk, G., 62, 95
Seidelin, P., 56f., 67f., 70–72, 109
Sellin, E., 26–28, 33, 108
Siegfried, K., 46
Sjöberg, E., 52, 60, 74, 110f.
Snaith, N. H., 108
Staerk, W., 48, 55, 61, 110
Stählin, G., 75, 97
Stamm, J. J., 20, 34, 108
Stäudlin, C. F., 28
Stauffer, E., 89
Stenning, J. F., 67f., 110
Strack, H. L., 73, 75f., 110
Strack-Billerbeck see Billerbeck
Surkau, H. W., 100

Taylor, V., 106, 111
Tödt, H., 90, 99
Torczyner, H., 14f.
Torrey, C. C., 51, 65, 75, 102, 110f.

de Vaux, R., 11
Vincent, H., 102
Violet, B., 51
de Voisin, D. J., 64
Volz, P., 26, 29f., 42, 108

Weber, F., 71, 110
Weiss, J. H., 73
Wellhausen, J., 26
Wiencke, G., 111
Wilcox, M. J., 81
Windisch, H., 97
Wolff, H. W., 33, 46, 60, 88, 95, 97, 99f., 108
Wrede, W., 78
Wünsche, A., 64, 70, 72f., 75, 77, 110

Zahn, T., 74
Ziegler, J., 31, 37, 43f., 63, 65, 81, 108
Zolli, I., 53, 83, 111
Zunz, L., 73

INDEX OF BIBLICAL REFERENCES

References to the Targum are included. References are according to the Revised Version unless otherwise stated, even when the reference in the text is to the LXX.

Bible Ref.	Page
Genesis	
4.2	11 n. 4
15.2	12 n. 10
17.13, 27	12 n. 9
18.3	15 n. 24, 38, 47 n. 156, 48 n. 164
18.5	15 n. 24, 38
18.17	50 n. 180
18.27	15 n. 25
20.14	11 n. 5
24	12, 29
24.2, 5, 9, 10	12 n. 10
24.12	12
24.14	21 n. 43
24.17	12 n. 10
24.20	98 n. 445
24.27	12
24.34	12 n. 10
24.35	11 n. 5
24.42, 48	12
24.52	12 n. 10
24.54ff.	12
24.59	12 n. 10
26.24	21 n. 43
30.43	11 n. 5
32.5	11 n. 5
32.10	38
45.16	38 n. 111
50.17	15 n. 22, 38 n. 111
Exodus	
4.10	15 n. 25, 38, 50 n. 183
5.16	38
12.44	12 n. 9
14.31	21, 23 n. 46, 38
20.2	12
20.5	16
20.10	12 n. 9
20.24	29 n. 78
21.2, 5, 7, 20	38
21.21	11 n. 5
21.26f.	12 n. 6, 38
21.32	38
23.13	29 n. 78
32.13	38
32.30	34 n. 98
34.14	16
Leviticus	
22.11	11 n. 5, 12 n. 9
25.39f.	11 n. 3
25.42	12
25.44	38
25.55	15 n. 23
Numbers	
11.11	15 n. 25
12.7f.	17, 21, 38
14.24	18 n. 29, 22 n. 44, 38
20.12	34 n. 58
Deuteronomy	
3.24	15 n. 25
3.26	34 n. 98
4.24	16
5.6	12
5.9	16
5.14	12 n. 9
6.12	12
6.15	16
12.12, 18	12 n. 9
23.16	12 n. 8
32	39
32.36	38f., 48 n. 169
32.43	38f.
34.5	45f., 50 n. 183
Joshua	
1.1	41 n. 119
1.2, 7	22
1.13	22, 38
1.15	22, 41 n. 119, 50 n. 183
8.31	22
9.8f.	38
9.11	14 n. 16, 38
9.23	14, 38
12.6	38
14.7	41 n. 119
23.7	29 n. 78
24.19	16
24.29	22 n. 44, 38
Judges	
2.8	22 n. 44, 38
I Samuel	
7.1	24 n. 57
8	32 n. 92
8.14f.	13 n. 13

Index of Biblical References

Bible Ref.	Page	Bible Ref.	Page	Bible Ref.	Page
I Samuel		*I Kings*		*I Chronicles*	
11.5, 10	24 n. 57	11.13	22 n. 45, 85 n. 370	17	42 n. 127
14.52	12 n. 11			18.6f.	42 n. 127
15.23	40 n. 117	11.26	13 n. 14	28.5	23 n. 46
16.15	13 n. 14	11.32	22 n. 45, 85 n. 370	29.23	23 n. 46
18.5	13 n. 12			*II Chronicles*	
21.7	13 n. 14	11.34	22, 85 n. 370	1.3	22
22.6f.	39 n. 113	11.36	22 n. 45, 50 n. 184	13.6	13 n. 14
22.7	13 n. 13			13.18	23 n. 46
22.8	39	14.8	50 n. 184	24.6	22, 24 n. 55, 42
22.9	13 n. 12	14.18	24		
22.14	39 n. 113	15.29	24	24.9	15 n. 22
25.10	39	16.2	49 n. 175	24.11	98 n. 445
30.13	39 n. 112	16.9	13 n. 14	32.16	23 n. 46
		18.36	23	34.20	13
II Samuel		19.16	26 n. 79		
2.12f., 15, 17	13 n. 12	20.32	14 n. 16	*Ezra*	
		22.19ff.	24 n. 53	2.55, 58	14 n. 21
3.18	22, 85 n. 370			5.11	15 n. 22, 41 n. 123, 47
7	42 n. 127	*II Kings*			
7.14	83 n. 354	2.9	29 n. 79	9.11	24 n. 52, 41 n. 123
8.6f.	42 n. 127	8.13	14 n. 18		
9.2	13 n. 14, 39 nn. 112–13	8.19	22 n. 45, 85 n. 370	*Nehemiah*	
				1.7f., 11	42
9.8	14 n. 18	9.7	24 n. 52	7.57, 60	14 n. 21
9.9	13 n. 14	9.36	24	9.14	42
9.10, 12	39 n. 112	10.5	14 n. 16	10.29	15 n. 22
10.2ff.	13 n. 14, 23	10.10	24	11.3	14 n. 21
10.19	14, 39	14.25	24		
11.9, 13	13 n. 14	16.7	14 n. 16, 16	*Job*	
12.18f.	39	17.13, 23	24 n. 52	1.8	25, 41 n. 121
15.34	13 n. 14, 39	17.27	32 n. 92	2.3	25
17.4, 7, 25f.	42 n. 127	18.12	22	4.18	23 n. 49, 24, 81
		18.24	14		
19.17	39 n. 112	19.23	13 n. 14	7.2	11 n. 2
21.22	39	19.34	22 n. 45, 85 n. 370	14.13–15	25
				30.4	75 n. 317
I Kings		20.6	22 n. 45, 85 n. 370	42.7f.	25
4.6	13 n. 14			42.8	41 n. 121
8.30	23 n. 47	21.10	24 n. 52		
8.34	49 n. 175	22.12	13, 39	*Psalms*	
8.36, 52	23 n. 47	24.2	24 n. 52	2	33 n. 96
8.53, 56	22			2.7	82 and n. 349, 83 n. 354
8.59	23 n. 47, 40 n. 114	*I Chronicles*			
		6.49	15 n. 22	15	18 n. 30
9.22	11 n. 2	16.13	21 n. 43	18 tit.	41 n. 122

Index of Biblical References

Bible Ref.	Page
Psalms	
22.2	82 n. 349
24	18 n. 30
34.22	19
36 tit.	50 n. 184
50	18 n. 30
69.36	19
79.2	19
80.8ff.	80
86.16	41 n. 122
89.3	23, 60 n. 249
89.19	60 n. 249
89.20	23
89.39, 50	23 n. 47
105.6	21 n. 43
105.25	19
105.26	22 n. 44
105.42	21 n. 43
109.28	18
113.1	18 n. 33, 41 n. 122
118.22	90 n. 406, 99 n. 448a
119.17, 23, 76, 135, 140, 176	18
132.10	85 n. 370
134.1	18 n. 33
135.1	18 n. 33
135.12	49 n. 175
135.14	19
136.22	20 n. 41, 49 n. 175
137.7	98 n. 445
141.8	98 n. 445
143.11f.	16 n. 26
149.6	93 n. 425
Proverbs	
12.11	11 n. 4
28.9	11 n. 4
Isaiah	
6.2	49 n. 174

Bible Ref.	Page
Isaiah	
6.7	29 n. 80
6.10	68 n. 290, 93
8.11	63 n. 263
9.3	35 n. 104
9.6	43
10.15	44
11.1	43
11.2	61
11.4	61, 93 n. 425
20.3	24 n. 51, 25 n. 58, 52
22.20	25 n. 58, 52
32.15	98 n. 445
33.10	44
37.24	13 n. 14
37.35	25 n. 58, 50 n. 184, 52, 85 n. 370
40ff.	53f., 71, 103
40.10f.	35 n. 104
40.27	31
41.1–5	32 n. 91
41.8	49 nn. 175–7, 52, 53 nn. 199 and 202, 54 and n. 207, 55, 58, 68 n. 291, 80
41.8ff.	19 n. 38, 20
41.9	49 nn. 175–6, 52, 53 nn. 199, 202, 54 and n. 207, 55 and n. 213, 68 n. 291, 80
41.21–29	32 n. 91
41.22f., 26f.	24 n. 50
42	67 n. 289, 94
42.1	26 n. 66, 27 n. 69, 28, 29 and n. 79, 32 n. 92, 42, 45, 49 n. 175, 51f., 53 nn.

Bible Ref.	Page
Isaiah	
	199, 202, 54 and nn. 206–7, 59, 60 and n. 249, 61ff., 68 and nn. 292–3, 80 and n. 345, 82 and n. 350, 83, 90
42.1f.	31, 61
42.1ff.	54 and n. 209, 56 n. 216, 60f., 68 n. 292, 72, 76 and n. 328, 78, 81, 95, 99
42.1–4	26, 27 n. 68, 29, 30 n. 82, 32 n. 92, 43, 63, 88, 90, 94
42.1–7	61
42.2f.	30 and n. 86, 32 n. 92
42.3f.	28
42.4	30, 32 n. 92, 42, 61, 81 and n. 346
42.4–9	27 n. 68
42.5–9	26 n. 63, 43
42.6	29, 31 n. 89, 60f., 63, 90 n. 403, 94
42.7	28, 30f., 61, 95 n. 428
42.9	24 n. 50
42.16	95 n. 428
42.19	20, 48 n. 169, 52, 53 nn. 199, 200, 54 and n. 207, 55, 56 and nn. 215, 219, 68 n. 291
42.23	53 n. 199
43.1–10	68 n. 293
43.8	20, 31

Index of Biblical References

Bible Ref.	Page	Bible Ref.	Page	Bible Ref.	Page
Isaiah		*Isaiah*		*Isaiah*	
43.8–13	32 n. 91	49.1f.	61, 78	50.10	48 n. 167, 52, 53 n. 199, 55f., 57 and n. 226, 58, 68 n. 291
43.10	20 n. 40, 32 n. 92, 51f., 53 n. 199, 58f., 68 and n. 293, 78 and n. 336	49.1–6	26, 27 n. 68, 43		
		49.2	28f., 30 n. 86, 60 and n. 252, 93 n. 425		
				50.10f.	27 n. 68
43.27	21 n. 42	49.3	26f., 27 n. 69, 29, 43, 49 nn. 175–6, 52, 53 n. 200, 55 and n. 213, 56f., 68 n. 291	51.8	35 n. 103
44.1	20, 49 nn. 175–6, 52, 53 n. 199, 55			52.13	29, 43, 44 and n. 136, 47 n. 156, 51, 52, 53 nn. 199, 202, 54 n. 207, 55, 59, 61, 68 and nn. 290 and 293, 69, 76 n. 328a, 83 n. 356, 97 n. 441, 98 and n. 446
44.1f.	19 n. 38, 68 n. 291				
44.2	20, 49 nn. 175–7, 52, 53 n. 199, 55 and n. 213	49.4	34		
		49.5	29, 52, 53 n. 200, 57		
		49.5f.	15 n. 23, 27, 30f., 55, 56 and n. 214, 68 n. 291		
44.4–6	32 n. 91				
44.8	32 n. 92				
44.21	15 n. 23, 19 n. 38, 20, 49 nn. 175–6, 52, 53 n. 199, 55, 68 n. 291	49.6	29, 31 n. 89, 52, 53 nn. 199, 202, 54 and n. 207, 59f., 63, 72 n. 305, 88 n. 390, 90 n. 403, 94, 99	52.13ff.	26, 34 n. 99, 35, 46, 54f., 56 n. 217, 60f., 72 n. 308, 76 nn. 328, 328a, 78 and n. 337, 86 and n. 380, 94f., 99
44.22	20, 31				
44.26	23 n. 49, 28 n. 71, 48 n. 169, 52, 53 n. 199, 54 n. 208, 56 n. 221, 57f., 68 n. 291	49.6f.	61, 78	52.13–53.1	27 n. 68
		49.7	26 and n. 63, 27 n. 68, 32f., 36, 43, 60	52.13–53.12	26 and nn. 65 and 67, 32f., 35, 43, 63, 67 n. 289, 69, 71f., 96 n. 434
45.4	19 n. 38, 20, 49 nn. 175–6, 52, 53 n. 199, 55, 68 n. 291	49.8	29, 31 n. 89, 72 n. 305		
		49.8ff.	30, 58	52.14	43, 44 nn. 134–5, 55, 61f., 69, 98 n. 446
45.9f.	33	49.8–13	26 n. 63, 43		
45.20	32 n. 91	49.9	28, 31		
45.23f.	31 n. 89	50.4	29, 59 n. 240		
48.20	19 n. 35, 20, 48 n. 166, 49 nn. 175–6, 52, 53 n. 200, 54 n. 208, 55, 68 n. 291	50.4ff.	28, 29, 56 n. 216, 57 and n. 226, 76 n. 328	52.14f.	36, 43
				52.15	33, 43, 55f., 61f., 69, 79 n. 340, 88f., 93, 95, 100 n. 454
		50.4–9	26, 27 n. 68, 32, 43		
		50.5	34 n. 100		
49.1	29 and n. 78, 58 n. 228, 60	50.6	57 n. 226	53	7, 33, 35, 44, 52, 54f., 56
		50.7ff.	35		

Index of Biblical References

Bible Ref.	Page
Isaiah	
	and n. 216, 60 n. 251, 62f., 65f., 67 and n. 289, 68 n. 290, 71, 72 n. 304, 73f., 75 n. 324, 76 and nn. 324, 328a, 77 and n. 329, 78 n. 331, 79 n. 338, 88 nn. 392, 392a, 89 and nn. 396, 398, 90 and n. 400, 91 n. 412, 92, 94 and n. 426, 95f., 97 and n. 444, 98, 99 and n. 448, 100 and n. 452, 101 n. 460, 103, 105f.
53.1	69, 88f., 93, 95
53.1ff.	43f.
53.1–10a	35
53.1–11a	26, 34 n. 99
53.1–12	69, 78
53.2	43 and nn. 129, 132, 62, 69, 75, 77 n. 328a, 86 n. 380, 98 n. 446
53.2–4	55
53.2–13	27 n. 68
53.3	55, 64 n. 274, 68 n. 290, 69, 70 n. 296, 71 n. 302, 77 n. 328a, 90, 99, 103
53.4	33 n. 93, 43 n. 132, 63 and n. 267, 64 and nn. 273–4, 65 and n. 275, 67

Bible Ref.	Page
Isaiah	
	and n. 289, 68 n. 290, 70, 74, 77 n. 328a, 88, 90, 92, 93, n. 424, 95, 96 n. 434, 98 n. 446
53.4–6	95 n. 431
53.5	62, 67 n. 283a, 68 n. 290, 70, 73, 75, 89 n. 397, 92, 96 and n. 434, 99, 105
53.6	34, 55, 70, 73, 89 n. 399d, 92f., 96
53.7	34, 68 n. 290, 70, 74, 98 n. 446, 100 and nn. 453 and 458
53.7f.	55, 58, 88, 91, 94
53.8	43 n. 132, 44 n. 138, 63, 67 n. 282a, 70
53.8–10	33
53.9	44 n. 140, 63, 65 and n. 285, 67 n. 288a, 68 n. 290, 70, 92, 97, 100, 103f.
53.10	34 and n. 98, 35 n. 105, 57, 67 n. 288a, 68 n. 290, 71, 92f., 95 n. 431, 96 and n. 434, 97 and n. 442, 100 and n. 455
53.10–12	55, 90 n. 401, 103
53.11	29, 44 n. 139, 52, 53 n. 200, 55ff., 59, 60 and n. 250,

Bible Ref.	Page
Isaiah	
	61, 68 n. 291, 71, 76 n. 324, 86 n. 380, 91f., 95 and n. 432, 100
53.11b–12	26, 34 n. 99
53.12	35, 55, 58 and n. 234, 65 and n. 283, 66f., 71 and n. 302, 76, 77 n. 329, 84, 88, 89 and nn. 397, 399, 90 and nn. 404 and 409, 92, 95, 96 and n. 434, 97 and n. 440, 98 and n. 100, 445–6 105
54.17	41
56.6	15 n. 23, 19, 42 n. 124
61.1	29 n. 79
61.1ff.	26 n. 67
63.17	42 n. 124
65.8	42 n. 124
65.8f.	19
65.9	42 n. 124
65.13ff.	19, 42 n. 124
66.14	42 n. 124, 49 n. 172
66.24	66 n. 286
Jeremiah	
1.5	31 n. 88
1.9	29 n. 80
1.10	31 n. 88
7.25	24 n. 52, 42
9.4	21 n. 42
11.19	34
12.1–6	31 n. 87
12.3	34 n. 101
12.7ff.	33 n. 97

Index of Biblical References

Bible Ref.	Page
Jeremiah	
15.16	29 n. 77
15.19	34 n. 100
20.14ff.	28 n. 75, 33 n. 97
23.5	60 n. 250
23.29	30 n. 86
25.4	24 n. 52, 42
25.9	23
26.5	24 n. 52, 42, 48 n. 167
26.27f. LXX	42, 49 n. 175
27–29	23
27.6	23
29.19	24 n. 52
30.10	19 n. 35, 20 n. 41, 45, 47 n. 156, 49 nn. 175–6
33.5 LXX	42, 48 n. 167
33.15	60 n. 250
33.21f., 26	23
35.15	24 n. 52, 42, 48 n. 167
42.15 LXX	42, 48 n. 167
43.10	23
44.4	24 n. 52, 42, 48 n. 167
45.4f.	33 n. 97
46.27f.	20 n. 41, 42, 49 n. 175
51.4 LXX	42, 48 n. 167
51.58	98 n. 445
Lamentations	
5.8	14
Ezekiel	
2.8	34 n. 100
3.1ff.	29 n. 80
28.25	20 n. 41, 49 n. 175

Bible Ref.	Page
Ezekiel	
34.23f.	23, 51
37.24f.	23, 51
37.25	20 n. 41, 49 n. 175
38.17	24 n. 52
Daniel	
3.26	15 n. 22
3.28	42 n. 125
3.33 LXX	48 n. 164
3.35 LXX	50 n. 187
3.44 LXX	48 n. 164
3.85 Θ	48 n. 169
3.93 LXX	48 n. 169
3.93 Θ	47, 51 n. 193
3.95 LXX	48 n. 169
3.95 Θ	45, 48 n. 169, 51 n. 193
6.20	51 n. 192
6.21	15 n. 22
9.6, 10	24 n. 52, 48 n. 167
9.11	15 n. 22, 50 n. 183
9.17	48 n. 164
12.3	56
Hosea	
12.3ff.	21 n. 42
Amos	
3.7	24 n. 52, 25 n. 58
Nahum	
1.2	16
Haggai	
2.23	23, 51 n. 195
Zechariah	
1.6	24 n. 52

Bible Ref.	Page
Zechariah	
3.8	23, 51
9.9	60 n. 250
12.10ff.	75 n. 318
12.12	75
13.5	11 n. 4
Malachi	
4.4	22
4.5f.	105
I Esdras	
4.59	47 n. 160, 48 n. 164
6.13	41 n. 123, 45, 47, 48 n. 166
6.27	45, 47, 51 n. 191
8.82	41 n. 123, 45f., 48 n. 167
II Esdras (IV Ezra)	
1.32	81
2.1, 18	81
3.11	50 n. 185
3.23	50 n. 184
5.45, 56	48 n. 164
6.12	48 n. 164
7.28f.	47 n. 163, 51
7.75, 102	48 n. 164
8.2, 24	48 n. 164
10.37	48 n. 164
12.8	48 n. 164
13.14	48 n. 164
13.32, 37, 52	47 n. 163, 51 and n. 196
14.9	47 n. 163, 51 and n. 196
14.31	50 n. 183
Wisdom of Solomon	
2.13	45 and n. 145, 46 and n. 152, 54f.
2.16	46
2.18	46 and n. 152
2.19f.	55

Index of Biblical References

Wisdom of Solomon

Bible Ref.	Page
4.18	55
4.20ff.	54f., 61, 78 n. 337
5.1ff.	46, 55
5.3f.	55
5.5	46 n. 151, 55
5.6f., 15f.	55
9.4	45 and n. 145
9.5	48 n. 164
9.7	45 n. 145
10.16	50 n. 183
12.7	45
12.19ff.	45 n. 145
12.20	45
19.6	45

Ecclesiasticus

Bible Ref.	Page
11.13	56
36.17(22)	47 n. 160, 48 nn. 164 and 169
48.10	58 n. 234, 59, 72 n. 305

Psalms of Solomon

Bible Ref.	Page
2.37	48 n. 169
10.4	48 n. 169
12.6	45, 47, 49 n. 177, 80
17.21	45, 47, 49 n. 177, 80
18.12	49 n. 174

Baruch

Bible Ref.	Page
1.20	45–7, 50 n. 183
2.20, 24	45–7, 48 n. 167
2.28	45–7, 50 n. 183
3.36	45, 46 n. 149, 47, 49 n. 177, 55 n. 213

I Maccabees

Bible Ref.	Page
4.30	50 n. 184, 85 n. 370

II Maccabees

Bible Ref.	Page
1.2	50 n. 186
7.6	48 n. 169
7.33	45 n. 148, 48 n. 169
7.34	45, 48 n. 166
7.37f.	104 n. 476
8.29	48 nn. 164, 166 and 169

IV Maccabees

Bible Ref.	Page
6.29	104 n. 476

Matthew

Bible Ref.	Page
1.22	93 n. 424
3.17	29 n. 81, 82
5.3f.	103
5.12	102 n. 467
8.17	88, 90, 91 n. 408, 93 n. 424, 95
9.34	101
11.5	103
12.18	80 and n. 341, 81, 82 and n. 352, 83, 84 n. 360, 86, 95 n. 429
12.18–20	81, 91 n. 408, 95
12.18–21	88, 90
12.21	81, 91, 93
17.5	29 n. 81, 82
17.12, 22	90 n. 405
20.19	101 n. 459
20.28	90, 95, 96 and n. 435, 97 n. 442, 99
21.35f.	102 n. 469
22.6	102 n. 469
23.29–35	102 n. 470
23.30–32	102 n. 469
23.33	93 n. 424
23.34–36	102 and n. 469
23.35	102
23.37	101 and n. 465, 102 and n. 469
23.37–39	102 n. 470
24.26	60 n. 252
24.30	75 n. 318
25.41, 46	66 n. 286
26.2	99, 105
26.28	95, 96 n. 435, 97
26.54	90 n. 405, 93 and n. 424
26.63	100
26.64	100 n. 454
27.12, 14	100
27.46	82 n. 349

Mark

Bible Ref.	Page
1.10	82
1.11	29 n. 181, 82f., 86, 90 and n. 402, 91 n. 408, 95 n. 429
2.7	101
2.23–3.7a	101f.
2.24	101 n. 463
3.1ff.	101
3.1–6	101 n. 464
3.6	101
3.7	101 and n. 464
3.22	101
4.12	68 n. 290
4.13, 40f.	78 n. 331
6.16	102
6.52	78 n. 331
7.18	78 n. 331
8.16–21	78 n. 331
8.31	90 nn. 405–6, 101 n. 459, 104
8.32	78 n. 331
8.33	104
9.7	29 n. 81, 81f.,

Index of Biblical References

Bible Ref.	Page
Mark	
	90 n. 402, 91 n. 408, 95 n. 429
9.11	105
9.12	90 and nn. 405–6, 91 n. 408, 99 and n. 448a, 103, 105
9.12f.	102
9.31	99, 101 n. 459, 103, 105
9.32	78 n. 331
10.32	90 n. 405
10.32–40	103
10.33	99, 105
10.33f.	101 n. 459
10.38	78 n. 331
10.39	103 n. 472
10.42–45	104 n. 474
10.45	90, 91 n. 408, 92, 95, 96 and nn. 435–6, 97 n. 442, 99, 103f., 106 and n. 487
11.17	103
14.3–9	104
14.5	104
14.6	105
14.8	100, 103f., 105 and n. 480
14.21	90 n. 405, 99, 105
14.22–5	106 n. 484
14.24	90, 91 n. 408, 95, 96 and n. 435, 97, 103, 106 and n. 484
14.29, 31	103 n. 472
14.41	99, 105
14.49	90 n. 405
14.58	104
14.61f.	100 and n. 454
15.5	100
15.34	82 n. 349

Bible Ref.	Page
Mark	
15.45f.	105 n. 480
Luke	
1.54	47, 49 n. 177, 55 n. 213, 80 and n. 341
1.69	47, 50 n. 184, 80 and n. 341
2.29–32	90, 99
2.32	90 and n. 403, 97
3.22	29 n. 81, 82 and n. 349
4.18ff.	103
4.29	102 n. 465
9.31	90 n. 405
9.35	29 n. 81, 62 n. 260, 82, 95 and n. 429
9.44	90 n. 405
9.45	78 n. 331
11.21f.	100 n. 454a
11.22	101 n. 460
13.31	102
13.32	104
13.33	90 n. 405, 101, 102 and n. 469, 103
14.25–33	103
17.25	90 n. 405
18.9	91 n. 406
18.31	90 n. 405, 91 n. 407
18.34	78 n. 331
22.19f.	96 n. 435, 106 n. 483
22.22	90 n. 405
22.24–7	104 n. 474
22.36	105
22.36f.	103
22.37	67, 88, 90 and n. 404, 91 n. 408, 100, 103, 105
22.38	105

Bible Ref.	Page
Luke	
23.9	100
23.11	91 n. 406
23.34	100 and n. 455, 103f.
23.35	62f.
24.7	90 n. 405, 99, 105
24.21	103 n. 472
24.25–7, 32, 44–6	90 n. 405
John	
1.29	83f., 92, 97 and n. 440
1.34	62 and n. 261, 82 n. 350, 83, 92, 95
1.36	83, 92
3.14	92, 97 n. 441
5.10	101 n. 463
5.18	101
6.51	96 n. 435
7.27	60 n. 252
7.39	97 n. 441
8.28	97 n. 441
8.59	102 n. 465
10.11, 15	92, 96 and n. 435, 100, 103f.
10.17f.	92, 96, 100, 103f.
10.31, 33	101 n. 461
10.31–6	102 n. 465
10.33–6	101
11.8	102 n. 465
11.51f.	96 n. 435
12.16, 23, 32	97 n. 441
12.34	92, 97 n. 441
12.37f.	93 n. 423
12.38	88f., 93 and n. 421, 95
12.40	93 and n. 421
15.13	96 n. 435
16.16	104
16.32	92

Index of Biblical References

Bible Ref.	Page
John	
17.1, 5	97 n. 441
17.19	96 n. 435
18.14	96 n. 435
19.9	100
19.37	75 n. 318
19.38ff.	105 n. 480
Acts	
1.6	103 n. 472
2.23	91 n. 414
2.33	97 n. 441
3	81, 91
3.13	80 and n. 341, 81, 86 nn. 379–80, 87 and nn. 384a–5, 97 n. 441
3.13f.	91 n. 412
3.13ff.	86
3.14	86 n. 380, 91
3.18	86 n. 380, 91 n. 414
3.26	80 and n. 341, 81, 87 and n. 385
4	81, 91
4.11	90 n. 406
4.24–30	81
4.25	50 n. 184, 80 n. 341, 85, 86 and n. 378, 87 and n. 385
4.27	80 and n. 341, 81, 85, 86 and n. 378, 87 and n. 385
5.31	97 n. 441
7.51f.	102 n. 469
7.52	91 and n. 414
8.5–40	91
8.12ff.	91 and n. 411
8.32f.	88, 91, 94
8.34	26 n. 67, 58
8.36, 38f.	91 and n. 411
9.17	91 and n. 413

Bible Ref.	Page
Acts	
10.43	91 n. 414
13.27, 29	91 n. 414
13.47	88 n. 390
17.2f.	91 n. 414
22.13f.	91
22.14	91 n. 413
26.18	88 n. 390, 95 n. 428
26.22f.	91 n. 414
Romans	
1.3	86
3.25	96 n. 435, 97 n. 442
4.25	66, 89 and n. 397, 96 and n. 435, 97
5.6, 8	96 n. 435
5.16, 19	89
8.3	96 n. 435, 97 n. 442
8.32	89 and n. 399d, 96 and n. 435
8.34	65, 89 and n. 399, 95
10.16	89, 93, 95
11.3	102 n. 469
14.15	96 n. 435
15.21	88f., 93, 95
I Corinthians	
1.13	96 n. 435
1.23	78 n. 331
5.7	96 n. 435
8.11	96 n. 435
11.23–5	89, 106
11.24	96 n. 435, 106 n. 484
11.24f.	106 n. 483
15.3	89, 91, 94f., 96 and nn. 433 and 435
15.3–5	88

Bible Ref.	Page
II Corinthians	
5.14f.	96 n. 435
5.21	96 n. 435, 97 n. 441
Galatians	
1.4	89, 96 and n. 435
2.20	89, 96 and n. 435
3.13	78 n. 331, 96 n. 435
Ephesians	
1.6	95 n. 429
5.2, 25	89, 96 and n. 435
Philippians	
2.5–11	99
2.6–9	98 and n. 446
2.6–11	89 and n. 398, 97, 98 n. 445
2.7	17, 97 n. 444, 98 and n. 445
2.8	98 n. 445
2.10f.	98
I Thessalonians	
2.15	102 n. 469
5.10	96 n. 435
I Timothy	
2.6	89, 96 and nn. 435–6, 97 and n. 442
Titus	
2.14	89, 96 and n. 435
Hebrews	
2.9	96 n. 435
2.10	45 n. 147
2.18	92
7.25	65, 92, 95
7.27	96 n. 435
9.24, 27ff.	92

Index of Biblical References

Bible Ref.	Page
Hebrews	
9.28	92, 97 and n. 440
10.12, 26	96 n. 435
11.35–8	102 n. 469
James	
5.10	102 n. 469
I Peter	
1.11	92
2.21	96 n. 435
2.21–5	92, 99
2.22	97
2.22–5	97, 99
2.24	97 and n. 440

Bible Ref.	Page
I Peter	
3.18	92, 96 n. 435
4.1	96 n. 435
II Peter	
1.17	82, 95 n. 429
I John	
2.1	92, 95 and n. 432
2.1f.	65
2.2	92, 95, 96 n. 435
2.29	92
3.5	92, 97 and n. 440
3.7	92

Bible Ref.	Page
I John	
3.16	96 and n. 435
4.10	92, 95, 96 n. 435
Revelation	
1.7	75 n. 318
1.16	93 n. 425
11.7	102 n. 469
11.18	48 n. 167
12.5	60 n. 252
14.10f.	66 n. 286
15.3	50 n. 183
16.6	102 n. 469
18.24	102 n. 469
19.15	93 n. 425

www.ingramcontent.com/pod-product-compliance
Lightning Source LLC
Chambersburg PA
CBHW050838160426
43192CB00011B/2074